The People of ARGYLL, BUTE, and DUNBARTON
at Home and Abroad
1800-1850

By David Dobson

CLEARFIELD

Copyright © 2022
by David Dobson
All Rights Reserved

Published for Clearfield Company by
Genealogical Publishing Company
Baltimore, Maryland
2022

ISBN: 9780806359427

INTRODUCTION

This book contains references to people of the counties of Argyll, Bute, and Dunbarton, at home and abroad, between 1800 and 1850. These counties lie roughly north-west of Glasgow from the Firth of Clyde to the Firth of Lorne, together with Mull and some smaller islands. Most of the people identified here were recorded in contemporary sources, such as court records, newspapers, journals, and monumental inscriptions. Most entries bring together emigrants, their places of origin and destination, especially in North America and Australasia, with their kin who remained in Scotland.

Argyll, Bute, and Dunbartonshire were to some extent still Gaelic speaking in the early nineteenth century. The first two counties had formed much of Dalriada a thousand years earlier, while Dunbarton, the fort of the Britons, had been part of Rheged. The major families or clans found in this region were the Campbells, McDonalds, McLeans, MacAulays, Galbraiths, McLachlans, Malcolms, McMillans, McEwans, McDougalls, McQuarries, McKinnons, McGregors, McIntyres, McFarlanes, Colquhouns, Lamonts, and Buchanans.

The early nineteenth century was a period of restructuring and development resulting from the Agricultural Revolution and the Industrial Revolution. Small farms were formed into larger, more efficient, units which created a labour surplus. Some of the displaced persons opted the emigrate to the colonies or the United States while other moved to the burgeoning factory towns and collieries of the nearby industrial districts. For example, Greenock, lying across the Firth of Clyde, had grown from a population of 2,000 in 1700 to 17,500 in 1800.

The rise in transatlantic trade in the eighteenth century, furthermore, generated industrial development in Scotland, especially in the vicinity of Glasgow. In Argyll, Bute, and Dunbartonshire, the economy remained largely based on farming and fishing, but there was an expansion of burghs functioning as market and administrative centres. A burgh was a semi-autonomous town which was run by burgh councils, elected by the burgesses. Burgesses were the social and economic elite of the town, constituting about 10 per cent of the male population. Only burgesses could vote, operate businesses, or train apprentices. To be a burgess one had to be the son of a burgess, or marry the daughter of a burgess, or serve an apprenticeship under a burgess. Occasionally, one could purchase the right or, rarely, obtain it as an honour. This book identifies many of the burgesses of the burghs of Dunbarton and Inveraray.

David Dobson

Dundee, Scotland, 2022

REFERENCES

ABR   Ayr Burgess Roll

AJ   Aberdeen Journal, series

AMC   Annals of Megantic County

ANY   St Andrew's Society of New York

AP   St Andrew's Society of Philadelphia

BA   Officers of the Bengal Army, London 1838

BM   Blackwood's Magazine, series

BPP   British Parliamentary Papers

BOA   Book of Arran, [Glasgow, 1914]

CCG   Charleston City Gazette, series

CG   City Gazette, St John, New Brunswick, series

CM   Caledonian Mercury, series

CMM   Clan McMillan Magazine, series

DBR   Dunbarton Burgess Roll

DC   Daily Courant, Edinburgh, series

DPCA   Dundee, Perth, and Cupar Advertiser, series

EA   Edinburgh Advertiser, series

EC   Edinburgh Courant, series

EEC   Edinburgh Evening Courant, series

F   Fasti Ecclesiae Scoticanae

GA   Glasgow Archives

GC   Glasgow Courant, series

GM   Gentleman's Magazine, series

IBR   Inveraray Burgess Roll

IC   Inverness Courier, series

LAC   Libraries & Archives, Canada

LGR   London Guildhall Records

MAGU   Matriculation Album, Glasgow University

NARA   National Archives, Records Administration

NBC New Brunswick Courier, series
NCPres. North Carolina Presbyterian, series
NCSA North Carolina State Archives, Raleigh
NSARM Nova Scotia, Archives, Records Managent
NLS National Library of Scotland, Edinburgh
NRS National Records of Scotland, Edinburgh
NWI New World Immigrants, Baltimore
PACAN Public Archives, Canada
PANS Public Archives, Nova Scotia
PAPEI Public Archives, Prince Edward Island
PC Perth Courier, series
QM Quebec Mercury, series
QCG Quebec City Gazette, series
SCA South Carolina Archives
SGen Scottish Genealogist, series
SHS Scottish History Society
SM Scots Magazine, series
SP Skye Pioneers and the Island, Charlottetown
TNA The National Archives, London
W The Witness, series

Iona Abbey

GRAN.

GLENCOE: THE ROAD.

THE PEOPLE OF ARGYLL, BUTE, AND DUNBARTON,
1800-1850

ADAM, ANDREW, a merchant, was admitted as a burgess and guilds-brother of Dunbarton on 3 October 1806. [DBR]

ADAM, JOHN, a baker, was admitted as a burgess of Inveraray on 13 March 1829. [IBR]

ADAM, MARY, born 1829, servant of John McLellan in Gallochelly, North Knapdale, was accused of rioting at a Highland clearance in 1848. [NRS.AD14.48.319]

ADAM, ROBERT, a baker, was admitted as a burgess of Dunbarton on 23 April 1830, by right of his wife the daughter of a burgess. [DBR]

ADAM, WILLIAM, a grain merchant, was admitted as a burgess of Dunbarton on 26 June 1832. [DBR]

AITKEN, JOHN, born 1806 in Cumbernauld, Dunbartonshire, a merchant in New York, died at 31 West 52nd St., N.Y., on 6 January 1879. [ANY]

ALEXANDER, ALEXANDER, an able seaman in Campbeltown in May 1795. [NRS.HCR.212]

ALEXANDER, ANDREW, a butcher, was admitted as a burgess and guilds-brother of Dunbarton on 7 August 1807. [DBR]

ALEXANDER, ANDREW, was admitted as a burgess of Dunbarton on 20 May 1842, as eldest son of a burgess. [DBR]

ALEXANDER, WILLIAM, from Campbeltown, a merchant in Bonavista, Newfoundland, admin. 1828. [Royal Gazette, Newfoundland Advertiser, 9 September 1828]

ALLAN, HUGH, born 1785, miller in Cumbrae, died 12 March 1832, husband of Margaret Orr, born 1775, died on 4 June 1856. [Cumbrae gravestone]

ALLAN, JAMES, a tallow chandler, was admitted as a burgess and guilds-brother of Dunbarton on 20 July 1820. [DBR]

ALLAN, JOHN, a tailor, was admitted as a burgess and guilds-brother of Dunbarton on 16 March 1814. [DBR]

ALLAN, ROBERT, born 1801, died 10 October 1865, husband of Margaret Crawford, born 1803, died 20 January 1849. [Cumbrae gravestone]

ANDERSON, ALEXANDER, a merchant, was admitted as a burgess of Inveraray on 21 June 1819. [IBR]

ANDERSON, Sir ALEXANDER, died 26 July 1842 in Campbeltown, grandfather of Gordon Anderson Gardner in Brisbane, Queensland, Australia. [NRS.S/H]

ANDERSON, ALEXANDER, born 1813, died in New Zealand on 20 April 1869. [Kilmun gravestone]

ANDERSON, JOHN, a vintner in Campbeltown, testament, 20 September 1791, Comm. Argyll. [NRS]

ANDERSON, JOHN, in Inveraray, was evicted by the Duke of Argyll on 28 March 1805. [NRS.B32.2.1.42]

ANDERSON, JOHN, Moderator of the Free Presbytery of Dunbarton, a letter dated 19 April 1844. [NRS.GD112.74.825.22]

ANNAN, ANDREW, was admitted as a burgess of Inveraray on 8 November 1837. [IBR]

ANNAN, JOHN, an innkeeper, was admitted as a burgess of Inveraray on 29 September 1806. [IBR]

ARBUTHNOT, HELEN, born 11 December 1800, married John McHaffie on 14 March 1826, died 11 December 1826. [Cumbrae gravestone]

ARBUTHNOT, ROBERT, born 1775, feuar in Millport, died 24 March 1832, husband of Jane Taylor, born 1780, died 11 October 1836. [Cumbrae gravestone]

ARCHIBALD, ANDREW, a mason, was admitted a a burgess of Dunbarton on 22 November 1790. [DBR]

ARCHIBALD, JAMES, from Little Cumbrae, Bute, died at River Bank on the Mohawk River, New York, on 3 August 1824. [Scots Magazine, 94.383]

ARMOUR, JOHN, a cooper in Campbeltown, testament, 20 January 1792, Comm. Argyll. [NRS]

ARNOTT, DANIEL, with his wife and children John, Daniel, David, Duncan born 1818, Andrew, Elizabeth, Agnes, Catherine, Jane, Mary born 1823, and Martha born 1825, from Campbeltown, emigrated via Londonderry on the brig Dispatch of Workington bound for Quebec on 28 May 1828, were shipwrecked off the Ile aux Mort, Newfoundland, but landed at Port aux Basque and taken to Halifax, Nova Scotia, on 26 July 1828. [NSARM]

ARNOTT, DONALD, an able seaman in Campbeltown in May 1795. [NRS.HCR.212]

ARROL, JAMES, born 1744, parochial schoolmaster of Rhu, Dunbartonshire, died in March 1823. [Rhu gravestone]

AUCHINVOLE, DAVID, a wright, was admitted as a burgess and guilds-brother of Dunbarton on 24 September 1813. [DBR]

BABTIE, WILLIAM, a shopkeeper, was admitted as a burgess and guilds-brother of Dunbarton on 5 November 1804. [DBR]

BABTIE, WILLIAM, a merchant, was admitted as a burgess and guilds-brother of Dunbarton on 25 January 1830. [DBR]

BAINE, GEORGE, born 1795 in Dunbarton, a printer who was drowned at Maugerville, New Brunswick, on 1 December 1824. [NBRG.7.12.1824]

BAIN, JOHN, jr., a shipmaster, was admitted as a burgess and guilds-brother of Dunbarton on 4 October 1791. [DBR]

BAIRD, ROBERT, a currier, was admitted as a burgess and guilds-brother of Dunbarton on 26 June 1834. [DBR]

BALLANTYNE, DANIEL, a merchant in Campbeltown, testament, 10 July 1792, Comm. Argyll. [NRS]

BALLANTINE, DAVID, born 1772 in Campbeltown, a mariner who was naturalised in South Carolina on 21 March 1798. [NARA.M1183.1]

BALLANTYNE. DUNCAN, a merchant in Campbeltown, testament, 26 May 1790, Comm. Argyll. [NRS]

BALLANTYNE, JAMES, eldest son of James Ballantyne a merchant in Campbeltown, died in Demerara on 21 April 1802. [Scots Magazine, 64.708]

BALLANTINE, WILLIAM, cottar in Tangy Cottage, Kintyre, was accused of looting a wrecked vessel in 1817. [NRS.AD14.17.86]

BANCKS, MARY JANE, born 1820, late of Bowldley, Coburg, Upper Canada, died 8 July 1840. [Rothesay gravestone, Bute]

BANNATYNE, ALEXANDER, a farmer at Kilmahalmag, Rothesay, Bute, testament, 7 October 1799, Comm. Isles. [NRS]

BANNATYNE, EBENEZER, a vintner in Blackwater, Arran, 1840. [BOA231]

BANNATYNE, JAMES, a merchant in Rothesay, Bute, formerly a farmer in Edinmore, Bute, testament, October 1792, Comm. Isles. [NRS]

BANNATYNE, JAMES, a grocer in Lamlash, Arran, 1840. [BOA230]

BANNATYNE, JAMES, an innkeeper in Lamlash, Arran, 1840. [BOA231]

BANNATYNE, JOHN, born 1823, in Birchburn, Kilmory, Arran, was accused of assault in 1842. [NRS.AD4.42.430]

BANNATYNE, MARGARET, died 12 August 1806, spouse of Patrick Davidson a tenant in Glen Rosa, Kilbride, Arran, edict of executry, 1806. [NRS.CC12.7.38.8]

BANNATYNE, NINIAN, a merchant in Rothesay, Bute, testament, 30 October 1799, Comm. Isles. [NRS]

BAYNE, JOHN, son of Edward Bayne feuar at the Bridgend of Crieff, a writer in Oban, was admitted as a Notary Public on 18 May 1790. [NRS.NP2.34.171]

BEATON, MALCOLM, from Tarbert, a shepherd in Portland, Victoria, Australia, by 1856. [NLS.Acc.6880]

BEATSON, ALEXANDER, a nailer and a spirit dealer, was admitted as a burgess of Dunbarton on 13 December 1838. [DBR]

BEATSON, JAMES, a smith, was admitted as a burgess and guilds-brother of Dunbarton on 25 December 1806. [DBR]

BEATSON, JAMES, a publican, son of a burgess, was admitted as a burgess of Dunbarton on 15 June 1833. [DBR]

BEITH, ALEXANDER, minister at Kilbrandon from 1826 to 1830. [F.4.90]

BEITH, ALEXANDER, Customs Collector at Campbeltown versus Peter Thomson or McTavish, at Orrogaig, Skipness, on board the wherry Bell of Rothesay, Bute, a smuggler, 4 November 1826. [NRS.JP36.5.69]

BEITH, JOHN, a carter in Campbeltown, was accused of rioting and attacking a ship loaded with grain attempting to sail from Campbeltown, a petition, 21 March 1801. [NRS.JP36.5.46]

BEITH, JOHN, a merchant in Rothesay, Bute, died 6 December 1872, father of John Beith in San Francisco, California, his heir, 9 March 1877. [NRS.S/H]

BELL, ARCHIBALD, a druggist, was admitted as a burgess and guilds-brother of Dunbarton on 12 March 1801. [DBR]

BELL, JOHN, jr., a butcher, was admitted as a burgess and guilds-brother of Dunbarton on 19 May 1824, as son of a burgess. [DBR]

BETHUNE, Reverend JOSEPH, formerly a Church of Scotland minister at Renton, Dunbartonshire, died on 5 June 1800. [Kingston Cathedral gravestone, Jamaica]

BELL, DUNCAN, born 1728, Mary born 1780, Dougald born 1781, Duncan born 1799, emigrated via Oban on board the Spencer of Newcastle bound for Prince Edward Island on 22 September 1806. [PAPEI.2702]

BELL, DUNCAN, a shopkeeper, was admitted as a burgess of Inveraray on 29 September 1806. [IBR]

BELL, DUNCAN, a shoemaker, was admitted as a burgess of Inveraray on 29 September 1806. [IBR]

BELL, DUNCAN, a merchant in Inveraray, versus James Rankin, a fisherman at Cladich re the fishing boat Kitty of Inveraray, 3 April 1816. [NRS.AC20.2.51]

BELL, DUNCAN, a shoemaker, was admitted as a burgess of Inveraray on 9 June 1842. [IBR]

BELL, HUGH, a herd in Killowcraw, a debtor to James McMillan a shoemaker in Killowcraw, 20 March 1811. [NRS.JP36.5.56]

BELL, JAMES, a shoemaker, was admitted as a burgess of Inveraray on 29 September 1806. [IBR]

BELL, JOHN, born 1766, Catherine McEachern born 1779, Flora born 1797, John born 1803, emigrated via Oban aboard the Spencer of Newcastle bound for Prince Edward Island on 22 September 1806. [PAPEI, 2702]

BELL, JOHN, a shoemaker in Inveraray, was evicted by the Duke of Argyll on 1 April 1802. [NRS.B32.2.1.41]

BELL, MALCOLM, born 1741, Archibald born 1781, Angus born 1782, emigrated via Oban aboard the Spencer of Newcastle bound for Prince Edward Island on 22 September 1806. [PAPEI, 2702]

BELL, MALCOLM, a butcher in Inveraray, was admitted as a burgess there, on 1 August 1843. [IBR]

BELL, MARGARET, relict of Alexander Duncanson, a workman at Cromalt, a petition of 1790. [NRS.NRAS.1209.198]

BELL, MARION, born 1772, emigrated via Oban aboard the <u>Spencer of Newcastle</u> bound for Prince Edward Island on 22 September 1806. [PAPEI, 2702]

BELL, WILLIAM, a butcher, was admitted as a burgess and guilds-brother of Dunbarton on 7 August 1807. [DBR]

BENN, WILLIAM, of Furnace, Argyll, was admitted as a burgess of Inveraray on 12 July 1802. [IBR]

BENNET, JAMES, son of John Bennett, [1764-1827], a farmer in Finnartbeg, and his wife Agnes Anderson, [1770-1830], died in the West Indies in 1820. [Kilmun gravestone]

BIRKMYRE, MARGARET, born 1768, wife of David Miller, died in Dunoon on 28 September 1842. [New Brunswick Courier, 12 November 1842]

BISSET, GEORGE, a mason, was admitted as a burgess and guilds-brother of Dunbarton on 31 July 1810. [DBR]

BLACK, ANGUS, born 1834, son of James Black [1807-1852] and his wife Isabel McBride [1810-1881], died in Winnipeg, Canada, in August 1882. [Kilbride gravestone, Arran]

BLACK, DAVID, clerk to Neil McGibbon a writer in Inveraray, a petition, 22 March 1808. [NRS.B32.2.1.44]

BLACK, DAVID, a merchant and a writer, was admitted as a burgess of Inveraray on 21 February 1822. [IBR]

BLACK, JAMES, born 1785 in Rothesay, Bute, a carpenter, died at Musquash, New Brunswick, on 18 March 1817. [New Brunswick Courier, 26 April 1817]

BLACK, JOHN, a seaman in Rothesay, Bute, testament, 28 October 1796, Comm. Isles. [NRS]

BLACK, JOHN, son of Duncan Black in Tarbert, a debtor of William Caldwell at Lochwinnoch, 5 November 1810. [NRS.JP36.5.55]

BLACK, PETER, a fisher in Largiebeg, Arran, was accused of running down a vessel and causing death in 1824. [NRS.AD14.24.262]

BLACK, ROBERT, a fisher in Largiebeg, Arran, was accused of running down a vessel and causing death in 1824. [NRS.AD14.24.262]

BLAIR, ALEXANDER, a shipmaster, was admitted as a burgess and guilds-brother of Dunbarton on 24 September 1813. [DBR]

BLAIR, ALEXANDER, a spirit dealer, was admitted as a burgess of Dunbarton on 24 January 1839. [DBR]

BLAIR, DUGALD, in Lochgilphead, died in 1812, grandfather of James Scott Blair in Detroit, Michigan, his heir, 18 May 1878. [NRS.S/H]

BLAIR, HUGH, a labourer in Lochgilphead, South Knapdale, was accused of assault by stabbing at Ardrissaig point, South Knapdale in 1835, found guilty and sentenced to imprisonment in Inveraray Tolbooth for two months. [NRS.AD14.35.165]

BLAIR, JOHN, formerly a distiller in Shannachill, later in Lead of Drymen, Dunbartonshire, testament, 1790, Comm. Glasgow. [NRS]

BLAIR, JOHN, born 1742, a shipmaster, died 29 July 1813. [Dunbarton gravestone]

BLAIR, JOHN, a weaver in Killarie, Kilchenzie, Kintyre, was accused of looting a wrecked vessel in 1816. [NRS.AD4.16.62]

BLAIR, ROBERT, a tenant in Ardochhill, was admitted as a burgess and guilds-brother of Dunbarton on 12 March 1801. [DBR]

BLAIR, ROBERT, a shipmaster, was admitted as a burgess and guilds-brother of Dunbarton on 10 March 1810. [DBR]

BLUE, CHARLES, miller at Lochend, a debtor of William Caldwell at Lochwinnoch, 5 November 1810. [NRS.JP36.5.55]

BLUE, DANIEL, born 1783, died 13 June 1853, wife Elizabeth Strachan, born 1786, died 15 August 1846. [Rothesay gravestone, Bute]

BLUE, DONALD, miller at Kilean Mill, a petition dated 13 July 1789. [NRS.NRAS.1209.518]

BLUE, DONALD, in Tayinloan, a decreet, 1811. [NRS.JP36.5.56]

BLUE, DUNCAN, born 1803 on Colonsay, emigrated to Prince Edward Island, Canada, in 1852, died 21 January 1881. [Little Sands gravestone, PEI]

BLUE, NEIL, at Marmonagach, a debtor to James McMillan a shoemaker in Killowcraw, 20 March 1811. [NRS.JP36.5.56]

BOAG, JOHN, a baker, was admitted as a burgess and guilds-brother of Dunbarton on 25 December 1828. [DBR]

BOGLE, JAMES, in Uigle, Kintyre, a petition in 1850. [NRS.CS279.259]

BOLIN, JAMES, born 1767 in Kintyre, died in Cumberland County, North Carolina, on 1 April 1843. [NCSA.2.23]

BONAR, ANDREW JAMES, a stone merchant, was admitted as a burgess of Dunbarton on 17 December 1833. [DBR]

BONTINE, ISOBEL, and Grizzell Bontine, in Ardoch, Dunbartonshire, testaments, 1800, Comm. Glasgow. [NRS]

BONTINE, JOHN, a boatman, was admitted as a burgess and guilds-brother of Dunbarton on 29 September 1825 by right of his father Alexander Bontine a burgess. [DBR]

BORDIS, BRYAN, Major of the 73rd Regiment, was admitted as a burgess of Inveraray on 17 July 1800. [IBR]

BORLAND, JOHN, a changekeeper, was admitted as a burgess and guilds-brother of Dunbarton on 25 May 1808. [DBR]

BOWIE, ROBERT, a slater, was admitted as a burgess and guilds-brother of Dunbarton on 5 October 1804. [DBR]

BOYD, JAMES, a mason in Lamlash, Arran, 1840. [BOA231]

BOYD, Captain JAMES, died at the Cape of Good Hope, South Africa, in 1841. [Cumbrae gravestone]

BRACKENRIDGE, HUGH HENRY, born 1748 in Campbeltown, emigrated to Pittsburgh, Pennsylvania, in 1782, an author and judge, died 1816. [SSA.84]

BRADLEY, PETER, born 1786 in Campbeltown, a mariner, was naturalised in South Carolina on 10 June 1806. [SCA]

BRAID, MATHEW, born 1779 in Cumbernauld, Dunbartonshire, son of Alexander Braid and his wife Barbara Allan, a carpenter in Charleston, South Carolina, was naturalised on 27 August 1813. [NARA.M1183.1]

BREAKINRIDGE, JOHN, in Campbelltown, brother and heir of Thomas Breakinridge a merchant in Jamaica, 1839. [NRS.S/H]

BROCK, ALEXANDER, a farmer in Kilmalid, was admitted as a burgess of Dunbarton on 26 June 1834, as son of a burgess. [DBR]

BROCK, JOHN, jr., in Kilmalid. was admitted as a burgess and guilds-brother of Dunbarton on 12 March 1801. [DBR]

BROCK, ROBERT, a merchant, was admitted as a burgess and guilds-brother of Dunbarton on 26 June 1834, as son of a burgess. [DBR]

BROCK, WILLIAM, formerly a farmer, later a spirit dealer, was admitted as a burgess and guilds-brother of Dunbarton on 28 April 1829. [DBR]

BROCK, WILLIAM, son of Christina Brock in Dunoon, settled in Australia by 1856. [NRS.S/H]

BRODIE, ANGUS, a tenant in Loggantwire, Arran, with his family of seven, emigrated via Lamlash bound to Quebec, landed there on 25 June 1829, settled in Inverness township. [TNA.CO384.22.fo.3-5] [AMC]

BRODIE, D., in Old Kilpatrick, Dunbartonshire, applied to settle in Canada, on 3 March 1815. [NRS.RH9]

BRODIE, HUGH, in Green, was admitted as a burgess and guilds-brother of Dunbarton on 12 March 1801. [DBR]

BROLOCHAN, LACHLAN, tenant of Achnaclach, Campbeltown, a memorandum, 1818. [NRS.NRAS.1209.1942]

BROWN, ALEXANDER, a wright at West Bridgend, Dunbarton, was admitted as a burgess and guilds-brother of Dunbarton on 19 April 1800. [DBR]

BROWN, ALEXANDER, a painter, was admitted as a burgess and guilds-brother of Dunbarton on 7 Septembr 1824, as son of Alexander Brown a wright, burgess. [DBR]

BROWN, ALEXANDER, a blacksmith in Brodick, Arran, 1840. [BOA231]

BROWN, DANIEL, a labourer and change-keeper at Castle Road, Dunbarton, was admitted as a burgess and guilds-brother of Dunbarton on 13 October 1829. [DBR]

BROWN, DAVID, a Church of Scotland missionary in Ardentinny 1846-1847. [F.4.21]

BROWN, DUNCAN, jr., a mariner in Rothesay, Bute, testament, 26 February 1790, Comm. Argyll. [NRS]

BROWN, DUNCAN, from Rothesay, Bute, settled in Port Adelaide, South Australia, before 1863. [NRS.NRAS.2365/DRI.36.6]

BROWN, EDWARD, tenant of Machrimore, Southend, Kintyre, a memorandum, 1800. [NRS.NRAS.1209.744]

BROWN, IVER, an able seaman in Argyll in June 1795. [NRS.HCR.213]

BROWN, JAMES, a wright, was admitted as a burgess of Dunbarton on 25 September 1829, as son of a burgess. [DBR]

BROWN, JAMES, born 1794, died 19 January 1833, son of Duncan Brown tenant in Kilchattan. [Kilchattan gravestone]

BROWN, MARY, a teacher in Brodick, Arran, 1840. [BOA231]

BROWN, NANCY, born 1783, emigrated via Oban aboard the <u>Spencer of Newcastle</u> bound for Prince Edward Island on 22 September 1806. [PAPEI, 2702]

BROWN, ROBERT, a seaman in Rothesay, Bute, testament, 3 April 1800, Comm. Isles. [NRS]

BROWN, ROBERT, and his wife Ann, in Dunoon, were victims of forgery in 1832. [NRS.JC26.588]

BROWN, ROBERT, born 1797, merchant and postmaster in Dunoon, died 21 January 1842. [Dunoon gravestone]

BROWN, WILLIAM, a wright at West Bridgend, Dunbarton, was admitted as a burgess of Dunbarton on 25 September 1822, as son of a burgess. [DBR]

BRUCE, ROBERT, Sheriff Depute of Argyll, was admitted as a burgess of Inveraray on 24 July 1818. [IBR]

BRYAN, WILLIAM, a sawyer, was admitted as a burgess and guilds-brother of Dunbarton on 24 April 1834. [DBR]

BRYCE, DAVID, was admitted as a burgess and guilds-brother of Dunbarton on 12 March 1801, as son of William Bryce in Boghead a burgess. [DBR]

BRYDIE, MARGARET, born 1838 on Arran, was accused of uttering base coin in Glasgow in 1856. [NRS.AD14.56.28]

BUCHANAN, ALEXANDER, formerly in Tobago, a deed, 19 September 1803, [NRS.RD2.289.1173]; later in Campbeltown, died 18 March 1811, testament and inventory, 20 December 1811. [NRS.CC2.5.11; CC2.3.58]; edict of executry, 1811. [NRS.CC2.8.115.13]

BUCHANAN, ALEXANDER, a shipmaster in New York, a deed,1811, later in Campbelltown, testament, 20 December 1811. Comm. Argyll. [NRS][NRS.CC2.8.115.13]

BUCHANAN, ALEXANDER, born 1814, Catherine born 1814, Mary born 1835, John born 1837, Malcolm born 1841, Kate born 1846, Ann born 1849, and Christy an infant, from Bormaskitaig, emigrated via Liverpool on board the <u>Priscilla</u> bound for Victoria, Australia, on 15 October 1852. [NRS.HD4/5]

BUCHANAN, ARCHIBALD SHANNAN, from Drumhead, Dunbarton, died in Antigua on 18 September 1791. [Scots Magazine.53.568][GC.35]

BUCHANAN, ARCHIBALD, born 1790 in Argyll, declared his intention to naturalise in Norfolk, Virginia, on 18 March 1823. [NARA]

BUCHANAN, CHRISTINA, born 1800, died 10 March 1835, wife of Donald Livingston at Slate Quarry. [Keil gravestone]

BUCHANAN, JOHN, a farmer in Little Kilcattan, Kingarth, Bute, testament, 16 July 1795, Comm. Isles. [NRS]

BUCHANAN, JOHN, born 1794 in Callander, son of John Buchanan, educated at Edinburgh University, minister at Kingarth from 1826 until his death on 26 May 1871. [F.4.35]

BUCHANAN, JOHN, a merchant, was admitted as a burgess of Inveraray on 11 November 1836. [IBR]

BUCHANAN, JOHN, in Auchentoshan, Dunbartonshire, father of John Buchanan who married Rosa Henrietta Jenken second daughter of Thomas Jenken, MD, of Zacatecas, Mexico, in the British Consulate in Mexico on 4 March 1865. [GM.ns.52.18.778]

BUCHANAN, MARGARET, daughter of William Buchanan of Torry, died 27 November 1812 in Campbeltown, inventory, 23 February 1814. [NRS.CC2.5.11]

BULLOCH, ARCHIBALD, and JOHN, of the Dunlocher Grain Mill, West Kilpatrick, Dunbartaonshire, were victims of theft in 1824. [NRS.AD14.34.7]

BULLOCH, JAMES, a mason, was admitted as a burgess of Dunbarton on 19 February 1841. [DBR]

BULLOCH, WALTER, a labourer in Dunoon, was accused of assault in 1835. [NRS.AD14.35.154]

BUNTAIN, ROBERT, a smith, was admitted as a burgess of Inveraray on 9 December 1840. [IBR]

BURNS, GEORGE, an ironmonger, was admitted as a burgess and guildsbrother of Dunbarton on 23 September 1825. [DBR]

BURNS, WILLIAM, born 1805, an apprentice calico printer in Renton, Cardross, Dunbartonshire, was accused of the murder of Alexander McFarlane in 1824. [NRS.AD14.24.201]

BUTT, GEORGE, a spirit dealer from Glasgow, was admitted as a burgess of Dunbarton on 24 March 1843. [DBR]

BYRKMYRE, MARGARET, born 1768, wife of David Miller, died in Dunoon on 28 September 1842. [NBC.12.11.1842]

CADENHEAD, DAVID, a joiner and cabinetmaker, was admitted as a burgess and guilds-brother of Dunbarton on 21 September 1827. [DBR]

CAIRD, JOHN, M.A., a Church of Scotland missionary in Ardentinny in 1844. [F.4.21]

CALDERWOOD, JAMES, son of James Calderwood in Rothesay, Bute, died 1819, cousin of John Calderwood in Illinois, his heir. [NRS.S/H]

CAMERON, Ensign ALEXANDER, of the Argyll Militia, was admitted as a burgess of Inveraray on 10 June 1803. [IBR]

CAMERON, ALEXANDER, born 1803, Sarah born 1828, and Allan born 1843, from Raneschoa, Ardnamurchan, emigrated via Liverpool on board the Allison bound for Melbourne, Victoria, Australia, on 13 September 1852. [NRS.HD4/5]

CAMERON, ALEXANDER, minister at Tarbert from 24 November 1819 until to 16 September 1824. [F.4.19]

CAMERON, ALLAN, tacksman of Inverscaddle, warrant of inventory, 24 February 1815. [NRS.CC2.6]

CAMERON, ALLAN, born 1817, Mary born 1820, Alexander born 1846, Peggy born 1848, James born 1850, from Arevaighig, emigrated via Liverpool on board the Marmion bound for Moreton Bay, Australia, on 28 August 1852. [NRS.HD4/5]

CAMERON, ANGUS, born 1768, a labourer from Auchleik, Ann his wife born 1781, Mary born 1803, Euphemia born 1805, emigrated on board the Clarendon of Hull bound for Prince Edward Island, Canada, on 6 August 1808. [PANS][TNA.CO226.23]

CAMERON, ANGUS, born in Argyll, a former Sergeant in the Canadian Fencibles, with his wife, two sons and two daughters, settled in Burgess, Upper Canada, in 1816, moved to Leeds, Upper Canada, in 1817. [PAO]

CAMERON, ANGUS, a publican, was admitted as a burgess and guilds-brother of Dunbarton on 18 June 1825. [DBR]

CAMERON, ANGUS, born 1820, Catherine born 1817, Janet born 1847, and Duncan an infant, from Laga, Ardnamurchan, emigrated via Liverpool on board the Allison bound for Melbourne, Victoria, Australia, on 13 September 1852. [NRS.HD4/5]

CAMERON, ARCHIBALD, born 18 June 1813 on Lismore, a machinist and engineer in Charleston, South Carolina, was naturalised on 15 April 1850, died in Charleston on 5 January 1881. [Second Presbyterian gravestone, Charleston.] [NARA.M1183.1]

CAMERON, DANIEL, a publican, was admitted as a burgess and guilds-brother of Dunbarton on 29 January 1803. [DBR]

CAMERON, DONALD, born 1809, his wife Susan born 1816, son John born 1838, and son Dugald born 1841, from Tobermory, emigrated via Liverpool aboard the Marmion bound for Moreton Bay, Australia, on 28 August 1852. [NRS.HD4/5]

CAMERON, HUGH, a day labourer in Old Kilpatrick, Dunbartonshire, testament, 1798, Comm. Glasgow. [NRS]

CAMERON, HUGH, a vintner, was admitted as a burgess of Inveraray on 28 April1846. [IBR]

CAMERON, HUGH, born 1822, Christy born 1828, Mary born 1846, Archibald born 1848, and Peter born 1851, from Ardnamurchan, emigrated
via Liverpool on board the Marmion bound for Moreton Bay, Australia, on 28 August 1852. [NRS.HD4/5]

CAMERON, JAMES, born 1786 in Argyll, died in Harnett County, North Carolina, on 27 February 1863. [North Carolina Presbyterian, 14.3.1863]

CAMERON, JAMES, a workman, was admitted as a burgess and guilds-brother of Dunbarton on 23 April 1830. [DBR]

CAMERON, JOHN, tacksman of Culchenna, died 19 May 1810, inventory, 14 March 1814. [NRS.CC2.5.11]

CAMERON, JOHN, a shoemaker, a former apprentice of a burgess, was admitted as a burgess and guilds-brother of Dunbarton on 25 September 1818. [DBR]

CAMERON, JOHN, of Barcaldine, born 27 June 1824, died in Berbice on 29 January 1857. [St Modans gravestone, Ardchattan]

CAMERON, JOHN, late in Berbice, then in Glen Nevis, a sasine, 1848. [NRS.RS.Inverness.291]

CAMERON, LUDOVIC, a writer in Inverary, was admitted as a burgess of Inveraray on 21 August 1821. [IBR]; subscribed to a bond of caution, 30 October 1820. [NRS.CC2.9.7]

CAMERON, MARGARET, born 1787, Donald born 1822, Mizi born 1824, Una born 1825, Hugh born 1826, Dugald born 1826, Catherine born 1831, Allan born 1832, Alexander born 1834, John born 1837, Ronald born 1840, from Strontein, Ardnamurchan, emigrated via Liverpool on board the Allison bound for Melbourne, Victoria, Australia, on 13 September 1852 [NRS.HD4/5]

CAMERON, MATTHEW, an innkeeper, was admitted as a burgess and guilds-brother of Dunbarton on 24 June 1793. [DBR]

CAMERON, NEIL, a draper, was admitted as a burgess of Dunbarton on 25 February 1842. [DBR]

CAMERON, PETER, a spirit dealer at East Bridgend, was admitted as a burgess and guilds-brother of Dunbarton on 28 July 1824. [DBR]

CAMPBELL, ALEXANDER, a writer in Dunbarton, son of Neil Campbell a writer in Dunbarton, was admitted as a Notary Public on 22 November 1798, died on 18 April 1843. [NRS.NP2.36.203]

CAMPBELL, ALEXANDER, of Ballochyle, testament, 1 November 1800. [NRS.CC2.3.12]

CAMPBELL, ALEXANDER, tenant in Strone, Kintyre, a bond, 1803. [NRS.CS271.589]

CAMPBELL, ALEXANDER, a Captain of the Argyll Militia, was admitted as a burgess of Inveraray on 11 June 1803. [IBR]

CAMPBELL, ALEXANDER, in Inveraray, heir to John Colquhoun, was evicted by the Duke of Argyll on 28 March 1805. [NRS.B32.2.1.42]

CAMPBELL, ALEXANDER, a merchant, was admitted as a burgess of Inveraray on 29 September 1806. [IBR]

CAMPBELL, Sir ALEXANDER, of Ardkinglass, died in Devon, England, on 19 September 1810, inventory, 26 February 1812. [NRS.CC2.5.11]

CAMPBELL, ALEXANDER, tenant at Strone, Kintyre, in 1803. [NRS.CS271.589]

CAMPBELL, ALEXANDER, a farmer at Havock, was admitted as a burgess and guilds-brother of Dunbarton on 28 March 1819, by right of his wife the daughter of a burgess. [DBR]

CAMPBELL, ALEXANDER, jr., a wright, was admitted as a burgess of Dunbarton on 25 September 1829, as son of a burgess. [DBR]

CAMPBELL, ALEXANDER, born 1766 in Argyll, died in Sydney, Nova Scotia, on 14 March 1834. [Halifax Journal, 7 April 1834]

CAMPBELL, ALEXANDER, born 1832, died in Belnahua on 27 July 1887. [Kilchattan gravestone]

CAMPBELL, ANGUS, a weaver, was admitted as a burgess of Inveraray on 25 October 1813. [IBR]

CAMPBELL, ANGUS, a fisherman in Lochgoilhead, Dunbartonshire, was accused of housebreaking in 1845. [NRS.AD14.45.251]

CAMPBELL, ANN, in Bracklet, Appin, relict of John MacDougall tenant of Upper Fernoch, died 11 April 1811, inventory 24 January 1812. [NRS.CC2.5.11]

CAMPBELL, ARCHIBALD, of Rohoy, testament, 23 October 1795, Comm. Argyll. [NRS]

CAMPBELL, ARCHIBALD, of Knockbuy, died in Minard, Jamaica, on 8 July 1798. [SM.60.652]

CAMPBELL, ARCHIBALD, town clerk of Inveraray, a petition to evict John Bell a shoemaker, and Robert MacKellar a merchant in Inveraray, 24 March 1804. [NRS.B32.2.1.42]

CAMPBELL, ARCHIBALD, a petition against William Turner, son of Colin Turner, late merchant in Inveraray, 24 May 1804. [NRS.B32.2.1.42]

CAMPBELL, ARCHIBALD, late post at Stronmillachan, driver of a horse and cart carrying unlicensed salt in Glenaray in 1804 petition, 14 November 1804. [NRS.JP36.5.49]

CAMPBELL, ARCHIBALD, born 1795, son of Lieutenant Colonel Campbell of Glendaruel, died on Golden Grove Estate, Tobago, on 27 March 1819. [Scotsman.126.19] [AJ.3731]

CAMPBELL, ARCHIBALD, born 1762, died 7 July 1831, of the Argyll and Bute Militia, [Rothesay gravestone, Bute]

CAMPBELL, ARCHIBALD, of Colonel Tarleton's Dragoons, was admitted as a burgess of Inveraray on 18 December 1800. [IBR]

CAMPBELL, ARCHIBALD, in Auchendain, Inveraray, a victim of crime in 1829. [NRS.AD14.29.302]

CAMPBELL, ARCHIBALD, from Askinish, born 1752, died in Hanover, Jamaica, on 18 June 1830. [Hanover gravestone]

CAMPBELL, ARCHIBALD, born 1746, formerly a Captain of the South Carolina Dragoons, died on 8 April 1834. [Inveraray gravestone]

CAMPBELL, ARCHIBALD, born 1748 in Kilmartin, son of Alexander Campbell, educated at the University of Glasgow, minister at North Knapdale from 14 July 1778, died 27 April 1810. [F.4.16]

CAMPBELL, ARCHIBALD, born 1791 in St Andrews, New Brunswick, a Lieutenant of the 59th Regiment, died in Taynuilt, Argyll, on 7 February 1824. [CG.6.5.1824]

CAMPBELL, ARCHIBALD, was served heir to his father Archibald Campbell in North Knapdale, on 1 March 1816. [NRS.SC54.7.6.4.5]

CAMPBELL, ARCHIBALD, a cattle dealer and grazier in Lochhead, Southend of Kintyre, sederunt books dated 1830-1831. [NRS.CS96.343-344]

CAMPBELL, ARCHIBALD, born 1781, third son of John Campbell of New Hope, Westmoreland, Jamaica, of the family of Auchenbreck, Argyll, died in Westmoreland parish, Jamaica, on 21 April 1833. [Auchendour gravestone, Jamaica]

CAMPBELL, ARCHIBALD, a feuar and shipowner in Lochgilphead, father of Charles Campbell, born 1853, died in Clarksonville, Alexandria, Jamaica, on 5 November 1878. [EC.29391]

CAMPBELL, AUGUSTA MURRAY, born 10 April 1816, daughter of Reverend George Campbell in Ardchattan, died in Caen, Normandy, France, on 20 December 1824. [F.4.82]

CAMPBELL, CATHERINE, daughter of Hugh Campbell of Lix, heir to her uncle Captain Colin Campbell a planter in South Carolina, in 1791. [NRS.SH]

CAMPBELL, CATHERINE, second daughter of Alexander Campbell in Campbeltown, married Walter Irvine of Tobago, in Deebank in August 1797. [EEC.12369]

CAMPBELL, CATHERINE, in Inveraray, was evicted by the Duke of Argyll on 1 April 1802. [NRS.B32.2.1.41]

CAMPBELL, CATHERINE, born 1831, daughter of Catherine McLachlan or Campbell in Bellanach, North Knapdale, was accused of rioting at a Highland clearance in 1848. [NRS.AD14.48.319]

CAMPBELL or MCLACHLAN, Mrs, born 1803, a widow in Ballanoch, North Knapdale, was accused of rioting at a Highland clearance in 1848. [NRS.AD14.48.319]

CAMPBELL, CHARLES, an able seaman in Campbeltown in June 1795. [NRS.HCR.213]

CAMPBELL, Colonel CHARLES, of Barbreck, testament, 19 December 1800. [NRS.CC2.3.12]

CAMPBELL, CHRISTINA, born 1833, daughter of Catherine McLachlan or Campbell, in Ballanoch, North Knapdale, was accused of rioting at a Highland clearance in 1848. [NRS.AD14.48.319]

CAMPBELL, COLIN, in Charleston, South Carolina, brother of Elizabeth Campbell in Straban, Argyll, admin. 1794. [TNA]

CAMPBELL, Captain COLIN, at Castleton, testament, 20 February 1798, Comm. Argyll. [NRS]

CAMPBELL, COLIN, of Stonefield, was admitted as a burgess and guilds-brother of Ayr on 7 July 1790. [Ayr Burgess Roll]

CAMPBELL, COLIN, Customs Controller in Campbeltown, testament, 12 April 1800. [NRS.CC2.3.12]

CAMPBELL, COLIN, a writer in Inveraray, a petition to evict James Wright, a wright in Inveraray, and Margaret Campbell, 29 May 1804. [NRS.B32.2.1.42]

CAMPBELL, COLIN, son of John Campbell the tacksman of Benmore, died in Charleston, South Carolina, on 17 July 1810. [Edinburgh Advertiser, 4880.223]

CAMPBELL, COLIN, of Auchinellan, born around 1785, eldest son of Dugald Campbell minister of Glassary, educated at the University of Glasgow, minister at North Knapdale from 1816 until his death on 27 February 1834. [F.4.17]

CAMPBELL, COLIN, the younger, was admitted as a burgess of Inveraray on 26 August 1823. [IBR]

CAMPBELL, COLIN, born 4 July 1777, son of Reverend Peter Campbell and his wife Margaret Scott in Glassary, Argyll, was educated at Glasgow University in 1791, a physician, died in Jamaica on 8 May 1824. [F.4.7][MAGU.163]

CAMPBELL, COLIN, from Oban, emigrated to South Australia in 1839. [NRS.GD174.2340]

CAMPBELL, COLIN FISHER, minister at Tarbert, from 1836 until13 April 1843. [F.4.19]

CAMPBELL, DANIEL, born 1787, a labourer from Rhu, Dunbartonshire, emigrated to Canada aboard a Hudson Bay Company vessel in 1811, and settled on the Red River. [PACAN.m155, 145]

CAMPBELL, DAVID, of Comby, died 5 April 1814, inventory, 31 March 1815. [NRS.CC2.5.11]

CAMPBELL, DAVID MONTGOMERY, a writer, was admitted as a burgess of Inveraray in 1841. [IBR]

CAMPBELL, DONALD, a boatman, was admitted as a burgess and guilds-brother of Dunbarton on 1 July 1807. [DBR]

CAMPBELL, DONALD, born 1772 in Ardchattan, son of John Campbell a farmer, was educated at the University of Glasgow, minister at Kilmodan from 1810 until his death on 29 December 1837. [F.4.32]

CAMPBELL, DONALD, a weaver, was admitted as a burgess of Inveraray on 29 September 1806. [IBR]

CAMPBELL, DONALD, of Sonachan, subscribed to a bond of caution re Duncan McLullich and Archibald MacArthur in Barbreck, Duncan Campbell and Alexander MacIntyre jr at Barachanvoir, who had been admitted as constables for Argyll, 26 May 1795. [NRS.JP36.6.1]

CAMPBELL, Ensign DONALD, of the Argyll Militia, was admitted as a burgess of Inveraray on 10 June 1803. [IBR]

CAMPBELL, DONALD, a merchant in Campbeltown, a memorandum, 1805. [NRS.NRAS.1209.940]

CAMPBELL, DONALD, a weaver, was admitted as a burgess of Inveraray on 25 October 1813. [IBR]

CAMPBELL, DONALD, second son of Archibald Campbell of Larags, Argyll, died in Lucea, Jamaica, on 21 June 1817. [Scots Magazine, 74.727]

CAMPBELL, DONALD, at Bellfield, was admitted as a burgess and guilds-brother of Dunbarton on 2 May 1822. [DBR]

CAMPBELL, DOUGALD, an innkeeper, was admitted as a burgess and guilds-brother of Dunbarton on 16 May 1822. [DBR]

CAMPBELL, DUGALD, of Dunstaffnage, Captain and Paymaster of the Argyll Fencible Regiment, residing in Glasgow, testament, 1797, Comm. Glasgow. [NRS]

CAMPBELL, DUGALD, a merchant in Kingston, Jamaica, son of Colin Campbell the Customs Controller in Campbeltown, an edict of executry, 1801. [NRS.CC2.8.105.9]

CAMPBELL, DUGALD, of Carradell, testament, 3 January 1801. [NRS.CC2.3.12]

CAMPBELL, DUGALD, of Auchinellan, born in Kilmodan about 1756, son of Patrick Campbell of Auchinellan and his wife Elizabeth Campbell, educated at Glasgow University, minister at Glassary from 28 September 1779 until his death on 5 December 1826. [F.4.7]

CAMPBELL, DUGALD, fourth son of Archibald Campbell of Larags, Argyll, died in Jamaica, in 1817. [Scotsman,15. 17]

CAMPBELL, DUGALD WILLIAM, born in Glassary, on 6 June 1779, son of Reverend Peter Campbell and his wife Margaret Scott, a merchant who died in Bahia, Brazil, on 11 August 1823. [F.4.7][BM.14.624]

CAMPBELL, DUGALD, of Auchinellan, born 1801, educated at Glasgow University, minister at Glassary from 1830 until his death on 14 February 1852. [F.4.7]

CAMPBELL, Captain DUGALD, of the Argyll Militia, admitted as a burgess of Inveraray on 10 June 1803. [IBR]

CAMPBELL, DUGALD NEIL, born 12 November 1802, son of Reverend Dugald Campbell minister at Kilfinichen, educated at Glasgow University, minister at Kilmore from 1835 to his deat on 2 April 1869. [F.4.95]

CAMPBELL, DUGALD, from Arran, emigrated with his family of six to Quebec, settled in Inverness in 1831. [AMC]

CAMPBELL, DUNCAN, Sheriff Substitute of Kintyre, was admitted as a burgess and guilds-brother of Ayr on 7 July 1790. [Ayr Burgess Roll]

CAMPBELL, DUNCAN, of Glenfeachan, the Customs Collector at Oban, testament, 16 January 1790, Comm. Argyll. [NRS]

CAMPBELL, DUNCAN, from Knapdale, died at Aux Cayes, St Domingo, in 1795. [Scots Magazine.57.818]

CAMPBELL, DUNCAN, tenant of Treshnish farm, Argyll, in 1795. [SHS.ns.1.184]

CAMPBELL, DUNCAN, born 12 May 1770, son of Reverend Peter Campbell and his wife Margaret Scott in Glassary, Argyll, died in Jamaica in January 1797. [F.4.7]

CAMPBELL, DUNCAN, of Barr, testament, 14 April 1801. [NRS.CC2.3.12]

CAMPBELL, DUNCAN, town officer, was admitted as a burgess of Inveraray on 29 September 1806. [IBR]

CAMPBELL, DUNCAN, from Culchenna, died in Campbeltown, Jamaica, in 1817. [Scotsman.15.17]

CAMPBELL, DUNCAN, son of Neil Campbell of Knap, died in Demerara in August 1826. [Blackwood's Magazine, 21.373]

CAMPBELL, DUNCAN, born in Kilmartin in 1794, son of Angus Campbell and his wife Christian McLellan, emigrated to North Carolina in 1804, settled in Robeson County, died on 18 September 1881. [St Paul's Presbyterian Church records]

CAMPBELL, DUNCAN, born 24 January 1812 in Ardchattan, son of Reverend George Campbell and his wife Jane McDiarmid, a physician in Toronto. [F.4.82]

CAMPBELL, DUNCAN, born 1823, died 18 October 1900, husband of Catherine McLachlan, born 1825, died 2 June 1907. [Kilchattan gravestone]

CAMPBELL, EDWARD, a wright in Campbeltown, testament. 11 March 1789, Comm. Argyll. [NRS]

CAMPBELL, EDWARD, born 1757 in Kintyre, emigrated via Greenock to South Carolina in 1788, settled in Florida in 1819, died in Escambia County, Florida, in February 1837, his wife Mary McLellan, died in South Carolina in 1816. [NCSA.2.70]

CAMPBELL, EDWARD, and his wife Mary, in Lochgilphead, were victims of crime in 1829. [NRS.AD14.29.302]

CAMPBELL, ELIZABETH, relict of Alexander Campbell a merchant in Inveraray, and their children, Alexander, Colin, Archibald, Agnes and Margaret, in Inveraray, were evicted by the Duke of Argyll on 28 March 1805. [NRS.B32.2.1.42]

CAMPBELL, ELIZABETH HARDWICK ROSS, only daughter of Dugald Campbell in Kildullaig, Argyll, died on Plas Farm, Canada West, on 22 January 1860. [DC.23476]

CAMPBELL, FREDERICK, born 1804, son of Lieutenant Donald Campbell of Fernicarry, Dunbartonshire, died at Estancia Macitas, province of Entre Rios, Argentina, in 1868. [Scotsman.7675]

CAMPBELL, GEORGE, the Marquis of Lorne and Provost of Dunbarton, was admitted as a burgess and guilds-brother of Dunbarton on 29 September 1790. [DBR]

CAMPBELL, GEORGE, born 17 May 1769, son of Peter Campbell the minister of Glassary, educated at Glasgow University, minister at Ardchattan from 1796 until his death in 1817. [F.4.82]

CAMPBELL, GEORGE, fourth son of John Campbell in Prospect, Argyll, died in Lucca, Jamaica, on 11 June 1822. [Blackwood's Magazine.12.519] [EEC.17350]

CAMPBELL, GEORGE, born 1807, son of John Campbell of Bragleenbeg, a medical student who died in Glasgow on 30 October 1828. [Kilchattan gravestone]

CAMPBELL, GEORGE JAMES, born in Ardchattan on 12 October 1814, son of Reverend George Campbell and his wife Jane McDiarmid, in the Service of the Honourable East India Company and later United States Vice Consul in Port Maria, Jamaica, died on 3 June 1841. [F.4.82]

CAMPBELL, GEORGE, born in Petersburg, Virginia, on 28 November 1859, died in Dunoon, Argyll, on 9 October 1864. [Inverallen gravestone]

CAMPBELL, GRACE, born 13 June1808, daughter of Reverend George Campbell in Ardchattan, wife of Alexander Campbell Stevens a Member of the Royal College of Surgeons of Edinburgh in Falmouth, Jamaica. [F.4.82]

CAMPBELL, HARRIET, youngest daughter of Duncan Campbell in Knapdale, St Ann's, Jamaica, married James P. Utton, a Member of the House of Assembly, in Jamaica on 31 January 1829. [DPCA.1395]

CAMPBELL, HARRIET, born 1793, daughter of Hugh Campbell of Killundon, Morvern, emigrated to Prince Edward Island, married Allan MacDougall, died 10 November 1863, buried at Belfast, P.E.I. [SP]

CAMPBELL, HECTOR, born 1776, Neil born 1803, and John born 1805, emigrated via Oban aboard the Spencer of Newcastle bound for Prince Edward Island on 22 September 1806. [PAPEI]

CAMPBELL, HENRY, a tailor, was admitted as a burgess of Inveraray on 29 September 1806. [IBR]

CAMPBELL, HUMPHREY TRAFFORD, an advocate, was admitted as a burgess of Inveraray on 27 September 1811. [IBR]

CAMPBELL, ISABELLA, daughter of John Campbell sr. in Campbeltown, married Charles MacLarty, an MD in Kingston, Jamaica, in Glasgow in June 1803. [E.A., 4118.03]

CAMPBELL, ISABEL, wife of Peter MacThellar in Sligrachan, testament, 10 June 1796, Comm. Argyll. [NRS]

CAMPBELL, Mrs ISABELLA, relict of Patrick Campbell of Knap, South Knapdale, an edict of executry, 1804. [NRS.CC2.8.108.13]

CAMPBELL, J., born 1770, a Captain of the 91st Regiment, died 29 January 1848, husband of Elizabeth Stevenson, died in January 1817. [Kilchattan gravestone]

CAMPBELL, JAMES, of Silver Craig, Provost of Inveraray, was admitted as a burgess and guilds-brother of Ayr on 17 June 1794. [Ayr Burgess Roll]

CAMPBELL, JAMES, from Kilmichael Glassary, a midshipman on board the frigate Dido in 1798. [NRS.S/H]

CAMPBELL, JAMES, in Grenada, later in Tobago where he died in 1805, possibly from Islay, testament, 1809, Comm. Edinburgh. [NRS]

CAMPBELL, JAMES, of Ormaig, Captain of a troop of native cavalry during the insurrection in St Vincent and Grenada, died on 21 April 1805. [EEC]

CAMPBELL, JAMES, from Argyll, emigrated to Canada in 1801, settled in Martintown North, Upper Canada. [CGS.506]

CAMPBELL, JAMES, from Argyll, was naturalised in South Carolina on 22 August 1810. [Circuit Court Journal.10.74]

CAMPBELL, JAMES, in Arumdarroch, was accused of profaning the Sabbath, 1814. [NRS.AD14.14.71]

CAMPBELL, JAMES, a mason, was admitted as a burgess and guilds-brother of Dunbarton on 4 September 1824. [DBR]

CAMPBELL, JAMES, jr., a mason, was admitted as a burgess and guilds-brother of Dunbarton on 25 September 1829, as son of a burgess. [DBR]

CAMPBELL, JAMES ROBERTSON, minister at Tarbert from 1843 until 28 February 1844. [F.4.19]

CAMPBELL, Major General JAMES, born 1731, died 25 January 1810. [Dunoon gravestone]

CAMPBELL, JANE ATHOL GORDON, daughter of John Campbell in Argyll, and widow of Major Thomas Fortye of the 8th Regiment, died in Toronto on 22 March 1864. [GM.ns2/16.805]

CAMPBELL, JANET, daughter of James Campbell of Ruddel, Argyll, widow of Dugald McDuffie a merchant in Kingston, Jamaica, she died in 1790, testament, 1794, Comm. Edinburgh. [NRS]

CAMPBELL, JANET, in New Kilpatrick, testament, 1796, Comm. Glasgow. [NRS]

CAMPBELL, JEAN, born 1756, died in June 1831, wife of Niel Campbell farmer in Kilchattan. [Kilchattan gravestone]

CAMPBELL, JOHN, a merchant in Tarbert, testament, 1793, Comm. Glasgow. [NRS]

CAMPBELL, JOHN, a grocer, was admitted as a burgess and guilds-brother of Dunbarton on 20 September 1813. [DBR]

CAMPBELL, JOHN, born 1764 in Perthshire, educated at the University of St Andrews, minister at North Knapdale from 9 May 1811 until his death on 7 May 1815. [F.4.16]

CAMPBELL, JOHN, born 23 April 1766, son and heir of Peter Campbell minister of Kilmichael Glassary and his wife Margaret Scott, a merchant in Virginia, died in December 1796. [F.4.7] [NRS.S/H]

CAMPBELL, JOHN, a wood-monger, was admitted as a burgess of Inveraray on 29 September 1806. [IBR]

CAMPBELL, JOHN, born on 18 February 1768 at Kilmelford, son of Reverend Patrick Campbell and his wife Ann Campbell, died in India in 1794. [F.4.97]

CAMPBELL, JOHN, of the Indiaman ship Ceres was admitted as a burgess of Inveraray in 1789. [IBR]

CAMPBELL, JOHN, born 1772, son of Duncan Campbell of Glenfeochan, educated at the University of St Andrews, minister at Dunoon from 18 September 1800 to his death on 28 April 1831. [F.4.24]

CAMPBELL, JOHN, minister at Kilfinan from 1809 to 1811. [F.4.30]

CAMPBELL, JOHN, jr., a writer in Inveraray, was admitted as a burgess and guilds-brother of Ayr on 7 July 1790. [ABR]

CAMPBELL, JOHN, Captain of the 57th Regiment of Foot, testament, 20 September 1791, Comm. Argyll. [NRS]

CAMPBELL, JOHN, a merchant in Virginia, son and heir of Reverend Peter Campbell in Kilmichael Glassary in 1792. [NRS.S/H]

CAMPBELL, JOHN, a writer in Edinburgh, son of Archibald Campbell of Jura, was admitted as a Notary Public on 9 July 1793, died 28 April 1826. [NRS.NP2.35.91]

CAMPBELL, JOHN, the younger, in Inveraray, was admitted as a burgess and guilds-brother of Ayr on 12 June 1794. [ABR]

CAMPBELL, JOHN, a merchant in Campbeltown, was admitted as a burgess and guilds-brother of Ayr on 12 June 1794. [ABR]

CAMPBELL, Lord JOHN, a Member of Parliament, was admitted as a burgess of Inveraray on 4 January 1800. [IBR]

CAMPBELL, JOHN, a cattle dealer and grazier in Lochhead, Southend of Kintyre, sederunt books dated 1830-1831. [NRS.CS96.344]

CAMPBELL, JOHN, born 1811 in Argyll, emigrated to Caledon, Peel County, Upper Canada, died there on 1 May 1890. [Caledon gravestone]

CAMPBELL, JOHN, son of Neil Campbell, a herd in Kerranmory, was accused of sheep stealing in 1813. [NRS.AD14.13.39]

CAMPBELL, JOHN, of Glen Saddell, testament, 1 November 1800. [NRS.CC2.3.12]

CAMPBELL, JOHN, youngest son of Dugald Campbell in Carradale, Argyll, died in Port Royal, Jamaica, on 12 June 1804. [Scots Magazine.65.720]

CAMPBELL, JOHN, Major of the Argyll Militia, was admitted as a burgess of Inveraray on 11 June 1803. [IBR]

CAMPBELL, JOHN, a Captain of the 6th Regiment of Foot, was admitted as a burgess of Inveraray on 10 June 1803. [IBR]

CAMPBELL, JOHN, late post at Stronmillachan, driver of a horse and cart carrying unlicensed salt in Glenaray in 1804 petition, 14 November 1804. [NRS.JP36.5.49]

CAMPBELL, JOHN, a baker, was admitted as a burgess of Inveraray on 29 September 1806. [IBR]

CAMPBELL, JOHN, a labourer, born 1752, Isabel born 1752, Roderick born 1778, Donald born 1783, Alexander born 1799, emigrated via Oban on board the Claredon of Hull bound for Charlottetown, Prince Edward Island on 6 August 1808. [TNA.CO226.23]

CAMPBELL, JOHN, a labourer, born 1758, Catherine born 1763, Margaret born 1788, Isabel born 1790, Mary born 1792, Janet born 1797, Elizabeth born 1799, Archibald born 1804, Christian born 1807, emigrated via Oban on board the Claredon of Hull bound for Charlottetown, Prince Edward Island on 6 August 1808. [TNA.CO226.23]

CAMPBELL, JOHN, in Achen, a decreet, 1811. [NRS.JP36.5.56]

CAMPBELL, JOHN, born in Auchenwillin, Argyll, former Lieutenant Colonel of the 78th Regiment, died at Becancour, Three Rivers, Quebec, on 11 October 1819. [Weekly Chronicle, 26 November 1819][Scotsman. 151.19]

CAMPBELL, JOHN, writer in Inveraray, versus Captain John Sime and James Duncan, 28 March 1805. [NRS.B32.2.1.42]

CAMPBELL, JOHN, of Coilessa, Lochgilphead, was admitted as a burgess of Inveraray on 25 January 1810. [IBR]

CAMPBELL, JOHN D., born 1758 in Campeltown, a shipmaster who settled in New York in 1798, died there on 6 June 1820. [ANY]

CAMPBELL, JOHN, jr., a writer in Inveraray, versus Donald McKinnon, a cooper in Ballibeg Lochowside, 30 May 1820. [NRS.AC2.52]

CAMPBELL, JOHN, a herd on the common moor of Largie, Kintyre, was accused of sheep stealing in 1820. [NRS.AD14.2.112]

CAMPBELL, JOHN, born 1772, son of Duncan Campbell of Glenfeochan, educated at the University of St Andrews, minister at Dunoon from 1800 until his death on 28 April 1831. [F.4.24]

CAMPBELL, JOHN, alias ALEXANDER, born 1787, a teacher and former examiner of the Scottish Society for the Promotion of Christian Knowledge schools, residing in Clachan, Kilcalmonell, was accused of fraud in 1822. [NRS.AD14.22.29]

CAMPBELL, JOHN, born 1764 in Argyll, emigrated to Canada in 1784, died in St Andrews, New Brunswick, on 9 August 1830. [New Brunswick Courier, 14 August 1830]

CAMPBELL, JOHN, a cattle dealer and grazier in Lochead, South Knapdale, sederunt books, 1830-1831. [NRS.CS96.343-344]

CAMPBELL, JOHN ALEXANDER, late of the 91st Regiment of Foot, died in Rothesay, Bute, on 21 September 1840. [Rothesay gravestone]

CAMPBELL, JOHN, a grocer, was admitted as a burgess of Inveraray on 9 June 1842. [IBR]

CAMPBELL, JOHN, fourth son of Neil Campbell of Sunipole, Argyll, a merchant in Monroe, Ouchita, Louisiana, died there in 1845. [W.VII.640][DGH.15.1.1846]

CAMPBELL, JOHN, minister of Kilbrandon from 1843 to 1850. [F.4.93]

CAMPBELL, Sir JOHN, of Ardnamurchan, father of a son who was born on St Vincent on 27 January 1845. [PC]

CAMPBELL, LACHLAN, born 1798, farmer at Upper Ardlarach, Luing, died at Ellenabeich on 8 October 1874, husband of Mary Campbell, born 1815, died 24 May 1897. [Kilchattan gravestone].

CAMPBELL, LAUCHLINE, Provost of Inveraray, was admitted as a burgess and guilds-brother of Ayr on 7 July 1790. [Ayr Burgess Roll]

CAMPBELL, LIVINGSTONE, son of Sir James Campbell of Ardinglas, Inveraray, died in Portugal in 1786. [Anglican Church Records, Lisbon]

CAMPBELL, LORNE, late Chamberlain of Argyll, was admitted as a burgess of Inveraray in 1843. [IBR]

CAMPBELL, LUDOVICK, a writer in Inveraray, a petition, 1820. [NRS.AC20.2.52]

CAMPBELL, MACMILLAN, born 21 January 1786 on Bute, a merchant in Charleston, South Carolina, died 3 December 1813. [Old Scots gravestone, Charleston]

CAMPBELL, MALCOLM, tenant of Penmore farm, Argyll, 1795. [SHS.ns.1.184]

CAMPBELL, MALCOLM, born 1781, a farmer in Argyll, emigrated with his wife and five children to America in September 1807, settled in Russia, Herkimer County, New York. [1812]

CAMPBELL, MALCOLM, a weaver, was admitted as a burgess of Inveraray on 29 September 1806. [IBR]

CAMPBELL, MALCOLM, youngest son of Archibald Campbell in Argyll, married Isabella, daughter of John Nicolson, Superintendent Engineer, Peninsular and Oriental Shipping Line, Sydney, Australia, at the Scotch Church there on 12 April 1864. [Aberdeen Journal.6075]

CAMPBELL, MARGARET, wife of Dugald Cameron of Ederline, heir of her uncle Captain Colin Campbell a planter in South Carolina in 1791. [NRS.S/H]

CAMPBELL, MARGARET, in Lochend, was accused of rioting and attacking a ship loaded with grain attempting to sail from Campbeltown, a petition, 21 March 1801. [NRS.JP36.5.46]

CAMPBELL, MARY, relict of Ronald McAlester in Tarbert, testament, 12 January 1801. [NRS.CC2.3.12]

CAMPBELL, MARY, wife of Duncan McAlpin in Kilmeral, Inverlissa, Knapdale, a victim of theft in 1831. [NRS.JC26.1831.499]

CAMPBELL, NEIL, an able seaman in Campbeltown in May 1795. [NRS.HCR.212]

CAMPBELL, NEIL, a shoemaker in Inveraray, was evicted by the Duke of Argyll on 1 April 1802. [NRS.B32.2.1.41]

CAMPBELL, Lieutenant NEIL, tacksman of Degnish, testament, 7 October 1799, Comm. Argyll. [NRS]

CAMPBELL, NEIL, in Cardyhouse, Kilmun, was accused of a hanging in 1828. [NRS.JC26.1828.400]

CAMPBELL, PETER, of Kilmory, Argyll, born 2 May 1766, settled in Petersville, Westmoreland parish, Jamaica, died in December 1821. [Petersville gravestone]; a disposition dated 8 October 1808. [NRS.RD3.331.202]

CAMPBELL, PETER, minister at Kilmichael Glassary, father of John Campbell a merchant in Virginia, his heir, 1792. [NRS.S/H]

CAMPBELL, PETER, born on 15 September 1775, son of Reverend Peter Campbell and his wife Margaret Scott in Glassary, Argyll, died in Jamaica on 6 November 1795. [F.4.7]

CAMPBELL, PETER, at Fish River, Jamaica, proprietor of Kilmory, Glassary, Argyll, a disposition of said lands to his son Peter Campbell, in 1808. [NRS.RD3.331.202]

CAMPBELL, PETER, a tailor, was admitted as a burgess of Inveraray on 29 September 1806. [IBR]

CAMPBELL, PETER, a piper at High Aird, Kintyre, testament, 4 December 1812, Comm. Argyll. [NRS]

CAMPBELL, PETER, a writer, was admitted as a burgess of Inveraray on 22 September 1814. [IBR]

CAMPBELL, PETER, of Askail, Kintyre, died in 1839. [NRS.GD542.10]

CAMPBELL, ROBERT, a writer in Edinburgh, son of Dougald Campbell in Argyll, was admitted as a Notary Public on 28 February 1798. [NRS.NP2.36.173]

CAMPBELL, Lieutenant ROBERT, of the Argyll Militia, was admitted as a burgess of Inveraray on 10 June 1803. [IBR]

CAMPBELL, ROBERT, in Rosneath, factor for the Duke of Argyll, letters to Lord John Campbell from 1802 to 1815. [NRS.NRAS.1209/41 & 461]; was admitted as a burgess of Inveraray on 4 January 1800. [IBR]

CAMPBELL, ROBERT, a mason, was admitted as a burgess of Dunbarton on 20 April 1811. [DBR]

CAMPBELL, ROBERT, in Raslie, was appointed Admiral Officer of the Admiralty Court of Argyll on 31 March 1825. [NRS.AC20.3.3]

CAMPBELL, ROBERT, an overseer, was admitted as a burgess of Inveraray on 1 November 1842. [IBR]

CAMPBELL, Mrs SARAH, born 1769 in Argyll, widow of Hugh Campbell, died in Richmond County, North Carolina, on 11 March 1859. [North Carolina Presbyterian.26.3.1859]

CAMPBELL, SUSANNA, daughter of Archibald Campbell in Succoth, testament, 8 September 1798, Comm. Argyll. [NRS]

CAMPBELL, SUSAN, daughter of Ronald Campbell of Auchenbreck, married John McDougall from Buenos Ayres, Argentina, in Drimsynie on 4 July 1827. [DPCA.1356]

CAMPBELL, SYLVESTER, was admitted as a burgess of Inveraray on 23 August 1824. [IBR]

CAMPBELL, Captain THOMAS, the road surveyor of Kintyre in 1849. [NRS.SC54.20.3.3710]

CAMPBELL, Captain WALTER, of the Argyll Militia as a burgess of Inveraray on 20 October 1821. [IBR]

CAMPBELL, WILLIAM, born 1741 in Argyll, settled in Worcester, Massachusetts, before 1776, a Loyalist who moved to Halifax, Nova Scotia, later to St John, New Brunswick, in 1786, mayor there for 20 years, died on 10 February 1823. [CG.13.2.1823]

CAMPBELL, WILLIAM, son of William Campbell of Glen Falloch, settled in Hanover, Jamaica, testament, 1794, Comm. Edinburgh. [NRS]

CAMPBELL, WILLIAM, an innkeeper in Inveraray, versus John Stewart an innkeeper, a petition, 27 August 1801. [NRS.JP36.5.46]

CAMPBELL, WILLIAM, born 1741 in Argyll, emigrated to Worcester, Massachusetts, in 1768, a Loyalist, moved to Saint John, New Brunswick, in 1786, died 10 February 1823. [City Gazette, 13 February 1823] [TNA.AO13.24.72.4]

CAMPBELL, WILLIAM, born 1760 in Argyll, emigrated in 1783, died in Cornwallis, Nova Scotia, on 26 May 1840. [The Nova Scotian, 4 June 1840]

CAMPBELL, WILLIAM, born 16 November 1760, son of William Campbell and his wife Rosanna Doughty in Stuckchaple, settled in Jamaica in 1778, a planter in Hanover parish, died there in October 1791, probate 8 June 1793. [Scots Peerage.2.195]

CAMPBELL, WILLIAM, in London, was admitted as a burgess of Inveraray on 23 September 1802. [IBR]

CAMPBELL, Colonel, tenant of Fidden farm, Argyll, 1795. [SHS.ns.1.184]

CARLINE, HUGH, a weaver, was admitted as a burgess of Dunbarton on 25 September 1818. [DBR]

CARLIN, ROBERT, born 1832, died at Bonny in West Africa on 9 November 1866. [Rhu gravestone]

CARMICHAEL, CHRISTIAN, wife of Dougal McIntyre in Lismore, emigrated to South Carolina in 1821, settled in Dillon, S.C. [Scottish Highlander Carmichaels of the Carolinas, Washington, 1935]

CARMICHAEL, DUNCAN, born 1733, tenant in Lockamor, died 29 October 1829. [Kilchattan gravestone]

CARMICHAEL, JAMES, a weaver, was admitted as a burgess of Dunbarton on 25 September 1818. [DBR]

CARMICHAEL, JAMES, born 1811, in Toberonochy, died 27 May 1884, husband of Annabella McLachlan, born 1813, died 31 January 1876. [Kilchattan gravestone]

CARMICHAEL, ROBERT, born 1816, son of D. Carmichael and his wife Mary Morison, died in Kingston, North America, on 22 August 1849. [Oban gravestone]

CARRICK, WILLIAM, a grocer, was admitted as a burgess and guildsbrother of Dunbarton on 28 April 1829. [DBR]

CARRICK, WILLIAM, jr., a spirit dealer, was admitted as a burgess of Dunbarton on 28 April 1829, by right of his wife the daughter of a burgess. [DBR]

CARSWELL, DONALD, a spirit dealer, was admitted as a burgess of Dunbarton on 22 April 1822. [DBR]

CASTLE, CHARLES, born 1801, a shipmaster, died on 28 December 1867, wife Helen Baillie, born 1805, died 14 February 1846. [Cumbrae gravestone]

CATHAY, SAMUEL, a spirit dealer, was admitted as a burgess and guilds-brother of Dunbarton on 18 November 1828. [DBR]

CATHCART, FRANCES ANN, born 20 January 1820 in Dunbarton, wife of Thomas Lang Bowman, died 27 April 1893. [St George's gravestone, Port Elizabeth, South Africa]

CHAPMAN, DAVID, late Provost of Airdrie, a merchant in Glasgow, was admitted as a burgess and guilds-brother of Dunbarton on 12 December 1839. [DBR]

CHAPMAN, DAVID, son of Daniel Chapman a manufacturer in Kirkintilloch, Dunbartonshire, was educated at Glasgow University, a minister in Girvan from 1860 to 1872, died in Virginia in 1893. [F.3.43]

CHAPMAN, GEORGE, a wright, was admitted as a burgess and guilds-brother of Dunbarton on 18 March 1802. [DBR]

CHAPMAN, JOHN, a shipmaster, was admitted as a burgess and guilds-brother of Dunbarton on 28 May 1828, as son of John Chapman a carrier burgess and guilds-brother. [DBR]

CHISHOLM, DONALD, a house carpenter and miller in Ardnafeuran, testament, 14 December 1797, Comm. Argyll. [NRS]

CHRISTIE, J. R. B, of the Dunbarton Glassworks, was admitted as a burgess of Dunbarton on 9 January 1840. [DBR]

CLARK, DANIEL, a merchant in Campbeltown, tacksman of Achnaleck, papers 1791 to 1825. [NRS.NRAS.1209.501]

CLARK, DANIEL, a woollens manufacturer in Kintyre, a petition, 11 April 1817. [NRS.NRAS.1209.520]

CLARKE, DUNCAN, minister of the Kilean Free Church, a letter dated 15 April 1844. [NRS.GD112.74.1825.16]

CLARK, FINLAY, an innkeeper and butcher, was admitted as a burgess and guilds-brother of Dunbarton on 26 August 1817. [DBR]

CLARK, JOHN, an able seaman in Campbeltown in May 1795. [NRS.HCR.212]

CLARK, JOHN, in Campbeltown, versus Malcolm Taylor a tenant in Dailmore, decreet, 5 November 1810. [NRS.JP36.5.55]

CLARK, PETER, with his wife, from Campbeltown, emigrated via Greenock on board the Portaferry bound for Quebec in May 1832. [QM.13.6.1832]

CLARK, ROBERT, tenant in Garrachra, Kilmun, testament, 18 November 1793, Comm. Argyll. [NRS]

CLARKE, ROBERT DUNCAN, from Dunbarton, married Margaret Crawford, fourth daughter of Andrew Crawford, in Halifax, Nova Scotia, on 14 May 1842. [HMP.17.5.1842]

CLARK, WILLIAM, a grocer, was admitted as a burgess and guildsbrother of Dunbarton on 8 August 1821. [DBR]

CLARK, CAMPBELL, and Company, merchants in Campbeltown, a letter, 1793. [NRS.NRAS.1209.1936]

COCHRANE, ALEXANDER, born 1763, a shipmaster in Dunbarton, was admitted as a burgess and guilds-brother of Dunbarton on 23 September 1825 by right of his father Alexander Cochrane a burgess and guildsbrother, [DBR]; he was drowned at sea on 20 November 1820. [Dunbarton gravestone]

COCHRANE, ALEXANDER, a boatman, was admitted as a burgess and guilds-brother of Dunbarton on 24 November 1791. [DBR]

COCHRANE, DANIEL, a shipmaster, was admitted as a burgess and guilds-brother of Dunbarton on 26 September 1806, [DBR]

COCHRAN, JAMES, born 1797, farmer in Balloch, died 1 October 1831, husband of Janet McDougald. [Cumbrae gravestone]

COCHRAN, MARGARET, born 1757 in Campbeltown, died 1 May 1837 in South Carolina. [Old Scots gravestone, Charleston]

COCHRAN, PETER, a shipmaster, was admitted as a burgess and guildsbrother of Dunbarton on 10 October 1801. [DBR]

COLLINS, CHARLES, a merchant, was admitted as a burgess of Inveraray on 18 April 1820. [IBR]

COLLINS, JAMES, born 1808, an apprentice glass maker in Dunbarton, a witness at the murder trial of Alexander McFarlane in 1824. [NRS.AD14.24.201]

COLLINS, ROBERT, was admitted as a burgess of Dunbarton on 25 September 1818, having served an apprenticeship under a burgess. [DBR]

COLQUHOUN, ADAM, a weaver, was admitted as a burgess and guildsbrother of Dunbarton on 25 May 1808. [DBR]

COLQUHOUN, ALEXANDER, a bleacher from Cochnyfield, Dunbartonshire, died in Cornwall, Canada, on 26 August 1811. [DPCA.1111]

COLQUHOUN, ANGUS, born 1782 in Argyll, settled in Montgomery County, Georgia, before 1812. [NCSA.2.71]

COLQUHOUN, ARCHIBALD, son of James Colquhoun in Dunbarton, educated at Glasgow University in 1783, died in Washington County, North Carolina, on 7 August 1786. [MAGU.138][SM.48.518]

COLQUHOUN, ARCHIBALD, a writer, was admitted as a burgess and guilds-brother of Dunbarton on 18 September 1802. [DBR]

COLQUHOUN, CATHERINE, wife of John Colquhoun, in Camstraddan, Dunbartonshire, niece and heir of Coll Turner a merchant in Tobago, 1817. [NRS.S/H]

COLQHOUN, JAMES, a weaver, was admitted as a burgess of Dunbarton on 17 September 1790. [DBR]

COLQUHOUN, JOHN, a weaver, was admitted as a burgess and guilds-brother of Dunbarton on 18 September 1806. [DBR]

COLQUHOUN, JOHN, a writer, was admitted as a burgess of Dunbarton on 27 January 1843, by right of his father a burgess. [DBR]

COLQUHOUN, LUDOVIC, of Luss, died in Pleasant City, Atacosco City, San Antonio, Texas, on 9 March 1873. [EC.27593]

COLQUHOUN, MALCOLM, pilot of the steamboat Leven, was admitted as a burgess of Dunbarton, on 6 February 1837, by right of his father a burgess. [DBR]

COLQUHOUN, ROBERT, a writer was admitted as a burgess of Dunbarton on 24 November 1791. [DBR]

COLQUHOUN, ROBERT, a weaver, was admitted as a burgess and guilds-brother of Dunbarton on 18 September 1806. [DBR]

COLQUHOUN, ROBERT, a proprietor, was admitted as a burgess of Dunbarton on 31 July 1846. [DBR]

COLQUHOUN, WALTER, of Camstradden, born 1750, a merchant, husband of Elizabeth McAlister, settled in Antigua, died in St John's, Antigua, on 13 February 1802. [SM.44.446]

COLQUHOUN, WALTER, born 1786, a labourer from Rhu, Dunbartonshire, emigrated from Scotland on a Hudson Bay Company vessel bound for Canada in 1811, settled on the Red River. [PACAN]

COLQUHOUN, WALTER, a weaver, was admitted as a burgess and guilds-brother of Dunbarton on 24 September 1818. [DBR]

COLTROP, JOSEPH, a wright, was admitted as a burgess of Dunbarton on 21 March 1836, who served an apprenticeship under a burgess. [DBR]

COLTROP, THOMAS, a weaver, was admitted as a burgess of Dunbarton on 25 September 1818. [DBR]

COLVIL, JOHN, in Barlea, a debtor to James McMillan a shoemaker in Killowcraw, 20 March 1811. [NRS.JP36.5.56]

COLVIN, DUGALD, a witness at the murder trial of Alexander McFarlane in 1824. [NRS.AD14.24.201]

CONNELL, DAVID, a shipmaster, was admitted as a burgess of Dunbarton on 3 March 1825 as the son of a burgess. [DBR]

CONNELL, JOHN, a shoemaker, was admitted as a burgess of Dunbarton on 24 September 1795. [DBR]

CONNELL, ROBERT, an innkeeper, was admitted as a burgess of Dunbarton on 6 June 1832, as son of a burgess. [DBR]

CONNELL, THOMAS, a shoemaker, was admitted as a burgess and guilds-brother of Dunbarton on 24 September 1795. [DBR]

CONNELLY, JAMES, an innkeeper, was admitted as a burgess and guilds-brother of Dunbarton on 11 December 1811. [DBR]

COOK, ALEXANDER, and family, from Cloined, Arran, settled in Inverness Township, Lower Canada, in 1831. [TNA.CO384.28.fos.24-26]

COOK, ARCHIBALD, and family, from Mid Kiscadale, Arran, settled in Inverness Township, Lower Canada, in 1831. [TNA.CO384.28.fos.24-26] [AMC]

COOK, JAMES, a blacksmith at Whiting Bay, Arran, 1840. [BOA231]

COOK, JOHN, from Arran, emigrated via Lamlash, Arran, on board the Caledonia bound for Quebec, landed there on 25 June 1829, settled in Inverness township. [AMC]

COOK, WILLIAM, a labourer, was admitted as a burgess and guilds-brother of Dunbarton on 18 May 1841. [DBR]

COOPER, WILLIAM, born 1802 in Tarbert, emigrated via Greenock to Charleston, South Carolina, in 1821, petitioned to naturalise in Marlboro County, S.C., on 9 March 1830. [SCA]

CRAIG, DANIEL, a teacher in Balmicheil, Arran, 1840. [BOA231]

CRAIG, JAMES, a butcher, was admitted as a burgess and guilds-brother of Dunbarton on 14 August 1812. [DBR]

CRAIG, JOHN, a butcher, was admitted as a burgess and guilds-brother of Dunbarton on 9 September 1800. [DBR]

CRAIG, WILLIAM, miller at Dunbarton Mill, was admitted as a burgess and guilds-brother of Dunbarton on 6 August 1795. [DBR]

CRAIG, WILLIAM, was admitted as a burgess and guilds-brother of Dunbarton on 20 October 1824 by right of his father William Miller . [DBR]

CRAWFORD, ALEXANDER, born 1785 on Arran, Bute, educated in Edinburgh from 1805 to 1808, settled in Yarmouth, Nova Scotia, and later inTryon, Prince Edward Island in 1815, died there on 15 May 1828, buried at Crafaud, P.E.I. [ST]

CRAWFORD, ALEXANDER, a barber, was admitted as a burgess and guilds-brother of Dunbarton on 6 August 1795. [DBR]

CRAWFORD, ALEXANDER, born 1811, died in Demerara in 1839, son of Ninian Crawford [1763-1849] and his wife Agnes Hunter [1761-1847]. [Cumbrae gravestone]

CRAWFORD, DONALD, from Arran, emigrated with his family of nine to Quebec, settled in Inverness township in 1831. [AMC]

CRAWFORD, DUGALD, born 15 May 1752 on Arran, son of David Crawford a farmer in Sisgan, Kilmorie, educated at Glasgow University, a minister in North Carolina from 1783 until 1790, then in Argyll from 1795 until his death on 22 March 1821. [F.4.63]

CRAWFORD, DUNCAN, and his son John Crawford, dyke-builders in Kintyre, a contract, 1824. [NRS.NRAS.1209.531]

CRAWFORD, ELIZABETH, spouse of Donald Shaw a tenant in Kildonan, Arran, a petition re Dugald Crawford minister of Kilmory, Arran, 1821. [NRS.CC12.6.9.6]

CRAWFORD, GEORGE, a wright, was admitted as a burgess of Dunbarton on 2 February 1836. [DBR]

CRAWFORD, JOHN, of Broadfield, born 1747, died at the Garrison, Cumbrae, in August 1813, wife Jean Tucker born 1760, died in Ardrossan in October 1840, son Joseph born 1792 British Consul General in Cuba, died in Havanna on 27 July 1864. [Cumbrae gravestone]

CRAWFORD, NEIL, a merchant in Inveraray, a petition, 7 March 1821. [NRS.JP36.5.65]

CRAWFORD, ROBERT, son of Andrew Crawford of Garelochhead, [1722-1798], settled in Jamaica by 1823. [Luss gravestone]

CRAWFORD, ROBERT, a weaver, was admitted as a burgess and guilds-brother of Dunbarton on 23 September 1818, by right of his father Alexander Crawford a burgess. [DBR]

CRAWFORD, ROBERT, born 1808, an apprentice calico printer in Milton, Cardross, a witness at the murder trial of Alexander McFarlane in 1824. [NRS.AD14.24.201]

CRAUFORD, SAMUEL, a writer on Islay, son of John Crauford on Arran, was admitted as a Notary Public on 12 June1792, died on Islay on 9 February 1792. [NRS.NP2.34.347]

CRAWFORD, WILLIAM, was admitted as a burgess of Dunbarton on 25 September 1818, by right of his father a burgess. [DBR]

CRAWFORD, WILLIAM, a tenant in Corrie, Arran, with his family of two, emigrated to Canada in 1829. [TNA.CO384.22.fo.3-5]

CRICHTON, AGNES, born 1828, died in Dunoon on 25 May 1855, wife of John Gibb. [Dunoon gravestone]

CRICHTON, ALEXANDER, an innkeeper, was admitted as a burgess and guilds-brother of Dunbarton on 6 August 1795. [DBR]

CROMBIE, ALEXANDER, a merchant, was admitted as a burgess of Inveraray on 25 May 1841. [IBR]

CROW, ALEXANDER, born 8 April 1812 in Campbeltown, emigrated to America in 1840, a textile manufacturer in Fairmount, Philadelphia, Pennsylvania, died there on 1 October 1889. [AP]

CRUICKSHANKS, GEORGE, was admitted as a burgess and guilds-brother of Dunbarton on 26 July 1804, by right of his father Alexander Cruickshanks a weaver burgess. [DBR]

CRUM. JOHN, a saddler, was admitted as a burgess and guilds-brother of Dunbarton on 28 May 1804. [DBR]

CRUM, ROBERT, a shoemaker, was admitted as a burgess and guilds-brother of Dunbarton on 21 July 1818 by right of his father Peter Crum a shoemaker, burgess and guildsbrother. [DBR]

CRUM, WILLIAM, a grocer, was admitted as a burgess and guilds-brother of Dunbarton on 21 July 1818, by right of his father Peter Crum a shoemaker, burgess and guildsbrother. [DBR]

CRUMBIE, CHARLES, a mason and innkeeper, was admitted as a burgess and guilds-brother of Dunbarton on 24 June 1793. [DBR]

CULBERTSON, JAMES, the younger, son of James Culbertson, late tenant in Bulloch, later in Cheskan, Campbeltown, was accused of theft and fire-raising in 1820. [NRS.AD14.20.173]

CULBERTSON, JANET, daughter of James Culbertson, late tenant in Bulloch, later in Cheskan, Campbeltown, was accused of theft and fire-raising in 1820. [NRS.AD14.20.173]

CULBERTSON, SAMUEL, born 1805, son of James Culbertson, late tenant in Bulloch, later in Cheskan, Campbeltown, was accused of theft and fire-raising in 1820. [NRS.AD14.20.173]

CUMMING, JAMES, a mason, was admitted as a burgess of Dunbarton on 25 September 1829. [DBR]

CUMMING, JOHN, with family, from Largymeanoch, Arran, settled in Inverness Township, Lower Canada, in 1831. [TNA.CO384.28.fos.24-26]

CUMMING, ROBERT, a grocer, was admitted as a burgess and guilds-brother of Dunbarton on 14 August 1812. [DBR]

CUNNINGHAM, JOHN, a wright at Cambusmoon, was admitted as a burgess of Dunbarton on 29 August 1796. [DBR]

CUNNINGHAM, JOHN, from Renton, Dunbartonshire, died in Streetsville, Hamilton, Canada West, on 8 March 1857. [Edinburgh Evening Courant.2106]

CUNNINGHAM, WILLIAM, a nailer, was admitted as a burgess and guilds-brother of Dunbarton on 22 October 1791. [DBR]

CURDIE, JAMES, MA, minister, French West Indies, at Tarbert from 30 November 1825 until 13 February 1827. [F.4.19]

CURRIE, ARCHIBALD, from Argyll, a merchant in New York, died in Martinique in 1802. [Edinburgh Advertiser.4048]

CURRIE, CATHERINE, born 1784, emigrated via Oban aboard the Spencer of Newcastle bound for Prince Edward Island on 22 September 1806. [PAPEI, 2702]

CURRIE, DANIEL, born 1797, son of Donald Currie and his wife Mary Nicol in Kilmory, Arran, died in Jamaica in 1822. [Kilmory gravestone]

CURRIE, DONALD, a merchant in Lochgilphead, testament, 15 February 1798, Comm. Argyll. [NRS]

CURRIE, DONALD, born 1850, died in Tobago in March 1868. [Clachan gravestone, Arran]

CURRIE, DUNCAN, born 1792, a sailor in High Ballevuline, Campbeltown, a prisoner in Campbeltown Tolbooth, was accused of assault in 1822. [NRS.AD14.22.147]

CURRIE, JAMES, born 1776, emigrated via Oban aboard the Spencer of Newcastle bound for Prince Edward Island on 22 September 1806. [PAPEI, 2702]

CURRIE, JAMES, born 1781, James born 1804, Mary born 1806, emigrated via Oban aboard the Spencer of Newcastle bound for Prince Edward Island on 22 September 1806. [PAPEI, 2702]

CURRIE, JEAN, at Roundbay, Kilbride, Arran, testament, 21 September 1798, Comm. Isles. [NRS]

CURRIE, JOHN, a teacher in Shaddog, Arran, 1840. [BOA231]

CURRY, NEILL, an able seaman in Campbeltown in May 1795. [NRS.HCR.212]

CURRIE, SAMUEL, an innkeeper, was admitted as a burgess and guilds-brother of Dunbarton on 9 June 1815. [DBR]

CUTHILL, ARCHIBALD, stamp-master in Kirkintilloch, Dunbartonshire, testament, 1792 Comm. Glasgow. [NRS]

CUTHILL, LAWRENCE, a mason, was admitted as a burgess and guilds-brother of Dunbarton on 17 September 1825. [DBR]

DALE, JOHN, a glassmaker, was admitted as a burgess of Dunbarton on 23 April 1830. [DBR]

DALES, ROBERT, a baker, was admitted as a burgess and guilds-brother of Dunbarton on 7 September 1824. [DBR]

DALLAS, ALEXANDER, born 1796 in Argyll, emigrated to Wilmington, North Carolina, on 10 November 1820, settled in Chesterfield, South Carolina, naturalised in S.C. on 8 November 1825. [Citizenship Book.109]

DARROCH, ANGUS, born 1746, Janet Currie born 1751, Rahel born 1769, James born 1774, Donald born 1772, Duncan born 1778 with John born 1803, Nancy born 1780, Malcolm born 1786, Archibald born 1786, emigrated via Oban aboard the Spencer of Newcastle bound for Prince Edward Island on 22 September 1806. [PAPEI, 2702]

DARROCH, MARY, in Campbeltown, was accused of rioting and attacking a ship loaded with grain attempting to sail from Campbeltown, a petition, 21 March 1801. [NRS.JP36.5.46]

DAVIDSON, ALEXANDER, a nurseryman at East Bridgend, was admitted as a burgess and guilds-brother of Dunbarton on 25 October 1810. [DBR]

DAVIDSON, ALEXANDER, born 1800, son of Thomas Davidson, [1758-1846], died in Savannah, Georgia, on 25 December 1825. [Kilbride gravestone, Arran]

DAVIDSON, JAMES, jr., a weaver, was admitted as a burgess of Dunbarton on 17 October 1793, by right of his father George Davidson a burgess. [DBR]

DAVIDSON, ROBERT, a shoemaker, was admitted as a burgess and guilds-brother of Dunbarton on 20 September 1810 by right of his father a burgess. [DBR]

DAVIDSON, THOMAS, MA, minister at Tarbert from 15 April 1829 until 30 March 1836. [F.4.19]

DAVIE, ARCHIBALD, a weaver, was admitted as a burgess of Dunbarton on 3 September 1798. [DBR]

DAVIE, JAMES, a boatman, was admitted as a burgess and guilds-brother of Dunbarton on 9 August 1790. [DBR]

DAVIE, JAMES, a gabbartman, was admitted as a burgess and guilds-brother of Dunbarton on 13 May 1794. [DBR]

DAVIE, JAMES, a tenant in Gooseholm, was admitted as a burgess and guilds-brother of Dunbarton, on 12 March 1801. [DBR]

DAVIE, JAMES, a baker, was admitted as a burgess and guilds-brother of Dunbarton on 10 October 1808. [DBR]

DAVIE, JAMES, a gardener, was admitted as a burgess and guilds-brother of Dunbarton on 28 April 1829. [DBR]

DAVIE, JAMES, jr., a wright, was admitted as a burgess of Dunbarton on 25 September 1829, by right of his father a burgess. [DBR]

DAVIE, JOHN, a boatman, was admitted as a burgess and guilds-brother of Dunbarton on 22 September 1825, by right of his father James Davie a boatman a burgess and guildsbrother. [DBR]

DAVIE, JOHN, a boatman, was admitted as a burgess of Dunbarton on 12 March 1836, by right of his father Archibald Davie a weaver burgess. [DBR]

DAVIE, ROBERT, a merchant, was admitted as a burgess and guildsbrother of Dunbarton on 18 November 1828. [DBR]

DENNISTOUN, JAMES, the younger of Colgrain, Dunbartonshire, was appointed the attorney of John Heugh in Montgomery County, Maryland, on 6 March 1789. [NRS.RD2.252.1227]

DENNY, ALEXANDER, a cooper, was admitted as a burgess and guildsbrother of Dunbarton on 20 March 1804, by right of his father John Denny at Braehead. [DBR]

DENNY, ALEXANDER, a shipbuilder, was admitted as a burgess of Dunbarton on 1 August 1845 by right of his father a burgess. [DBR]

DENNY, JAMES, a ship's joiner, was admitted as a burgess and guildsbrother of Dunbarton on 25 September 1829, by right of his father a burgess. [DBR]

DENNY, JAMES, a merchant, was admitted as a burgess of Dunbarton on 2 February 1836, by right of his father a burgess. [DBR]

DENNY, JOHN, a ship's carpenter, was admitted as a burgess and guildsbrother of Dunbarton on 19 May 1824 by right of his father a burgess. [DBR]

DENNY, JOHN, a writer, was admitted as a burgess of Dunbarton on 9 February 1836, by right of his father a burgess. [DBR]

DENNY, PETER, a merchant, was admitted as a burgess of Dunbarton on 15 February 1825, by right of his father a burgess. [DBR]

DENNY, PETER, a shipbuilder, was admitted as a burgess of Dunbarton on 1 August 1845 by right of his father a burgess. [DBR]

DENNY, ROBERT, in Greenhead, was admitted as a burgess and guildsbrother of Dunbarton on 12 March 1801. [DBR]

DENNY, ROBERT, an innkeeper, was admitted as a burgess and guildsbrother of Dunbarton on 28 March 1804. [DBR]

DENNY, WILLIAM, a ship's carpenter, was admitted as a burgess and guildsbrother of Dunbarton on 17 October 1822 by right of his father a burgess. [DBR]

DENNY, WILLIAM, a shipbuilder, was admitted as a burgess of Dunbarton on 1 August 1845 by right of his father a burgess, [DBR]

DENOON, JAMES, MA, minister at Kingarth from 1822 until 1824. [F.4.35]

DEOR, PETER, a wright, was admitted as a burgess of Inveraray on 29 September 1806. [IBR]

DEWAR, DUNCAN, in Strathlachlan, versus John Crawford a fish-curer there, 16 January 1821. [NRS.AC20.2.53]

DEWAR, HUGH, born 1771 in Perthshire, educated at the University of St Andrews, minister at Kilmartin from 17 April 1804 until his death on 19 April 1836, father of Duncan Dewar of Hopewell and St John's in Jamaica. [F.4.14]

DEWAR, JOHN, a weaver, was admitted as a burgess of Inveraray on 29 September 1806. [IBR]

DEWAR, JOHN, a grocer, was admitted as a burgess of Dunbarton on 27 December 1838. [DBR]

DEWAR, PATRICK, minister at Glencoe from 1829 to 1843. [F.4.85]

DIAMOND, WILLIAM, a boatman, was admitted as a burgess and guildsbrother of Dunbarton on 24 November 1791. [DBR]

DICK, ADAM, in Rothesay, Bute, a letter dated 2 January 1846. [NRS.NRAS.332.C4.351]

DICK, JAMES, owner and master of the SS Rosneath Castle was admitted as a burgess and guildsbrother of Dunbarton on 20 August 1825. [DBR]

DICK, JOHN, a nailer, was admitted as a burgess of Inveraray on 29 September 1806. [IBR]

DIXON, ANTHONY, a merchant, was admitted as a burgess and guildsbrother of Dunbarton on 27 September 1828 by right of his father a burgess and guildsbrother. [DBR]

DIXON, JACOB, jr., a merchant, was admitted as a burgess and guildsbrother of Dunbarton on 17 September 1819 by right of his father Jacob Dixon a merchant burgess. [DBR]

DIXON, JOHN, of the Dunbarton Glassworks, was admitted as a burgess and guildsbrother of Dunbarton on 15 November 1791. [DBR]

DIXON, JOHN, jr., a merchant, was admitted as a burgess and guildsbrother of Dunbarton on 27 September 1820 by right of his father John Dixon of Levengrove a burgess and guildsbrother. [DBR]

DIXON, JOSEPH, was admitted as a burgess and guildsbrother of Dunbarton on 1 October 1825, son of Provost Jacob Dixon [DBR]

DOBIE, THOMAS, an innkeeper and mason, was admitted as a burgess and guildsbrother of Dunbarton on 22 July 1816. [DBR]

DONALD, JAMES, an innkeeper, was admitted as a burgess and guildsbrother of Dunbarton on 3 September 1798. [DBR]

DONALD, JAMES, a slater, was admitted as a burgess and guildsbrother of Dunbarton on 18 March 1802. [DBR]

DONALD, JAMES, a grocer and spirit dealer, was admitted as a burgess and guildsbrother of Dunbarton on 9 June 1823 by right of his father a burgess. [DBR]

DONALDSON, JAMES, a slater, sometime in Down, was admitted as a burgess and guildsbrother of Dunbarton on 10 April 1812. [DBR]

DONALDSON, JAMES, a slater and a merchant, was admitted as a burgess and guildsbrother of Dunbarton on 23 September 1826. [DBR]

DOUGLAS, ALEXANDER, a baker, was admitted as a burgess and guildsbrother of Dunbarton on 21 July 1818, as married to the daughter of a burgess. [DBR]

DOUGLAS, JAMES, a tailor, was admitted as a burgess of Dunbarton on 22 September 1834 by right of his father a burgess. [DBR]

DOUGLAS, JOHN, an innkeeper, was admitted as a burgess and guildsbrother of Dunbarton on 25 May 1808. [DBR]

DOUGLAS, JOHN, a watchmaker, was admitted as a burgess and guildsbrother of Dunbarton on 8 March 1825. [DBR]

DOUGLAS, JOHN, born 1818 on Arran, a surgeon in Duntochter, West Kilpatrick, Dunbartonshire, was accused of housebreaking in 1846, also in 1851. [NRS.AD14.4.148; AD14.51.72]

DOUGLAS, JOHN, born 1830, son of Archibald Douglas and his wife Helen Bain, died in California on 18 March 1889. [Sannox gravestone, Bute]

DOUGLAS, ROBERT, a grocer in Currie, Arran, 1840. [BOA230]

DOUGLAS, WILLIAM, an innkeeper near Dunbarton Mill, was admitted as a burgess of Dunbarton on 13 October 1829. [DBR]

DOWNIE, DUNCAN, a smith, was admitted as a burgess of Inveraray on 29 September 1806. [IBR]

DOWNIE, DUNCAN, a tailor, was admitted as a burgess of Inveraray on 29 September 1806. [IBR]

DOWNIE, ROBERT, born 1773 near Campbeltown, settled in Charleston, South Carolina, before 1806, died 17 November 1856. [Old Scots gravestone, Charleston]

DREW, ROBERT, a grocer, was admitted as a burgess of Dunbarton on 19 September 1839. [DBR]

DUFF, JOHN, born 1790, late of Helensburgh, died 13 October 1851, his wife Jane, born 1797, died 7 December 1878. [Rhu gravestone]

DUNCAN, DANIEL, born 1733, a merchant and shipmaster in Rothesay, Bute, died 12 June 1799, testament, 12 June 1799, Comm. Isles. [NRS][Rothesay gravestone]

DUNCAN, EBENEZER, a quarrier at West Bridgend, was admitted as a burgess of Dunbarton on 12 December 1839. [DBR]

DUNCAN, JEAN, spouse of John Duncan a merchant in Rothesay, testament, 2 November 1800, Comm. Isles. [NRS]

DUNCAN, JOHN, sr., a mariner in Rothesay, Bute, testament, 16 March 1790, Comm. Isles. [NRS]

DUNCAN, JOHN, master of the Isabella of Rothesay, testament, 17 November 1798, Comm. Isles. [NRS]

DUNCAN, ROBERT, a mariner in Rothesay, Bute, testament, 1789, Comm. Isles. [NRS]

DUNCANSON, JAMES, son of Walter Duncanson the town-clerk of Dunbarton, died in Jamaica on 5 April 1797; his sister Catherine Duncanson was served as his heir in 1798. [Edinburgh Evening Courant.12335] [CM.11824][GM.67.528][NRS.S/H]

DUNCANSON, MATILDA, daughter of John Duncanson a physician in Inveraray, died in Washington, America, on 2 August 1799. [AJ.2700][EA.3732][GC.1268]

EAGLESIM, ROBERT, a cloth merchant, was admitted as a burgess of Dunbarton on 8 October 1834. [DBR]

EASTON, GEORGE, was admitted as a burgess of Dunbarton on 19 March 1836 as married to the daughter of a burgess. [DBR]

EDMISTONE, ARCHIBALD, an able seaman in Campbeltown in May 1795. [NRS.HCR.212]

ELDER, ROBERT, MA, minister of Kilbrandon from 1831 to 1834. [F.4.90]

ELLIS, GEORGE, a mariner in Inveraray, was evicted by the Duke of Argyll on 1 April 1802. [NRS.B32.2.1.41]

EWING, ALEXANDER, a glasscutter, was admitted as a burgess of Dunbarton on 7 February 1839. [DBR]

EWING, JAMES, a cooper in Doveholm, was admitted as a burgess and guildsbrother of Dunbarton on 24 August 1810 having served an apprenticeship under a burgess. [DBR]

EWING, JOHN, was admitted as a burgess and guildsbrother of Dunbarton on 17 September 1819 by right of his father William Ewing a wright burgess. [DBR]

EWING, JOHN, a crate maker, was admitted as a burgess and guildsbrother of Dunbarton on 4 September 1824 by right of his father a burgess. [DBR]

EWING, PETER, a tailor, was admitted as a burgess of Dunbarton on 24 September 1801. [DBR]

EWING, PETER, jr., a tailor, was admitted as a burgess and guildsbrother of Dunbarton on 16 June 1828. [DBR]

EWING, ROBERT, in Townend, was admitted as a burgess and guildsbrother of Dunbarton on 20 March 1819 by right of his wife daughter of a burgess. [DBR]

EWING, ROBERT, a wright, was admitted as a burgess of Dunbarton on 25 September 1822 by right of his father a burgess. [DBR]

EWING, WILLIAM, a wright at West Bridgend, was admitted as a burgess of Dunbarton on 13 August 1802. [DBR]

EWING, WILLIAM, a wrightwas admitted as a burgess of Dunbarton on 25 September 1829 as the son of a burgess. [DBR]

FAIRIE, JAMES, an innkeeper was admitted as a burgess and guildsbrother of Dunbarton on 9 August 1790. [DBR]

FAIRLY, ALEXANDER, born 1753 in Argyll, died in North Carolina on 25 December 1827. [Fairly gravestone, N.C.]

FERGUS, DAVID, son of James Fergus in Campsie, educated at Glasgow University in 1779, minister in Campbeltown from 1805 to 1822, emigrated to America, died in Cincinatti, Ohio. [MAGU.125]

FERGUSON, ALEXANDER, born 1791 in Argyll, settled in Caledon, Peel County, Upper Canada, died on 28 July 1870; Janet, his wife, born 1805 in Argyll, died on 29 April 1877. [Caledon gravestone]

FERGUSON, ALEXANDER, a merchant, was admitted as a burgess and guildsbrother of Dunbarton on 1 July 1807. [DBR]

FERGUSON, ALEXANDER, minister of Tobermory, married Catherine Macdonald, daughter of Allan Macdonald of Dairoch, Mull, in Edinburgh on 1 December 1825. [SM.97.126]

FERGUSON, ARCHIBALD, born 1791 in Argyll, settled in Caledon, Peel County, Upper Canada, died 9 January 1882, his wife Sarah, born 1810 in Argyll, died 5 August 1870. [Caledon gravestone]

FERGUSON, ARCHIBALD, a smith, was admitted as a burgess and guildsbrother of Dunbarton on 4 September 1824. [DBR]

FERGUSON, ARCHIBALD, a painter, was admitted as a burgess of Dunbarton on 10 January 1839. [DBR]

FERGUSON, CATHERINE, born 1795 in Argyll, wife of Alexander Stewart, settled in Caledon, Peel County, Upper Canada, died 26 July 1870. [Caledon gravestone]

FERGUSON, COLIN, a merchant, was admitted as a burgess of Inveraray on 19 October 1802. [IBR]

FERGUSON, DANIEL, an able seaman in Campbeltown in May 1795. [NRS.HCR.212]

FERGUSON, DANIEL, a merchant tailor, was admitted as a burgess and guildsbrother of Dunbarton on 16 May 1827. [DBR]

FERGUSON, DONALD, a butcher in Inveraray, and his wife Elisabeth McFie, versus Agnes Kennedy, a petition, 6 August 1801. [NRS.B32.2.1.40]

FERGUSON, DUGALD, son of Neil Ferguson in Fernoch, Glassrie, victim of an assault in 1832. [NRS.AD14.32.161]

FERGUSON, DUNCAN, born 1749 in Kilmichael Glassary, settled in Caledon, Peel County, Upper Canada, died in September 1835. [Caledon gravestone]

FERGUSON, JOHN, in Kinachruchkan, driver of a horse and cart carrying unlicensed salt in Glenaray in 1804, petition, 14 November 1804. [NRS.JP36.5.49]

FERGUSON, WILLIAM, a slater, was admitted as a burgess of Dunbarton on 26 October 1831 by right of his wife the daughter of a burgess. [DBR]

FERRIER, ALEXANDER, of Bloomhill, Dunbartonshire, late in Surinam, died on 20 April 1848, testament, 1849, Edinburgh. [NRS]

FERRIER, Major General ILAY, Governor of Dunbarton Castle from 1796 to 1824, papers. [NRS.NRAS.4159]

FERRIER, WILLIAM, from Dunbarton, applied to settle in Canada on 27 February 1815. [NRS.RH9]

FINDLATOR, ERIC JOHN, born 5 April 1813, son of Reverend William Findlator in Durness, educated at the University of Aberdeen, minister at Ardentinny from 1838 to 1843, joined the Free Church, Argyll, died 2 May 1886. [F.4.21]

FISHER, ARCHIBALD, born in Hulmechal, Glassary, Argyll, died in Bladen County, North Carolina, on 25 September 1820. [Brown Marsh gravestone, N.C.]

FISHER, DANIEL, a writer in Edinburgh, was admitted as a burgess and guildsbrother of Dunbarton on 8 May 1818. [DBR]

FISHER, DONALD, son of James Fisher in Kilchrennan, Argyll, emigrated to America in 1816, Principal Instructor at Jefferson College in Washington, Mississippi, from 1821 to 1823, died in Jamaica in 1826. [Scottish Genealogist.1.4.21]

FISHER, JOHN, in Lamlash, Arran, in 1812, formerly a teacher at Kerrycroy, Bute. [NRS.NRAS.2177, bundle 5245]

FISHER, JOHN, a tobacconist, was admitted as a burgess and guildsbrother of Dunbarton on 19 January 1828. [DBR]

FLEEK, WILLIAM, a butcher in Brodick, Arran, 1840. [BOA231]

FLEMING, DONALD, a merchant in Campbeltown, testament, 20 October 1798, Comm. Argyll. [NRS]

FLEMING, PETER, a slater, was admitted as a burgess and guildsbrother of Dunbarton on 17 September 1804. [DBR]

FLETCHER, ALEXANDER, a butcher was admitted as a burgess of Dunbarton on 15 June 1833. [DBR]

FLETCHER, ANGUS, born 1786, schoolmaster of Dunoon, died 8 August 1852. [Dunoon gravestone]

FLETCHER, DONALD, a grocer, was admitted as a burgess and guildsbrother of Dunbarton on 20 September 1813. [DBR]

FLETCHER, DUNCAN, a spirit dealer, was admitted as a burgess of Dunbarton on 3 May 1838. [DBR]

FLETCHER, JOHN, a butcher, was admitted as a burgess of Inveraray on 29 September 1806. [IBR]

FLETCHER, ROBERT, born 1798, son of Angus Fletcher schoolmaster in Dunoon, died on 28 October 1824 on Diamond Estate, St Lucia. [Scotsman]

FOGO, ROBERT, a writer, was admitted as a burgess of Inveraray on 22 September 1814. [IBR]

FORBES, Lieutenant ARTHUR, of the Argyll Militia, admitted as a burgess of Inveraray on 10 June 1803. [IBR]

FORREST, ALEXANDER, an innkeeper in Castle Road, was admitted as a burgess and guildsbrother of Dunbarton on 22 June 1825, as married to a daughter of a burgess. [DBR]

FORREST, ARCHIBALD, a shoemaker, was admitted as a burgess of Dunbarton on 24 September 1818 having served his apprenticeship under a burgess. [DBR]

FRAIL, PETER, a wright, was admitted as a burgess of Dunbarton on 25 September 1829. [DBR]

FRASER, ALEXANDER, minister of Kilmally, died 1 November 1812, inventory, 11 July 1814. [NRS.CC2.5.11]

FRASER, or FERGUSON, BARBARA, born 1814 at the Mull of Kintyre, a house cleaner, was accused of theft in 1849. [NRS.AD14.49.406]

FRASER, COLIN ALEXANDER, born 11 December 1833 in Ardchattan, son of Reverend Hugh Fraser and his wife Maria Campbell, a Legislature Assemblyman in New South Wales, Australia. [F.4.83]

FRASER, DUNCAN ALEXANDER, born 27 December 1831 in Ardchattan, son of Reverend Hugh Fraser and his wife Maria Campbell, Surgeon General of Malta, died 28 August 1912. [F.4.83]

FRASER, HUGH, born 1780 in Croy, Inverness-shire, son of Alexander Fraser, was educated at the universities of Aberdeen and of Edinburgh, minister at Oban Chapel in 1807, at Kilmore in 1809, and at Ardchattan from 18 October 1817 until 1843 when he became a Free Church minister there until 1851. He died in Edinburgh on 6 October 1865. [F.4.83]

FRASER, JOHN, a cloth merchant, was admitted as a burgess and guildsbrother of Dunbarton on 12 January 1828. [DBR]

FRASER, JOHN, a merchant in St John, Antigua, cousin and heir of Elizabeth Mary Gregory in Laurel Green, Helensburgh, Dunbartonshire, who died 16 July 1860. [NRS.S/H]

FRASER, JOHN, born 1753, late of Campbeltown, died 1838, husband of Isobel Clark, born 1757, died 1796, parents of Donald Fraser a merchant in Quebec by 1845. [Petty, Old, gravestone]

FRASER, WILLIAM, a clothier at Ascog Mill, Kingarth, testament, 17 August 1797, Comm. Isles. [NRS]

FRASER, WILLIAM, [I], born 9 July 1753, son of William Fraser of Downie, educated at Aberdeen University, minister at Kintra in 1787, at Gigha from 1791 to 1802, at Kilchrenan from 1802 until his death on 28 April 1829. [F.4.92]

FRASER, WILLIAM, [II], born 11 January 1801, son of the above, educated at the University of Glasgow, minister of Kilchrenan from 1827 until 1843, joined the Free Church, minister of the Kilbrandon Free Church, from 1843 until 1852, emigrated to Australia, minister of Bulla Presbyterian Church near Melbourne, Victoria, died 7 December 1872. [F.4.93]

FRASER, WILLIAM WILBERFORCE, born 24 August 1830 in Ardchattan, son of Reverend Hugh Fraser and his wife Maria Campbell, died in Australia in 1918. [F.4.83]

FREELAND, WILLIAM, an innkeeper, was admitted as a burgess and guildsbrother of Dunbarton on 12 March 1801. [DBR]

FULLARTON, ALEXANDER, and family, from South Blairmore, Arran, settled in Inverness Township, Lower Canada, in 1831. [TNA.CO384.28.fos.24-26]

FULLARTON, ARCHIBALD, an able seaman in Campbeltown in May 1795. [NRS.HCR.212]

FULLARTON, ARCHIBALD, and family, from Brodick, Arran, settled in Inverness Township, Lower Canada, in 1831. [TNA.CO384.28.fos.24-26]

FULLARTON, ELIZABETH RAE, daughter of Lewis Fullarton of Kilmichael, Arran, versus John Goldie a Lieutenant of the Royal Navy, residing in Kilmarnock, Ayrshire, a process of divorce, 1817. [NRS.CC8.6.1660]

FULLARTON, FERGUS, a tailor in Lamlash, Arran, 1840. [BOA231]

FULLARTON, JAMES, a sailor in Charleston, South Carolina, son of William Fullarton a sailor burgess of Rothesay, Bute, in 1801. [NRS.CS17.1.9/252]

FULLARTON, JAMES, a tenant in Corrie, Arran, with his family of seven, emigrated on the Albion to Quebec in 1829, settled in Inverness township. [TNA.CO384.22.fo.3-5][AMC]

FULLARTON, JAMES, a carpenter in Lamlash, Arran, 1840. [BOA230]

FULLARTON, JOHN, of Kilmichael in the parish of Kilbride, Arran, a tack, 1810. [NRS.NRAS.2177, bundle 2083]

FULLARTON, JOHN, postmaster at Lamlash, Arran, 1840. [BOA230]

FULLARTON, NEIL, a grocer in Brodick, Arran, 1840. [BOA230]

GALBRAITH, ALEXANDER, son of John Galbraith a tenant in Cuilnasharmaig, South Argyll, was accused of murder in 1826, he failed to turn up at his trial in Inveraray in 1826. [NRS.AD14.26.334; JC26.1826.202]

GALBREATH, DUGALD, a tenant in New Ulva, North Knapdale, was tried for assault but found not guilty in 1821. [NRS.JC13.50]

GALBREATH, DUNCAN, born 1823, tenant of Fernoch, North Knapdale, was accused of assault in 1821. [NRS.AD14.21.152]

GALBRAITH, ELIZABETH, married John Turner from Savannah, Georgia, in Luss, Dunbartonshire, on 17 August 1821. [EA.6025.127]

GALBREATH, JAMES, a miller, was admitted as a burgess of Dunbarton, on 19 Septembr 1839, as son of a burgess. [DBR]

GALBREATH, JOHN, [1], an able seaman in Campbeltown in May 1795. [NRS.HCR.212]

GALBREATH, JOHN, [2], an able seaman in Campbeltown in in May 1795. [NRS.HCR.212]

GALBRAITH, JOHN, a miller at Dunbarton Mill, was admitted as a burgess of Dunbarton on 19 February 1836, asson of a burgess. [DBR]

GALBRAITH, WILLIAM, a miller at Dunbarton Mill, was admitted as a burgess and guildsbrother of Dunbarton on 19 November 1821. [DBR]

GALBRAITH, WILLIAM, jr., a miller, was admitted as a burgess of Dunbarton on 19 September 1839. As son of a burgess. [DBR]

GARDNER, ALEXANDER, a weaver, was admitted as a burgess and guildsbrother of Dunbarton on 25 September 1818, having served his appenticeship under a burgess. [DBR]

GARDNER, Mrs ANN, in Inveraray versus Duncan Milloy, master of the Lark of Inveraray, 1809. [NRS.AC20.2.50]

GARDNER, JAMES, a tailor, was admitted as a burgess of Dunbarton on 17 September 1799, by right of his father James Gardner a shoemaker burgess. [DBR]

GARDNER, WILLIAM, a wheelwright, was admitted as a burgess and guilds-brother of Dunbarton on 10 October 1808. [DBR]

GARROW, WILLIAM, a mason, was admitted as a burgess and guilds-brother of Dunbarton on 18 April 1808. [DBR]

GAY, JOHN, a cooper, was admitted as a burgess and guilds-brother of Dunbarton on 26 April 1793. [DBR]

GEMMILL, ELLEN, born 1832, died 1850, daughter of John Gemmill, of the British Army, in Berryburn Cottage, Dunoon. [Dunoon gravestone]

GIBSON, JAMES, eldest son of Major James Gibson of the Dunbarton Fencibles, and grandson of James Gibson a surgeon in Edinburgh, died in Berbice on 7 November 1807. [Scots Magazine.70.398]

GIBSON, ROBERT, a brewer, was admitted as a burgess and guilds-brother of Dunbarton on 30 March 1791. [DBR]

GILFILLAN, JAMES, a tenant in Barr, was admitted as a burgess and guilds-brother of Dunbarton on 12 March 1801. [DBR]

GILLESPIE, JOHN, born 1797 in Arrochar, son of Reverend John Gillespie [1739-1816] and his wife Bethia Erskine, [1764-1842], a merchant on St Vincent, died 24 September 1833. [Arrochar gravestone] [F.3.326]

GILMOUR, THOMAS, a mason, was admitted as a burgess and guilds-brother of Dunbarton on 13 May 1794. [DBR]

GLEN, ALEXANDER, a plumber, was admitted as a burgess and guilds-brother of Dunbarton on 27 April 1835. [DBR]

GLEN, ARCHIBALD, a wright, was admitted as a burgess of Dunbarton on 25 September 1829, as son of a burgess. [DBR]

GLEN, ARCHIBALD, a cowfeeder, was admitted as a burgess of Dunbarton on 4 August 1843, as son of a burgess. [DBR]

GLEN, JAMES, sr., a weaver, was admitted as a burgess of Dunbarton on 27 September 1805, as son of a burgess. [DBR]

GLEN, JAMES, jr., a weaver, was admitted as a burgess of Dunbarton on 27 September 1805, as son of a burgess. [DBR]

GLEN, JAMES, a seaman in Washington, USA, son and heir of Elizabeth Weir, wife of Walter Glen a spirit dealer in Bonhill. Dunbartonshire, who died on 15 September 1848; also, heir to his uncle James Weir a mason in Bonhill, who died 13 September 1857. [NRS.S/H]

GLEN, JOHN, a shoemaker, was admitted as a burgess and guilds-brother of Dunbarton on 20 September 1810. [DBR]

GLEN, JOHN, a farmer in Ross, parish of Luss, was admitted as a burgess and guilds-brother of Dunbarton on 2 June 1828. [DBR]

GLEN, JOHN, a tailor, was admitted as a burgess of Dunbarton on 12 June 1834 as son of a burgess. [DBR]

GLEN, JOHN, an engraver in Alexandria, Dunbartonshire, died 24 July 1852, father of John Francis Gardner Glen in Port Elizabeth, Cape of Good Hope, South Africa. [NRS.S/H]

GLEN, ROBERT, in Townend, was admitted as a burgess and guilds-brother of Dunbarton on 20 March 1819 as son of a burgess. [DBR]

GLEN, ROBERT, a butcher and spirit dealer, was admitted as a burgess and guilds-brother of Dunbarton on 2 June 1828 by right of his father a burgess. [DBR]

GLEN, WALTER, a carter, was admitted as a burgess of Dunbarton on 13 December 1838. [DBR]

GOLDIE, JAMES, a mason at West Bridgend, was admitted as a burgess of Dunbarton on 21 July 1843 as married to the daughter of a burgess. [DBR]

GORDON, CATHERINE, second daughter of Alexander Gordon in Campbeltown, married Walter Irvine from Tobago, in Deebank in August 1797. [EEC.12369]

GORDON, JAMES, Excise officer at Campbeltown, died 16 February 1811, inventory, 17 February 1812. [NRS.CC2.5.11]

GORDON, Mrs PETER, from Arran, with her family of two, emigrated on board the Albion bound for Quebec in 1829, settled in Inverness township. [AMC]

GOURLAY, PETER, in Kirkcudbright, later in Lochgilphead, Argyll, sister of Samuel Gourlay in Jamaica, 1851. [NRS.S/H]

GOVAN, JAMES, a shoemaker, was admitted as a burgess and guilds-brother of Dunbarton on 5 May 1823 as son of Robert Govan a carter burgess. [DBR]

GOVAN, JAMES, a mason, was admitted as a burgess of Dunbarton on 25 September 1829. [DBR]

GOVAN, ROBERT, a carter, was admitted as a burgess of Dunbarton on 19 November 1821 as son of a burgess. [DBR]

GOVAN, WALTER, a tailor, was admitted as a burgess of Dunbarton on 20 September 1803. [DBR]

GRAHAM, ALEXANDER, an able seaman in Campbeltown in May 1795. [NRS.HCR.212]

GRAHAME, ARCHIBALD, a writer in Glasgow, was admitted as a burgess and guilds-brother of Dunbarton on 3 December 1828. [DBR]

GRAHAME, DUNCAN, a crofter in Ashfield, North Knapdale, in 1819, accused of an assault. [NRS.AD14.19.28]

GRAHAM, Colonel HUMPHREY, Provost of Campbeltown, was admitted as a burgess and guilds-brother of Ayr on 7 July 1790. [ABR]; in Inveraray, a letter, 23 May 1801. [NRS.NRAS]; letters, 1807. [NRS.NRAS.1209.744]

GRANT, DAVID, a merchant in Lochgilphead, was accused of assault in 1818. [NRS.AD14.18.252]

GRANT, JOHN, a distiller in Campbeltown, 1845. [NRS.NRAS.1209.1941]

GRANT, JOSEPH, was admitted as a burgess of Dunbarton on 25 July 1792. [DBR]

GRANT, LEWIS, of the Argyll Militia, stationed in Campbeltown, was appointed as a constable of the Justice of the Peace Court on 4 September 1815. [NRS.JP36.6.3]

GRANT, WILLIAM, an innkeeper, was admitted as a burgess and guilds-brother of Dunbarton on 21 June 1793. [DBR]

GRANT, WILLIAM, born 11 June 1812, minister at Kilmodan from 1843 until 1851. [F.4.32]

GRAY, JOHN, a merchant, was admitted as a burgess and guilds-brother of Dunbarton on 14 July 1831. [DBR]

GRAY, WILLIAM, a merchant, was admitted as a burgess of Dunbarton on 19 February 1841. [DBR]

GREENLEES, JAMES, in Campbeltown, a letter, 1818. [NRS.NRAS.1209.1936]

GREENLEES, JANE, eldest daughter of the late William Greenlees a farmer at Ardnacross, Argyll, married James Wyllie, of Toledo, USA, second son of Alexander Wyllie, a distiller in Campbeltown, on 18 December 1852 in Haarlem, Winnegago County, Illinois. [W.XIII.1301]

GREENLEES, MATTHEW, in Campbeltown, 1795, [NRS.NRAS.1209.1931]; a merchant in Campbeltown, 1835. [NRS.NRAS.1209.1941]

GREGORSON, ANGUS, tenant of Ardtorinish farm, Argyll, in 1795. [SHS.ns.1.184]

GREY, ROBERT, a teacher in Brodick, Arran, 1840. [BOA231]

GRIEVE, ROBERT, a writer, was admitted as a burgess of Dunbarton on 25 January 1830. [DBR]

GUTHRIE, ALEXANDER, a baker, was admitted as a burgess of Inveraray on 14 December 1844. [IBR]

HALL, CHARLES, a rope maker, was admitted as a burgess and guildsbrother of Dunbarton on 21 May 1803. [DBR]

HALL, THOMAS, sr., in Inveraray, testament, 24 February 1801. [NRS.CC2.3.12]

HALLY, ROBERT, a slater, was admitted as a burgess of Inveraray on 12 November 1813. [IBR]

HAMILTON, Mrs ELISABETH, born 1773, died 24 May 1847. [Rothesay gravestone, Bute]

HAMILTON, JAMES, born on Arran, a mariner who was naturalised in South Carolina on 24 July 1797. [NARA.M1183.1]

HAMILTON, JAMES, the Commander of the Revenue Cutter Prince William Henry, in Lamlash, Arran, died in Kilbride on 25 April 1812, an edict of executry, 1812. [NRS.CC12.7.41.9]

HAMILTON, JAMES, a tailor in Brodick, Arran, 1840. [BOA231]

HAMILTON, JOHN, born 1757, died 25 August 1843. [Dunoon gravestone]

HAMILTON, JOHN, a merchant, was admitted as a burgess and guildsbrother of Dunbarton on 5 June 1808. [DBR]

HAMILTON, JOHN, in Runahorine, a debtor to James McMillan a shoemaker in Killowcraw, 20 March 1811. [NRS.JP36.5.56]

HAMILTON, JOHN, in Ardrissaig Point, South Knapdale, was victim of an assault in 1835. [NRS.AD14.35.165]

HAMILTON, JOHN, a vintner in Brodick, Arran, 1840. [BOA231]

HAMILTON, PETER, a merchant, was admitted as a burgess and guildsbrother of Dunbarton on 29 January 1803. [DBR]

HAMILTON, PETER, from Monyguil, Arran, settled in Inverness township, Megantic County, Quebec, in 1831. [TNA.CO384.28.24-26]

HAMILTON, ROBERT, tidewaiter in Tarbert, testament, 23 July 1801. [NRS.CC2.3.13]

HAMILTON, THOMAS, a seaman in Mossend, Arran, crewman on the Customs cutter Prince William Henry, testament, 6 April 1796, Comm. Argyll. [NRS]

HAMILTON, WILLIAM H., born 1813, died 26 October 1836, husband of Agnes Robertson. [Rothesay gravestone, Bute]

HAMILTON, WILLIAM, from Cloined, Arran, settled in Inverness township, Megantic County, Quebec, in 1831. [TNA.CO384.28.24-26]

HAMILTON, WILLIAM, from Glenloig, Arran, settled in Inverness township, Megantic County, Quebec, in 1831. [TNA.CO384.28.24-26]

HAMILTON, WILLIAM, a vintner in Currie, Arran, 1840. [BOA231]

HAMILTON, WILLIAM, a mason in Currie, Arran, 1840. [BOA231]

HAMMAN, WILLIAM, a labourer, was admitted as a burgess of Dunbarton on 7 April 1830. [DBR]

HANNAH, JAMES, a jeweller, was admitted as a burgess and guildsbrother of Dunbarton on 9 June 1815. [DBR]

HARKNESS, Captain JAMES, born 1829, son of Gregor Harkness MD, son of Dr Gregor Harkness, died in Galveston, Texas on 17 August 1872. [Kilmun gravestone]

HARKNESS, THOMAS, in Garrachoran, a Justice of the Peace for Argyll, born 1790, died 3 March 1855, spouse Jean Currie. [Kilmun gravestone]

HARKNESS, THOMAS, of Ballimore, a wool and timber merchant in Garrochan, Cowal, in 1820. [NRS.CS96.3381]

HARRIS, JAMES, a draper, was admitted as a burgess of Dunbarton on 1 February 1836. [DBR]

HART, Sir WILLIAM, was admitted as a burgess of Inveraray on 29 September 1802. [IBR]

HARTLEY, BENJAMIN, a grocer, was admitted as a burgess and guildsbrother of Dunbarton on 1 August 1809. [DBR]

HARTLEY, JOHN, a glassmaker, was admitted as a burgess and guildsbrother of Dunbarton on 18 October 1808. [DBR]

HARVIE, ARCHIBALD, an able seaman in Campbeltown in May 1795. [NRS.HCR.212]

HARVEY, EDWARD, from Campbeltown, was admitted as a member of the Scots Charitable Society of Boston in 1819. [NEHGS/SCS]

HARVEY, ROBERT, a surgeon, plans, 1828. [NRS.NRAS.1209.1966]

HARVEY, WILLIAM, lighthouse-keeper at the Mull of Kintyre, testament, 28 December 1804. Comm. Argyll. [NRS]; edict of executry, 1804. [NRS.CC2.8.108.17]

HATLY, JAMES, born 1805, an employee of the Dunbarton Glassworks, was accused of the murder of Alexander McFarlane in 1824. [NRS.AD14.24.201]

HAWIE, JOHN, an able seaman in Campbeltown in May 1795. [NRS.HCR.212]

HEGGIE, ANDREW, a heritable proprietor, was admitted as a burgess of Dunbarton on 4 June 1834 [DBR]

HENDERSON, DUNCAN, a grocer, was admitted as a burgess of Inveraray in 1842. [IBR]

HENDERSON, DUNCAN, a grocer and spirit dealer, was admitted as a burgess of Dunbarton on 1 December 1843 by right of his father a burgess. [DBR]

HENDERSON, HUGH, born 1731 in Argyll, died on 26 June 1834 near St Andrews, New Brunswick, on 26 June 1834. [New Brunswick Courier, 12 July 1834]

HENDERSON, JAMES, a shipowner in Glasgow, was admitted as a burgess of Dunbarton on 26 September 1834 as married to the daughter of a burgess. [DBR]

HENDERSON, JOHN, a mason, was admitted as a burgess of Dunbarton on 25 September 1829. [DBR]

HENDERSON, JOHN, a dyer and spirit dealer, was admitted as a burgess of Dunbarton on 10 May 1830. [DBR]

HENDERSON, WILLIAM, born 1800, died 15 June 1864, his daughter Agnes Henderson, born 1831, died 12 November 1845. [Dunoon gravestone]

HENDRIE, DANIEL, born 17 June 1835 in Dunbartonshire, emigrated to America in 1851, a merchant in Philadelphia, Pennsylvania, died there on 13 December 1892. [AP]

HENDRY, DONALD, a farmer in Allgolach, Kilmory, Arran, testament, 12 May 1796, Comm. Isles. [NRS]

HENDRY, DONALD, a Congregationalist preacher from Arran, emigrated to Lower Canada in April 1831, [TNA.CO384.28.341/2]; settled in Inverness Township, Lower Canada, in 1831. [TNA.CO384.28.fos.24-26]

HENDRY, DONALD, and family of two, from Corrygills, Arran, emigrated to Lower Canada in April 1831. [TNA.CO384.28.341/2]; settled in Inverness Township, Lower Canada, in 1831. [TNA.CO384.28.fos.24-26][died 1847] [AMC]

HENDRY, WILLIAM, from Arran, emigrated via Lamlash, Arran, on board the Caledonia bound for Quebec, landed there on 25 June 1829, settled in Inverness township. [AMC]

HENDRY, WILLIAM, from Penrioch, Arran, settled in Quebec by 1834. [NLS.Acc.9479]

HENNEY, JOSEPH, an innkeeper, was admitted as a burgess and guildsbrother of Dunbarton on 25 May 1808. [DBR]

HENRY, EDWARD, an able seaman in Campbeltown in May 1795. [NRS.HCR.212]

HILL, WILLIAM, a smith in Tarbert, a debtor of William Caldwell at Lochwinnoch, 5 November 1810. [NRS.JP36.5.55]

HISLOP, DUGALD, the Customs surveyor in Inveraray, was admitted as a burgess of Inveraray on 29 September 1802. [IBR]; his wife died in Glenaray on 27 November 1825. [SM.97.127]

HODGE, DANIEL, a teacher in Lamlash, Arran, 1840. [BOA231]

HOGG, DAVID, minister of the Associate Congregation in Rothesay, testament, 24 July 1800, Comm. Isles. [NRS]

HOPE, WILLIAM, a currier in Campbeltown, a memorandum, 1801. [NRS.NRAS.1209.940]

HOPKINS, CHARLES, an innkeeper, was admitted as a burgess and guilds-brother of Dunbarton on 14 May 1827. [DBR]

HOUSTON, ALEXANDER, of Clerkington, was admitted as a burgess and guilds-brother of Dunbarton on 26 July 1802. [DBR]

HOUSTON, JAMES, a shoemaker, was admitted as a burgess of Dunbarton on 25 September 1816 as son of a burgess. [DBR]

HOUSTON, JOHN, an innkeeper, was admitted as a burgess and guilds-brother of Dunbarton on 18 October 1808. [DBR]

HOWAT, JOHN, an innkeeper, was admitted as a burgess and guilds-brother of Dunbarton on 9 June 1823. [DBR]

HUDSON, WILLIAM, a grocer, was admitted as a burgess and guilds-brother of Dunbarton on 14 August 1812. [DBR]

HUDSON, WILLIAM, a cooper, was admitted as a burgess and guilds-brother of Dunbarton on 8 August 1821, as son of a burgess. [DBR]

HUMPHREYS, Mrs DOROTHEA, widow of Reverend William Humphreys in Antigua, niece and heir of Robert Ferguson of Finnart, 1813. [NRS.S/H]

HUNTER, ARCHIBALD, born 1815, son of Thomas Hunter, [1775-1851], and his wife Elizabeth, died in Barbados in 1839. [Cumbrae gravestone]

HUNTER, DUNCAN, was admitted as a burgess and guilds-brother of Dunbarton on 2 January 1827. [DBR]

HUNTER, JAMES, born 1774 in Dunoon, formerly a partner in Hunter and Company in St John's. Newfoundland, died in Scotland in February 1834. [NFD.Times.30.4.1834]

HUNTER, ROBERT, a smith, was admitted as a burgess and guilds-brother of Dunbarton on 4 September 1824. [DBR]

HUNTER, WILLIAM, born 1752, bosun on the cutter Royal George died in June 1828. [Cumbrae gravestone]

HUTCHESON, JAMES, an innkeeper, was admitted as a burgess and guilds-brother of Dunbarton on 16 May 1822. [DBR]

HUTCHESON, JOHN, shipmaster in Campbeltown, inventory 12 May 1814. [NRS.CC2.5.11]

HUTCHESON, JOHN, a shoemaker, was admitted as a burgess of Dunbarton on 19 February 1836, by right of his father a burgess. [DBR]

HUTCHISON, MATTHEW, in America, brother and heir of Isabella Hutchison, widow of Archibald Black a cooper in Rothesay, Bute, 1839. [NRS.S/H]

HUTCHISON, ROBERT, a shoemaker, was admitted as a burgess and guilds-brother of Dunbarton on 5 June 1808, by right of his father Robert Hutchison a shoemaker burgess. [DBR]

HUTCHISON, WILLIAM, died June 1832, wife Sarah Baird born 1786, died 4 January 1877, [Rothesay gravestone, Bute]

HUTTON, JAMES, a sawyer and spirit dealer, was admitted as a burgess of Dunbarton on 29 October 1833. [DBR]

HYNDMAN, DANIEL, born 1742 in Rothesay, Bute, educated at Glasgow University, minister at South Knapdale from 23 April 1771 until his death on 11 February 1805. [F.4.18]

HYNDMAN, GEORGE, an able seaman in Campbeltown in June 1795. [NRS.HCR.213]

INGRAM, ARCHIBALD, son of Archibald Ingram of Cloberhill, East Kilpatrick, Dunbartonshire, [1699-1770], a merchant in St Kitts before 1769. [SRA]

INGRAM, JAMES, son of Archibald Ingram of Cloberhill, East Kilpatrick, Dunbartonshire, [1699-1770], a merchant in Glasgow later in Virginia. [SRA]

INGRAM, WILLIAM FORBES, a writer, was admitted as a burgess of Inveraray on 4 November 1840. [IBR]

INNES, DANIEL, born in Argyll, a mariner who was naturalised in South Carolina on 10 August 1797. [NARA.M1183.1]

INNES, DUNCAN, a sawyer in Brodick, Arran, was accused of assault in 1845. [NRS.AD14.45.247]

IRELAND, HENRY, sr., slater in Campbeltown, died 28 July 1814, inventory, 27 May 1815. [NRS.CC2.5.11]

IRONS, GEORGE, from Old Kilpatrick, Dunbartonshire, applied to settle in Canada on 3 March 1815. [NRS.RH9]

IRVING, ALEXANDER, a carrier, was admitted as a burgess of Dunbarton on 2 June 1846. [DBR]

IVOR, JOHN, born 1759, a wright in Dunoon, died 1826, husband of Isabella McArthur, born 1757, died 1829, parents of Alexander [1794-1866], Peter [1800-1821], Ann [1807-1833]. [Dunoon gravestone]

IRVINE, ALEXANDER, was admitted as a burgess of Inveraray on 15 October 1841. [IBR]

IRVINE, ALEXANDER, late from Australia, died in Ascog House, Bute, on 4 January 1856. [AJ.5636]

JACK, JOHN, a stocking maker, was admitted as a burgess and guilds-brother of Dunbarton on 22 July 1818. [DBR]

JAFFRAY, WILLIAM, minister of Dunbarton, was admitted as a burgess and guilds-brother of Dunbarton on 4 October 1823 as married to the daughter of a burgess. [DBR]

JAMIESON, JOHN, a wright, was admitted as a burgess and guilds-brother of Dunbarton on 22 November 1813. [DBR]

JAMIESON, ROBERT, a wright, was admitted as a burgess and guilds-brother of Dunbarton on 25 April 1790. [DBR]

JAMIESON, ROBERT, an innkeeper in Brodick, Arran, 1840. [BOA231]

JARDINE, ANDREW, a sawyer, was admitted as a burgess and guilds-brother of Dunbarton on 6 October 1819 by right of his fathe James Jardine at Gooseholm. [DBR]

JARDINE, DANIEL, a grocer and spirit dealer, was admitted as a burgess and guilds-brother of Dunbarton on 10 December 1817. [DBR]

JARDINE, JAMES, at Gooseholm, was admitted as a burgess and guilds-brother of Dunbarton on 29 January 1803. [DBR]

JARDINE, ROBERT, a butcher, was admitted as a burgess and guilds-brother of Dunbarton on 8 August 1821 by right of his father a burgess. [DBR]

JOHNSON, DUNCAN, [1761-1826], a farmer at Gariob, Knapdale, father of Archibald Johnson, settled at Mount Muirhead, Australia. [Kilmichael, Inverlussa, gravestone]

JOHNSTON, CATHERINE, in Tarbert, a debtor of William Caldwell at Lochwinnoch, 5 November 1810. [NRS.JP36.5.55]

JOHNSTON, JAMES, cottar in Drumalea, Kintyre, was accused of looting a wrecked vessel in 1817. [NRS.AD14.17.86]

JOHNSTON, JOHN, a shipmaster in Rothesay, Bute, husband of Ann Cunningham, 1789. [NRS.S/H]

JOHNSTONE, WILLIAM, a merchant, was admitted as a burgess and guilds-brother of Dunbarton on 21 June 1825. [DBR]

JONES, RICHARD, a blacksmith in Lamlash, Arran, 1840. [BOA231]

KEITH, PETER, an able seaman in Campbeltown in May 1795. [NRS.HCR.212]

KELLY, JOHN, an able seaman in Campbeltown in May 1795. [NRS.HCR.212]

KELLY, JOHN, sr., tenant in Darlochan, Kintyre, was accused of looting a wrecked vessel in 1816. [NRS.AD4.16.62]

KELLY, JOHN, jr., tenant in Darlochan, Kintyre, was accused of looting a wrecked vessel in 1816. [NRS.AD4.16.62]

KELLY, JOHN, a merchant, petitioned for a tenement to be used as a Masonic Lodge in 1832. [NRS.NRAS.1209.1977]

KELLY, PETER, son of John Kelly a tenant farmer in Darlochan, Kintyre, was accused of looting a wrecked vessel in 1816. [NRS.AD4.16.62]

KELSO, ALEXANDER, with a family of eight persons, in North Sannox, Arran, bound via Lamlash, Arran, aboard the brigantine *Caledonia* for Canada, 1829, landed in Quebec on 25 June 1829, settled in Inverness township. [TNA.CO384.22.3-5] [AMC]

KELSO, ARCHIBALD, with a family of eight persons, in Glen, Arran, bound for Canada, 1829. [TNA.CO384.22.3-5]

KELSO, or MCKILLOP, CATHERINE, with a family of four persons, from Corrie, Arran, bound for Canada, 1829. [TNA.CO384.22.3-5]

KELSO, JOHN, and family of five, from Corrie, Arran, settled in Inverness township, Megantic County, Quebec, in 1831. [TNA.CO384.28.24-26] [AMC]

KELSO, or MCMILLAN, MARGARET, with a family of three persons, from Loggantwine, Arran, bound for Canada, 1829. [TNA.CO384.22.3-5]

KELSO, ROBERT, with a family of eight persons, from Loggantwine, Arran, bound via Lamlash, Arran, aboard the brigantine Caledonia for Canada, 1829, landed in Quebec on 25 June 1829, settled in Inverness township. [TNA.CO384.22.3-5]

KELSO, WILLIAM, with a family of seven persons, from Mid Sannox, Arran, bound via Lamlash, Arran, aboard the brigantine Caledonia for Canada, 1829, landed in Quebec on 25 June 1829, settled in Inverness township. [TNA.CO384.22.3-5] [AMC]

KENNEDY, J. F., of Denure, was admitted as a burgess of Inveraray on 2 January 1818. [IBR]

KENNEDY, NIALL, a sailor in Cumbrae around 1796. [Cumbrae gravestone]

KERR, DONALD, and family from Nanachar, Arran, emigrated to Lower Canada in April 1831, [TNA.CO384.28.341/2]; settled in Inverness Township, Upper Canada, in 1831. [TNA.CO384.28.fos.24-26]

KERR, ALEXANDER, tacksman of Catacol, Kilmory, Arran, versus Finlay Kerr in Catacol, a summons, 2 December 1802. [NRS.CC12.2.13.5]

KERR, DUNCAN, at Tarbert, testament, 2 June 1800. [NRS.CC2.3.12]

KERR, HUGH, and family of ten, from Urinbeg, Arran, settled in Inverness Township, Lower Canada, in 1831. [AMC] [TNA.CO384.28.fos.24-26]

KERR, JOHN, and family of two, from Urinbeg, Arran, emigrated to Lower Canada in April 1831, [TNA.CO384.28.341/2]; settled in Inverness Township, Lower Canada, in 1831. [TNA.CO384.28.fos.24-26][AMC]

KERR, JOHN, a joiner and carpenter in Lamlash, Arran, 1840. [BOA230]

KERR, ROBERT, son of Robert Kerr in Campbeltown, a student at Marischal College, Aberdeen, in 1837. [MCA]

KINLOCH, CHRISTINA, born 1842, daughter of John Kinloch and his wife Ann David, died in Patterson, New Jersey, on 17 February 1881. [Alexandria gravestone, Dunbartonshire]

KINNINMONT, WILLIAM, a miller in Albion, Orleans County, New York, grandson and heir to William Kinninmont in Rothesay, Bute, who died 9 November 1856. [NRS.S/H]

KIRKWOOD, ROBERT, born 1804, from Kirkintilloch, Dunbartonshire, died in Montreal, Quebec, on 15 May 1840. [GA.5621]

KNOX, WALTER, born 1771 in Kilpatrick, Dunbartonshire, died in South Carolina on 9 June1838. [Old Scots gravestone, Charleston]

LAIDLER, ROBERT, a tailor, was admitted as a burgess of Dunbarton on 23 September 1818. [DBR]

LAING, JAMES, Adjutant of the Argyll Militia, was admitted as a burgess of Inveraray on 10 June 1803. [IBR]

LAING, ROBERT, born 1766, a shipmaster, died 29 July 1822. [Dunbarton gravestone]

LAING, ROBERT, a mason, was admitted as a burgess of Dunbarton on 19 September 1804. [DBR]

LAING, ROBERT, a merchant, was admitted as a burgess and guildsbrother of Dunbarton on 23 September 1825 as son of a burgess. [DBR]

LAIRD, WILLIAM, a butcher, was admitted as a burgess and guildsbrother of Dunbarton on 6 August 1795. [DBR]

LAMBIE, JOHN, a mason, was admitted as a burgess of Dunbarton on 23 April 1830. [DBR]

LAMBIE, WILLIAM, born 28 December 1758 in Kilmas in Argyll, son of Reverend Archibald Lambie and his wife Catherine McLachlan, was educated at the University of Glasgow around 1771, died in Jamaica on 29 July 1794. [F.4.14][Car.4.15]

LAMONT, DUGALD, born on 17 March 1762 in Kilfinan, son of Reverend Alexander Lamont and his wife Margaret Campbell, a Captain of the 8th Regiment who was killed at Seringapatam, India, in 1799. [F.4.29]

LAMONT, DUNCAN, in Barinlongart, eldest son of John Lamont tenant there and his wife Margaret McTavish, a petition dated 16 April 1807. [NRS.SC54.6.4.2.8]

LAMONT, HUGH, a workman in Askommelmore, was accused of rioting and attacking a ship loaded with grain attempting to sail from Campbeltown, a petition, 21 March 1801. [NRS.JP36.5.46]

LAMONT, JAMES, in Rothesay, Bute, a letter dated 18 March 1803. [NRS.NRAS.332.C4.432]

LAMONT, JOHN, Lieutenant Colonel of the Argyll Militia, was admitted as a burgess of Inveraray on 11 June 1803. [IBR]

LAMOND, JOHN, born 1782 at Gortansaig, son of James Lamond of Knockdow, emigrated to Trinidad in 1801, a planter at Cedargrove, Trinidad, died in 1850. [Trinidad History Society]

LAMONT, MARGARET, in Dergbrugh, widow of James Campbell of Kaims, testament, 23 November 1795, Comm. Argyll. [NRS]

LAMONT, MARY, born 1820, wife of John MacLean, died 20 August 1864. [Kilchattan gravestone]

LAMONT, MATTHEW, youngest son of James Lamont of Knockdaw, died in Kingston, Jamaica, on 2 April 1825. [BM.18.267]

LAMONT, ROBERT, son of Archibald Lamont tenant in Inverchaolain, emigrated on board the Caledonia on 25 May 1810 bound for New York, died there on 15 January 1820. [Lamont Clan]

LANG, ALEXANDER, a grocer, was admitted as a burgess and guilds-brother of Dunbarton on 15 February 1825 as son of a burgess. [DBR]

LANG, ALEXANDER, ship's joiner, was admitted as a burgess and guilds-brother of Dunbarton on 23 September 1829, as son of William Lang a merchant burgess. [DBR]

LANG, ALEXANDER, a calico printer, was admitted as a burgess of Dunbarton on 3 May 1844, as son of a burgess. [DBR]

LANG, JAMES, jr., in Townend, was admitted as a burgess of Dunbarton on 12 March 1801 as son of James Lang a burgess. [DBR]

LANG, JAMES, a merchant, was admitted as a burgess and guilds-brother of Dunbarton on 21 May 1803. [DBR]

LANG, JAMES, a weaver, was admitted as a burgess of Dunbarton on 25 September 1818, as son of a burgess. [DBR]

LANG, JAMES, master of the SS Leven, was admitted as a burgess and guilds-brother of Dunbarton on 7 August 1828 as son of a burgess. [DBR]

LANG, JAMES, a farmer at Murroch, was admitted as a burgess of Dunbarton on 3 May 1844. [DBR]

LANG, JOHN, a wright, was admitted as a burgess and guilds-brother of Dunbarton on 21 September 1802. [DBR]

LANG, JOHN, a distiller, was admitted as a burgess and guilds-brother of Dunbarton on 23 September 1829 as son of a burgess. [DBR]

LANG, ROBERT, born 1764, a shipmaster in Dunbarton, died on 29 July 1822. [Dunbarton gravestone]

LANG, ROBERT, tenant of Murroch, was admitted as a burgess and guilds-brother of Dunbarton on 25 January 1802. [DBR]

LANG, ROBERT, a shoemaker, was admitted as a burgess of Dunbarton on 25 September 1818, by right of his father a burgess. [DBR]

LANG, ROBERT, jr., a shoemaker, was admitted as a burgess of Dunbarton on 14 July 1831, as son of a burgess. [DBR]

LANG, ROBERT, a blacksmith, was admitted as a burgess of Dunbarton on 6 September 1834 as son of a burgess. [DBR]

LANG, ROBERT, a clerk, was admitted as a burgess of Dunbarton on 7 February 1839 as son of a burgess. [DBR]

LANG, WALTER, a farmer in Townend, was admitted as a burgess of Dunbarton on 18 March 1836 as son of James Lang of Chapelton a burgess. [DBR]

LANG, WILLIAM, a shipmaster, was admitted as a burgess of Dunbarton in 1794. [DBR]

LANG, WILLIAM, jr., a shoemaker, was admitted as a burgess of Dunbarton on 31 January 1821 having served an apprenticeship under a burgess. [DBR]

LANG, WILLIAM, of Cambusmoon, a ship's joiner, was admitted as a burgess and guilds-brother of Dunbarton on 23 September 1829 as son of William Lang a merchant burgess. [DBR]

LANGLANDS, ALEXANDER, a surveyor in Campbeltown, 1793. [NRS.NRAS.1209.534]

LANGLANDS, DONALD, born 1776, son of George Langlands a land surveyor in Campbeltown, died in Trinidad in 1803. [Caledonian Mercury.121866]

LANGLANDS, GEORGE, a land surveyor in Kintyre, erected houses, machinery, and a bleachfield for his eldest son Ralph Langlands in Strathbeg, Campbeltown, a memorandum in 1792. [NRS.NRAS.1209.1943]

LANGLANDS, RALPH, a bleacher in Campbeltown, 1818. [NRS.NRAS.1209.1942]

LANGWILL, ALEXANDER, an able seaman in Campbeltown in June 1795. [NRS.HCR.213]

LATHAM, JOSEPH, late of Furnace in Argyll, a contract, 1804. [NRS.NRAS.1209.44]

LATTA, JOHN, a butcher, was admitted as a burgess and guilds-brother of Dunbarton on 20 September 1813. [DBR]

LATTA, JOHN, a carter, was admitted as a burgess and guilds-brother of Dunbarton on 5 October 1816 as son of a burgess. [DBR]

LATTA, ROBERT, a tailor, was admitted as a burgess and guilds-brother of Dunbarton on 20 September 1803. [DBR]

LATTA, WILLIAM, a shipmaster, was admitted as a burgess of and guilds-brother of Dunbarton on 24 June 1793. [DBR]

LATTA, WILLLAM, a shipmaster, was admitted as a burgess and guilds-brother of Dunbarton on 1 February 1836, by right of his father a burgess. [DBR]

LAVERTON, JAMES, born 1785, served in the 71st Regiment of Foot from 1798 to 1822, died 24 September 1854, husband of Helen Baird, born 1798, died 17 April 1881. [Cumbrae gravestone]

LAUDER, JAMES, a bricklayer, was admitted as a burgess of Dunbarton on 27 September 1792. [DBR]

LAW, MARGARET, in Rothesay, Bute, received a letter requesting information on named people who emigrated from Glengarry to America in 1773-1774, dated 27 September 1859. [NRS.NRAS.4291]

LAWTHER, JOHN, a bricklayer. was admitted as a burgess of Dunbarton on 1 September 1792. [DBR]

LAWTHER, ROBERT, a mason, was admitted as a burgess of Dunbarton on 19 September 1804. [DBR]

LECKIE, JOHN, a wright, was admitted as a burgess and guilds-brother of Dunbarton on 24 September 1818, by right of his father Peter Leckie a carter burgess. [DBR]

LECKIE, WILLIAM, a farmer, was admitted as a burgess and of Dunbarton on 30 November 1837. [DBR]

LEITCH, ANGUS, an assistant Excise officer in Dunmore, Lochgilphead, was accused of fraud in 1815. [NRS.AD14.15.10]

LEITCH, DONALD, a fisherman at Stronchulline, versus John McAlpine, son of Andrew McAlpine at Strondour, 4 March 1823. [NRS.AC20.2.54]

LEITCH, JOHN, a tailor, was admitted as a burgess of Dunbarton on 10 September 1800. [DBR]

LEITCH, MALCOLM, from North Knapdale, emigrated aboard the Mars of Glasgow to Canada in 1818. [TNA.CO384.3]

LEITCH, WILLIAM, born 1814 in Rothesay, Bute, educated at Glasgow University, BA in 1837, MA in 1838, DD in 1860, Principal of Queen's College in Canada from 1859 to 1864, died in Kingston, Upper Canada, on 9 May 1864. [RGU]

LENNOX, DONALD, a grocer, was admitted as a burgess and guilds-brother of Dunbarton on 7 August 1807. [DBR]

LENNOX, JAMES, born 1790, son of Alexander Lennox in Helensburgh, Dunbartonshire, and his wife Helen Wilson, [1765-1821], a surgeon in Jamaica, died 15 September 1814. [Rhu gravestone]

LENNOX, JOHN, a bookseller, was admitted as a burgess and guilds-brother of Dunbarton on 8 March 1825. [DBR]

LENNOX, ROBERT MARTIN, a grocer, was admitted as a burgess of Dunbarton on 10 May 1830 by right of his father a burgess. [DBR]

LENNOX, WALTER, jr., an innkeeper, was admitted as a burgess and guilds-brother of Dunbarton on 12 January 1802. [DBR]

LENNOX, WALTER, a merchant, was admitted as a burgess and guilds-brother of Dunbarton on 3 March 1825 as son of a burgess. [DBR]

LIDDAL, WILLIAM, jr., a cloth merchant, was admitted as a burgess and guilds-brother of Dunbarton on 31 July 1810. [DBR]

LILLIE, THOMAS, a wright in Dunbarton, brother and heir of Alexander Lillie in Jamaica, 1842. [NRS.S/H]

LINDSAY, LAWRENCE, a mariner in Largiemore, Kilbride, Arran, was accused of assault in 1839. [NRS.AD14.39.13]

LINDSAY, PETER, a tailor, was admitted as a burgess of Dunbarton on 20 September 1803. [DBR]

LINDSAY, THOMAS, a wright, was admitted as a burgess and guilds-brother of Dunbarton on 25 September 1829, by right of his father a burgess. [DBR]

LINDSAY, WILLIAM, a wright, at West Bridgend, was admitted as a burgess and guilds-brother of Dunbarton on 6 January 1809. [DBR]

LINDSAY, WILLIAM, an innkeeper, was admitted as a burgess and guilds-brother of Dunbarton on 16 September 1814. [DBR]

LITTLE, JOHN, a spirit dealer, was admitted as a burgess of Dunbarton on 22 April 1842. [DBR]

LIVINGSTONE, ALEXANDER, born 1815 in Argyll, emigrated via Liverpool to New York bound for Charleston, South Carolina, in 1835, settled in Marlboro County, SC, petitioned for naturalisation on 14 October 1850. [SCA]

LIVINGSTONE, ANGUS, a son of John Livingstone in Appin, was apprenticed to Thomas Crawford a shipmaster in Greenock as a sailor for 3 years on 28 April 1790. [NRS.B41.7.9]

LIVINGSTONE, ANGUS, an innkeeper in Inveraray, versus James McNuier, 27 February 1808. [NRS.B32.2.1.44]

LIVINGSTONE, DONALD, in Oban, was appointed Admiral Officer of the Admiralty Court of Argyll 26 December 1818. [NRS.AC20.3.3]

LIVINGSTONE, DOUGALD, a shipmaster in Greenock, was admitted as a burgess of Dunbarton on 4 December 1846. [DBR]

LIVINGSTONE, HUGH, born 1779 in Argyll, a mariner in Charleston, was naturalised in South Carolina on 12 May 1819. [NARA.M1183.1]

LIVINGSTONE, JOHN, jr., a shipmaster, was admitted as a burgess of Dunbarton on 4 December 1846. [DBR]

LIVINGSTONE, MARGARET, born 1774, emigrated via Oban aboard the <u>Spencer of Newcastle</u> bound for Prince Edward Island on 22 September 1806. [PAPEI, 2702]

LIVINGSTONE, WILLIAM, a steamboat master, was admitted as a burgess and guilds-brother of Dunbarton on 4 December 1846. [DBR]

LIVESON, WILLIAM, in West Tarbert, a debtor of William Caldwell at Lochwinnoch, 5 November 1810. [NRS.JP36.5.55]

LOCKHART, JOHN, a butcher, was admitted as a burgess and guilds-brother of Dunbarton on 9 June 1815. [DBR]

LOCKIE, JOHN, son of John Lockie who died in 1835, died in Tuapeka, Otago, New Zealand, on 9 February 1860. [Rothesay gravestone, Bute]

LOGAN, FRANCIS, a tenant in North Sannox, Arran, with his family of six, emigrated to Canada in 1829. [TNA.CO384.22.fo.3-5]

LOGAN, JOHN, born 1746, of the Inland Revenue in Dunoon, died in March 1818. [Dunoon gravestone]

LOTHIAN, JOHN, born 3 May 1842 in Campbeltown, son of James Lothian a minister, emigrated to New Zealand in 1877, died in 1925. [F.4.604]

LOUDOUN, WILLIAM, in Louisiana, heir to his cousin Agnes Loudoun in Helensburgh, Dunbartonshire, who died on 19 September 1847. [NRS.S/H]

LOVE, JAMES, an able seaman in Campbeltown in May 1795. [NRS.HCR.212]

LOVE, JOHN, shipmaster in Campbeltown, died August 1810, inventory 13 February 1812. [NRS.CC2.5.11]

MACADAM, JAMES, born 1769 in Drymen, Dunbartonshire, a merchant, was admitted as a citizen of South Carolina on 25 June 1812. [NARA.M1183.1]

MCADAM, JAMES, a gardener, was admitted as a burgess and guilds-brother of Dunbarton on 24 June 1793. [DBR]

MCADAM, JAMES, at Barr Toll, was admitted as a burgess and guilds-brother of Dunbarton on 1 July 1807. [DBR]

MCADAM, PETER, a wright, was admitted as a burgess and guilds-brother of Dunbarton on 18 June 1825, as his wife was daughter of a burgess. [DBR]

MCALDRIDGE, GILBERT, born 1768, John born 1799, Alexander born 1801, Peter born 1803, and John born 1805, emigrated via Oban aboard the Spencer of Newcastle bound for Prince Edward Island on 22 September 1806. [PAPEI, 2702]

MCALLAN, DOUGALD, from Lochranza, Arran, emigrated to Lower Canada, in April 1831. [TNA.CO384.28.341/2]

MCALLAN, DUGALD, and family, from Lochranza, Arran, settled in Inverness Township, Upper Canada, in 1831. [TNA.CO384.28.fos.24-26]

MCALLISTER, A., of Torresdale Castle, father of Katherine Elizabeth McAllister who married William Rose, son of John Rose, in Montreal, Quebec, on 2 January1868. [GM.NS3/5.385]

MCALLISTER, ALEXANDER, with his family of ten, from Campbeltown, emigrated via Greenock on board the Portaferry bound for Quebec in May 1832. [QM.13.6.1832]

MCALLISTER, ALEXANDER, a merchant and late baillie of Paisley, was admitted as a burgess and guilds-brother of Dunbarton on 3 March 1809. [DBR]

MCALISTER, ALEXANDER, of Loup, papers re Tangy Mill dated 1830. [NRS.NRAS.1209.1854]

MCALESTER, CHARLES, born 5 April 1765 in Campbeltown,a shipmaster and merchant in Philadelphia, Pennsylvania, died in Willow Grove, Montgomery County, Philadelphia, on 29 August 1832. [AP.254]

MACALISTER, DONALD, born 16 February 1790, son of Alexander MacAlister of Strathaird and his wife Janet McLeod, a Captain of Artillery in Bengal, India, died in 1828. [BA.3.104]

MCALLISTER, DUNCAN, a innkeeper, was admitted as a burgess and guilds-brother of Dunbarton on 9 June 1815. [DBR]

MCALESTER, EFFY, born 1746, emigrated via Oban aboard the Spencer of Newcastle bound for Prince Edward Island on 22 September 1806. [PAPEI, 2702]

MCALLISTER, HECTOR, a merchant in New Providence in the Bahamas, died 22 August 1788, uncle of Hector McAllister in Medlaig, Cowal, testament, 1801, Comm. Edinburgh. [NRS]

MCALESTER, ISABELLA, born 1793, daughter of Charles McAlester born 1765 in Campbeltown died in Philadelphia, Pennsylvania, in 1832, wife of Anthony Slater from Derbyshire, died in Philadelphia on 4 January 1851. [GM.NS36.216]

MCALLISTER, JAMES, a wright, was admitted as a burgess and guilds-brother of Dunbarton on 12 January 1797. [DBR]

MCALLISTER, JAMES, a merchant, was admitted as a burgess and guilds-brother of Dunbarton on 23 September 1825 as son of a burgess. [DBR]

MCALLISTER, JAMES, was admitted as burgess of Dunbarton on 25 September 1829 as son of a burgess, [DBR]

MCALLISTER, JOHN, a wright, was admitted as a burgess and guildsbrother of Dunbarton on 6 March 1795. [DBR]

MCALLISTER, JOHN, a shoemaker, was admitted as a burgess of Dunbarton on 24 September 1795. [DBR]

MCALISTER, JOHN, in Tarbert, a debtor of William Caldwell at Lochwinnoch, 5 November 1810. [NRS.JP36.5.55]

MACALISTER, Colonel MATTHEW, of Rosshill, a petition, 8 January 1810. [NRS.JP36.5.55]

MCALLISTER, PETER, a shopkeeper, was admitted as a burgess and guildsbrother of Dunbarton on 13 June 1800. [DBR]

MCALLISTER, WILLIAM, a writer, was admitted as a burgess and guildsbrother of Dunbarton on 1 February 1836. [DBR]

MCALLUM, ARCHIBALD, possibly from Glendruar, probate, 1800, Cumberland County, North Carolina, [NCSA]

MACALPINE, ANGUS, born 1802, master mariner, drowned at the Calf of Man on 25 September 1843, wife Elizabeth Cleland, born 1817, died 6 July 1895. [Rothesay gravestone, Bute]

MCALPINE, CHARLES, a grocer, was admitted as a burgess and guildsbrother of Dunbarton on 21 July 1818. [DBR]

MCALPINE, DAVID, a tailor, was admitted as a burgess of Dunbarton on 16 September 1795. [DBR]

MCALPINE, DONALD, from North Knapdale, emigrated on board the Mars of Glasgow to Canada in 1818. [TNA.CO384.3]

MCALPINE, DUNCAN, a druggist, was admitted as a burgess and guilds-brother of Dunbarton on 1 July 1807. [DBR]

MCALPINE, PETER, an innkeeper on Castle Road, was admitted as a burgess and guilds-brother of Dunbarton on 20 July 1820. [DBR]

MCALPINE, ROBERT, a sailor and a tailor, was admitted as a burgess and guilds-brother of Dunbarton on 24 September 1818, by right of his father Robert McAlpine a tailor burgess. [DBR]

MCARTHUR, ALEXANDER, a packet-master, was admitted as a burgess of Inveraray on 4 May 1837. [IBR]

MCARTHUR, ANN, widow of Malcolm Fisher, in Inveraray, was evicted by the Duke of Argyll on 1 April 1802. [NRS.B32.2.1.41]

MCARTHUR, CHARLES, a sawyer in Inveraray, was evicted by the Duke of Argyll on 1 April 1802. [NRS.B32.2.1.41]; also on 28 March 1895. [NRS.B32.2.1.42]

MCARTHUR, DANIEL, an able seaman in Campbeltown in May 1795. [NRS.HCR.212]

MCARTHUR, DONALD, son of John McArthur of Ardgavannan, Argyll, died on voyage home from Demerara in July 1800 [NRS.CC2.8.105]; edict of executry, 1801. [NRS.CC2.8.105.1]

MCARTHUR, Ensign DONALD, of the Argyll Militia, was admitted as a burgess of Inveraray on 10 June 1803. [IBR]

MCARTHUR, DONALD, a shoemaker in Lochgoilhead, and family, emigrated to America in 1812, a farmer in Pennsylvania. ['History of Cowal' 1908]

MACARTHUR, DONALD, a fish curer in Inveraray, versus Duncan Milloy master of the Lark of Inveraray 9 August 1816. [NRS.AC20.2.51]

MCARTHUR, DUGALD, a merchant, was admitted as a burgess of Inveraray on 1 May 1846. [IBR]

MCARTHUR, DUNCAN, in Cladyhouse, versus Alexander MacAlpine, a boatman at Lochgilphead, and Duncan MacTavish in Fernoch, 22 July 1800. [NRS.AC20.2.48]

MCARTHUR, DUNCAN, a spirit dealer, was admitted as a burgess of Dunbarton on 22 April 1843. [DBR]

MCARTHUR, JAMES, in West Tarbert, a debtor of William Caldwell at Lochwinnoch, 5 November 1810. [NRS.JP36.5.55]

MCARTHUR, JAMES, a grocer, was admitted as a burgess of Dunbarton on 12 October 1837. [DBR]

MCARTHUR, JAMES, born 15 August 1832 in Bute, son of Reverend John McArthur, was educated at Glasgow University, minister at Kilmodan from 1869 until 1877, later an Episcopalian minister in Victoria and in New South Wales, Australia. [F.4.32]

MCARTHUR, JOHN, a grocer, was admitted as a burgess and guilds-brother of Dunbarton on 9 June 1815. [DBR]

MCARTHUR, JOHN, a fisherman in Culchurilan, versus John Black a fisherman in Inveraray, a petition, 1801. [NRS.AC20.2.48]

MCARTHUR, JOHN, born in Argyll, died in St Croix, Danish West Indies, in 1808. [Edinburgh Advertiser.4700]

MCARTHUR, KATHERINE, daughter of John McArthur a weaver in Dunbarton, spouse of James Gardiner a wheelwright, a sasine, 14 August 1807. [NRS.NRAS.4367.1.11]

MCARTHUR, PETER, of the 60th Regiment of Foot, testament, 17 October 1798, Comm. Argyll. [NRS]

MCARTHUR, PETER, a merchant, was admitted as a burgess of Inveraray on 29 April 1805. [IBR]

MCARTHUR, PETER, miller at Kyllypole Mill, a petition, 1808. [NRS.NRAS.1209.1945]

MCAULAY, ARCHIBALD, a shoemaker, was admitted as a burgess of Dunbarton on 14 July 1831 as son of a burgess. [DBR]

MCAULAY, JOHN, a shoemaker in Renton, was admitted as a burgess and guilds-brother of Dunbarton on 14 March 1800. [DBR]

MCAULAY, WILLIAM, a cooper, was admitted as a burgess and guilds-brother of Dunbarton on 1 July 1807. [DBR]

MCAULAY, WILLIAM, a weaver, was admitted as a burgess and guilds-brother of Dunbarton on 25 September 1818 as son of John McAulay a cooper burgess. [DBR]

MCAUSLAND, DANIEL, a ropemaker, was admitted as a burgess of Dunbarton on 19 January 1833 as husband of the daughter of a burgess. [DBR]

MCAUSLANE, ALEXANDER, a painter. was admitted as a burgess and guilds-brother of Dunbarton on 30 June 1827 as married to the daughter of a burgess. [DBR]

MCAUSLIN, JOHN, born 1761 in Dunbartonshire, died in Wilmington, North Carolina, on 23 February 1836. [Wilmington Advertiser, 26 February 1836]

MCAUSLANE, JOHN, an innkeeper, was admitted as a burgess and guilds-brother of Dunbarton on 24 June 1793. [DBR]

MCAUSLANE, JOHN, an innkeeper, was admitted as a burgess and guilds-brother of Dunbarton on 25 June 1808. [DBR]

MCAUSLANE, JOHN, a weaver and gardener, was admitted as a burgess and guilds-brother of Dunbarton on 24 September 1818 as son of John McAuslane a gardener, burgess and guilds-brother. [DBR]

MACBOAG, JOHN, in Cathadal, Southend, Kintyre, a victim of theft in 1830. [NRS.AD14.30.107]

MCBRADDAN, DONALD, wigmaker in Inveraray, warrant of inventory, 11 March 1806. [NRS.CC2.6]

MCBRIDE, ALEXANDER, parochial schoolmaster at Lochranza, Arran, 1840. [BOA231]

MCBRIDE, ARCHIBALD, born in Campbeltown, 'many years in the Bahamas', died on 5 October 1809. [Bahamas Royal Gazette, 7.10.1809]

MCBRIDE, ARCHIBALD, born in Argyll, settled in Caledon, Peel County, Upper Canada, died in February 1890. [Caledon gravestone]

MCBRIDE, DUGALD, born 1793, a farmer from Auchalaskin, Killean in Kintyre, son of Janet McKinven or McBride, emigrated from Campbeltown on the Monarch bound for Charleston, South Carolina, landed there on 20 November 1820. [NRS.AD14.20.112][NARA]

MCBRIDE, JAMES, born 1809 in Argyll, settled in Caledon, Peel County, Upper Canada, died 13 September 1887; his wife Catherine Campbell, born 1819 in Argyll, died 29 September 1901. [Caledon gravestone]

MCBRIDE, JOHN, a shipmaster in Lamlash, Arran, died in Kilbride, Arran, on 3 March 1813, husband of Mary Adams, an edict of executry in 1813. [NRS.CC12.7.42.2]

MCBRYDE, JOHN, a tailor, was admitted as a burgess and guilds-brother of Dunbarton on 22 October 1817 as married to the daughter of a burgess. [DBR]

MCBRIDE, MALCOLM, born 1791, a farmer from Auchalaskin, Killean in Kintyre, son of Janet McKinven or McBride, emigrated from Campbeltown on the Monarch bound for Charleston, South Carolina, landed there on 20 November 1820. [NRS.AD14.20.112][NARA]

MCBRIDE, MATTHEW, a vintner in Lamlash, Arran, 1840. [BOA231]

MCBRIDE, NEIL, born 1819, son of Alexander McBride [1774-1848], a farmer in Moniemore, and his wife Mary [1782-1867], died in South Hampton, Canada West, on 6 April 1853. [Kilbride gravestone, Arran]

MCBRIDE, NEIL, born in Argyll, settled in Caledon, Peel County, Upper Canada, died in August 1847, his wife Annie McKellar, born in Argyll, died in February 1840. [Caledon gravestone]

MCBRIDE, PETER, of the Free Presbytery of Dunoon and Inveraray, a letter dated 24 April 1844. [NRS.GD112.74.825.27]

MCCALL, JOHN, born 1780 in Argyll, a grocer who was naturalised in Charleston, South Carolina, on 19 September 1780. [NARA.M1183.1]

MACCALLUM, ANN, widow of Archibald McIntyre a shipmaster in Oban, died 27 April 1812, inventory, 30 October 1812. [NRS.CC2.5.11]

MCCALLUM, ARCHIBALD, a surgeon in Campbeltown, a bond, 1803. [NRS.CS271.589]

MCCALLUM, ARCHIBALD, ground officer to Stonefield, a debtor of William Caldwell at Lochwinnoch, 5 November 1810. [NRS.JP36.5.55]

MCCALLUM, ARCHIBALD, a weaver in South Killicraw, Kintyre, was accused of assaulting Revenue Officers in 1817. [NRS.JC26.1817.143]

MCCALLUM, DONALD, master of the Katty of Oban, versus John Livingstone, master of the Molly of Oban, 3 July 1799. [NRS.AC20.2.48]

MCCALLUM, DONALD, a shoemaker, was admitted as a burgess of Inveraray on 29 September 1806. [IBR]

MCCALLUM, DUNCAN, a merchant and dealer in Tarbert, 1816-1819. [NRS.CS96.4116]

MCCALLUM, DUNCAN, a merchant, was admitted as a burgess of Inveraray on 11 November 1818. [IBR]

MCCALLUM, DUNCAN, a shoemaker, was admitted as a burgess of Inveraray on 22 December 1840. [IBR]

MCCALLUM, HUGH, born 1814, a shepherd, with his wife born 1818, from Kilmorie, Ardnamurchan, bound for South Australia in 1848. [BPP.11.164]

MCCALLUM, JAMES, in Clachbreck, South Knapdale, deceased, an edict of curator re his children – Christian, Janet, and Duncan McCallum, dated 8 October 1814. [NRS.SC54.6.4.3.6]

MCCALLUM, JAMES, a butcher, was admitted as a burgess and guildsbrother of Dunbarton on 23 September 1826. [DBR]

MCCALLUM, JOHN, merchant in Campbeltown, testament, 5 February 1801. [NRS.CC2.3.12]

MCCALLUM, JOHN, a Lieutenant of the Marines, was admitted as a burgess of Inveraray on 29 September 1802. [IBR]

MCCALLUM, JOHN, in Campbeltown, accused of cattle theft in Kintyre in 1833. [NRS.AD14.33.160]

MCCALLUM, JOHN, born 1793, died 2 September 1855, husband of Elizabeth McFarlane, born 1785, died 21 November 1864. [Luss gravestone]

MCCALLUM, JOHN, and John MacPherson, carpenters in Oban, and Duncan Cameron, in Salachan, Lochaber, an agreement re the sloop Ferrit of Oban, 23 June 1825. [NRS.AC20.3.2]

MCCALLUM, MALCOLM, a tidewaiter in Campbeltown, a bond, 1803. [NRS.CS271.589]

MCCALLUM, NEIL, a wright in Inveraray, versus Mary McCallum a resident, decreet 28 June 1800. [NRS.B32.2.1.40]; a petition to evict William Johns a merchant, Alexander MacLachlan a clerk to Archibald Bell a writer, Malcolm Campbell a weaver, and Donald Campbell a weaver, 28 March 1803; versus Peter Gardner a stone cutter, 12 October 1803. [NRS.B32.2.1.41]

MCCALLUM, PETER, tenant of Crosshill, later in Dunskaig, 1848. [NRS.SC50.5.1848.25]

MCCALLUM, ROBERT, a carpenter, was admitted as a burgess of Dunbarton on 3 May 1844. [DBR]

MCCALMAN, DONALD, minister at Kilmartin from 1836 to 25 April 1844. [F.4.14]

MCCALMAN, DUNCAN, son of Dr McCalman in Islay, died in Jamaica in March 1795. [GM.65.791]

MCCALVIAN, Mrs FLORENCE, on Danna, daughter of Duncan Campbell of Knap, testament, 14 June 1794, Comm. Isles. [NRS]

MCCAMBRIDGE, DANIEL, an able seaman in Campbeltown in May 1795. [NRS.HCR.212]

MCCAMBRIDGE, JANET, versus James Hart, servant to Peter Langwill a tenant in Kilkivan, 11 March 1802. [NRS.JP36.5.47]

MCCAPAN, DUGALD, in Whitehouse, a debtor of William Caldwell at Lochwinnoch, 5 November 1810. [NRS.JP36.5.55]

MACCARNIE, NEILL, tenant in Monidrain, versus John MacCallum, a brewer in Fernach, a petition, 6 February 1792. [NRS.JP36.5.39]

MACARTNEY, ALEXANDER, second son of Reverend William MacArtney in Old Kilpatrick, Dunbartonshire, died in Arequibo, Puerto Rico, on 3 December 1833. [SG.3.241]

MACARTNEY, WILLIAM, son of Reverend William MacArtney in Old Kilpatrick, Dunbartonshire, died in Gualaguaychiu, Entre Rios, Argentina, on 30 August 1862. [Scotsman.2462]

MCCALLUM, DUGALD, born 1812, son of Hugh McCallum in Kirnan, Glassrie, was accused of assault in 1832. [NRS.AD14.32.161]

MCCALLUM, DUNCAN, was accused of the theft of cattle in Kintyre in 1833. [NRS.JC26.1833.279]

MCCALLUM, HUGH, born 1780, father of Dugald and John, in Kirnan, Glassrie, was accused of assault in 1832. [NRS.AD14.32.161]

MCCALLUM, JOHN, son of Hugh McCallum in Kirnan, Glassrie, was accused of assault in 1832. [NRS.AD14.32.161]

MCCALLUM, JOHN, was accused of the theft of cattle in Kintyre in 1833. [NRS.JC26.1833.279]

MCCLURE, ROBERT, a carter, was admitted as a burgess of Dunbarton on 23 April 1834. [DBR]

MCCOIG, DONALD, an able seaman in Campbeltown in May 1795. [NRS.HCR.212]

MCCOIG, NEIL, an able seaman in Campbeltown in May 1795. [NRS.HCR.212]

MCCOLL, DONALD, born 15 December 1799 son of Archibald McColl minister of Tiree, minister in Glenorchy from 29 February 1844 until his death on 3 March 1864. [F.4.87]

MCCOLL, DONALD, sr. and jr. in Glasdrim, were accused of offences under the Excise Act, 12 October 1804. [NRS.JP36.5.49]

MCCOLL, DOUGALD, a shopkeeper, was admitted as a burgess and guilds-brother of Dunbarton on 11 December 1811. [DBR]

MCCOLL, DUGALD D., born 1770, a landed proprietor in Caledonia, New York, died on 29 October 1818. [Keil Chapel, Appin, gravestone]

MCCOLL, DUGALD, a ferryman in Inveraray, was evicted by the Duke of Argyll on 1 April 1802. [NRS.B32.2.1.41]

MCCOLL, DUNCAN, born June 1774 in Appin, died in Stewartsville, Laurinburg, North Carolina, on 15 July 1850. [Stewartsville gravestone]

MCCOLL, JOHN, born near Loch Etive in 1761, died in Stewartsville, Laurinburg, North Carolina, on 20 June 1815. [Laurinburg gravestone]

MCCOLL, JOHN, a shopkeeper, was admitted as a burgess and guilds-brother of Dunbarton on 1 August 1810. [DBR]

MCCOLL, JOHN, born 1780 in Appin, died in Esquesing, Ontario, on 16 December 1854. [QCG]

MCCOLL, JOHN, in Glasdrim, was accused of offences under the Excise Act, 12 October 1804. [NRS.JP36.5.49]

MCCOLL, JOHN, from Invercolla, Appin, emigrated on board the Mary Currie to South Carolina in 1790. [SCA]

MCCOLL, JOHN, born before 1755 in Argyll, a former soldier of the 74th Regiment, fought in the American War of Independence, settled on the Digdeguash River, New Brunswick, died at Highland Hill, N.B. on 4 July 1839. [New Brunswick Courier, 13 July 1839]

MCCOLL, SOLOMAN, born 1746 at Inverfolla, Appin, emigrated to South Carolina in 1790, a merchant and a schoolmaster, was naturalised in 1809, died in 1814. [Stewartsville gravestone, S.C.]

MCCOLL, WILLIAM, a glassmaker and spirit dealer, was admitted as a burgess of Dunbarton on 28 October 1842. [DBR]

MCCOMIE, JOHN, a mason, was admitted as a burgess and guilds-brother of Dunbarton on 20 September 1813. [DBR]

MCCONACHIE, ARCHIBALD, an able seaman in Campbeltown in May 1795. [NRS.HCR.212]

MCCONACHIE, DANIEL, born 1773, a seaman on board HMS Diadem died on 13 April 1798. [Cumbrae gravestone]

MCCONACHIE, JOHN, shipmaster of the Peggy of Rothesay, Bute, testament, 1793, Comm.Isles, 1793. [NRS]

MCCONACHIE, MARGARET, daughter of Alexander McConachie [1784-1840] and his wife Janet Stobo [1790-1856], died in Melbourne, Victoria, Australia, on 15 September 1858. [Rothesay gravestone]

MCCONNELL, ARCHIBALD, a merchant in Glasgow, was admitted as a burgess of Dunbarton on 12 December 1839. [DBR]

MCCORMICK, DUNCAN, born 18 December 1758 in Appin, husband of Katherine Carmichael, emigrated to Wilmington, North Carolina, on 10 August 1791, settled in Richmond County, N.C., died 18 June 1845, buried in Stewartsville Cemetery, Laurinburg, Scotland County, N.C.

MCCORMICK, JOHN, born 20 March 1738 in Kintyre, husband of Barbara McEachern born in Kintyre on 22 October 1747, died in North Carolina on 1 October 1851, emigrated to America in 1768, settled in Robeson County, N.C., died 8 February 1814, buried in McCormick Cemetery, Rowan County, North Carolina.

MCCORMACK, JOHN, born 1756 in Appin, emigrated to Wilmington, North Carolina, on 10 September 1791, settled in Richmond County, N.C., a farmer, died 19 September 1831, buried in Stewartsville Cemetery, Laurenburg, Scotland County, N.C.

MCCORMACK, MARY, born 1751 in Knapdale, wife of Alexander Graham, died in North Carolina on 2 October 1826, buried in Longstreet Presbyterian cemetery, Hoke County, N.C.

MCCORQUADALE, ARCHIBALD, from Kilbride, Argyll, married Laura Jones, in St Johns, Newfoundland, on 7 November 1813. [GM.83.20]

MCCORQUADALE, BARBARA, widow of Sergeant William Campbell in Inveraray, a petition, 4 February 1816. [NRS.NRAS.1209.198]

MCCORQUADALE, JOHN, a labourer in Inveraray, versus John Campbell a workman in Inveraray, 11 September 1812. [NRS.B32.2.1.47]

MCCRACKEN, DAVID, a shopkeeper, was admitted as a burgess and guilds-brother of Dunbarton on 31 July 1810. [DBR]

MCCULLY, THOMAS, a grocer and spirit dealer, was admitted as a burgess and guilds-brother of Dunbarton on 20 January 1824. [DBR]

MCDAID, JAMES, a smith, was admitted as a burgess of Dunbarton on 25 September 1829 as married to the daughter of a burgess. [DBR]

MCDERMID, ARCHIBALD, a ship's carpenter at Bridgend, was admitted as a burgess of Dunbarton on 27 April 1835. [DBR]

MCDERMID, JOHN, a shoemaker, was admitted as a burgess of Dunbarton on 22 October 1791. [DBR]

MCDIARMID, ARCHIBALD, a shepherd in Ballychoillie, versus John MacCallum in Eriden, now at Barnakill in Knapdale, a petition, 25 May 1819. [NRS.JP36.5.63]

MCDIARMID, DIARMID, born on Islay around 1799, died in North Carolina on 30 January 1874. [Longstreet, Fort Bragg, gravestone]

MCDIARMID, JOHN, at Mucklach, a debtor of John McSporran a shoemaker in Campbeltown, a decreet, 3 June 1811. [NRS.JP36.5.56]

MCDIARMID, PETER, born in 1804, a shepherd, wife Margaret, born 1804, from Ardnamurchan, emigrated via Liverpool aboard the Marmion bound for Moreton Bay, Australia, on 28 August 1852. [NRS.HD4/5;RH2.4.87, 66-71]

MCDONALD, ALEXANDER, of Glenaladale, testament, 7 October 1799, Comm. Argyll. [NRS]

MCDONALD, ALEXANDER, a labourer from Appin, with Ann McDonald a spinner, emigrated via Fort William on board the Sarah of Liverpool bound for Pictou, Nova Scotia, in 1801. [NRS.RH2.4.87/66-71]

MCDONALD, ALEXANDER, of Glenalladale, testament, 24 August 1801. [NRS.CC2.3.13]

MCDONALD, ALEXANDER, a coal dealer, was admitted as a burgess and guilds-brother of Dunbarton on 28 March 1804. [DBR]

MCDONALD, ALEXANDER, born 1803, a crofter in Tobermory, Mull, with his wife Flora, and children Coll born 1835, Lachlan born 1837, Donald born 1839, Mary born 1844, Christy born 1846, Marion born 1848, and Julian born 1852, emigrated via Liverpool aboard the Panama bound for Van Diemen's Land, [Tasmania], Australia, on 8 January 1853. [NRS.HD.4/5]

MACDONALD, ALEXANDER, was appointed Deputy Vice Admiral of Cara in Kintyre on 5 March 1804. [NRS.AC20.3.4]

MCDONALD, ALEXANDER, born 1762 in Argyll, a Lieutenant Colonel, settled in Miramachi in 1784, died in Bartibog, New Brunswick, on 11 December 1834. [Gleaner, 30 December 1834]

MACDONALD, ALEXANDER, born 1786, miller at Milton, died 12 January 1833, father of Robert MacDonald, born 1812, died 25 December 1832. [Dunoon gravestone]

MCDONALD, ALEXANDER, minister at Tarbert from 1845 to 1847. [F.4.19]

MCDONALD, ARCHIBALD, an able seaman in Campbeltown in May 1795. [NRS.HCR.212]

MCDONALD, CATHERINE, born 1792 on Arran, died at Sydney Mines, Cape Breton, on 18 May 1869. [McArthur gravestone, Cape Breton]

MCDONALD, CHRISTIAN, born 1770, Mary Bell born 1791, Nelly Bell born 1794, Catherine Bell born 1796, Janet Bell born 1801, and Margaret Bell born 1806, emigrated via Oban aboard the Spencer of Newcastle bound for Prince Edward Island on 22 September 1806. [PAPEI, 2702]

MCDONALD, DONALD, a merchant in Auchinsaul, testament, 6 April 1790, Comm. Argyll. [NRS]

MCDONALD, DONALD, [1], an able seaman in Campbeltown in May 1795. [NRS.HCR.212]

MCDONALD, DONALD, [2], an able seaman in Campbeltown in May 1795. [NRS.HCR.212]

MCDONALD, DONALD, merchant in Campbeltown, testament, 26 June 1801. [NRS.CC2.3.13]

MCDONALD, DONALD, and family, from Glaister, Arran, Bute, emigrated to Lower Canada in April 1831, [TNA.CO384.28.341/2]; settled in Inverness Township, Lower Canada, in 1831. [TNA.CO384.28.fos.24-26]

MCDONALD, DONALD, a merchant in Drimintorran near Strontian, Argyll, a sederunt book, 1837-1838. [NRS.CS96.722.1]

MCDONALD, DONALD, born 1814, Catherine born 1823, Angus born 1844, Mary born 1846, Jane born 1848, and Peggy born 1851, from Clash,

Ardnamurchan, Argyll, emigrated via Liverpool to Australia in September 1852. [NRS.HD4/5]

MACDONALD, FRANCIS, born 1825 in Helensburgh, Dunbartonshire, settled in New York by 1848, a shipping agent who died on Staten Island, N.Y., on 7 November 1878. [ANY]

MCDONALD, GIVENY, an able seaman in Campbeltown in May 1795. [NRS.HCR.212]

MCDONALD, JOHN, born in Argyll in February 1773, died in Mississippi in June 1865. [Carolina Parish Church, Mishoba County, Mississippi]

MCDONALD, JOHN, a mason, was admitted as a burgess of Dunbarton on 6 May 1796. [DBR]

MCDONALD, JOHN, in Drimnatran, Ardnamurchan, testament, 20 June 1801. [NRS.CC2.3.13]

MCDONALD, JOHN, born on 8 June 1808 in Borrodale, Ardnamurchan, son of John McDonald of Borrodale and his wife Jane McNab, a Lieutenant Colonel of the 66th Bengal Native Infantry, India, died in Aberdeen on 16 February 1892. [BA.3.125]

MACDONALD, PATRICK, born 22 April 1729, son of Murdoch Macdonald minister at Durness, educated at University of Aberdeen, minister of Kilmore and Kilbride from 1757 until his death on 25 September 1824. [F.4.94]

MCDONALD, WILLIAM, an able seaman in Campbeltown in May 1795. [NRS.HCR.212]

MCDONNELL, JOHN, an Excise Riding Officer in Lochgilphead, was accused of assault in 1821. [NRS.AD14.21.151]

MCDOUGALD, ALEXANDER B., born in Argyll, son of William and Catherine McDougald, settled in Moore County, North Carolina, a Lieutenant of Company of the 56th Regiment, died in Peterburg, Virginia, on 2 July 1864. [NCPres.7.12.1864]

MCDOUGALD, DONALD, born in Argyll, son of William and Catherine McDougald, settled in Moore County, North Carolina, a prisoner at Fort Lookout in 1864. [NCPres.7.12.1864]

MCDOUGALD, DUNCAN, born 1838 in Argyll, son of William and Catherine McDougald, settled in Moore County, North Carolina, died of wounds at Fredericksburg, Virginia, in 1864. [NCPres.7.12.1864]

MCDOUGALD, PETER, born 1773, emigrated via Oban aboard the Spencer of Newcastle bound for Prince Edward Island on 22 September 1806. [PAPEI, 2702]

MCDOUGALL, ALEXANDER, a tailor, was admitted as a burgess of Inveraray on 29 September 1806. [IBR]

MACDOUGALL, ALEXANDER, at Ardchuple, died 11 February 1810, inventory,2 August 1811. [NRS.CC2.5.11]

MCDOUGALL, ALEXANDER, an innkeeper, was admitted as a burgess of Dunbarton on 28 December 1833. [DBR]

MACDOUGALL, ALEXANDER, a shoemaker, was admitted as a burgess of Inveraray on 12 October 1818. [IBR]

MACDOUGALL, ALEXANDER, late tacksman of Achtemmy, Ardnamurchan, with family, emigrated on board the Louisa of Aberdeen bound for Pictou, Nova Scotia, on 28 July 1819, landed there on 31 August 1819. [EA.5813/5382]

MCDOUGAL, ALEXANDER, from Dunbarton, mate of the brigantine Elizabeth of Halifax died in Kingston, Jamaica, on 16 November 1827. [Acadian Recorder, 21 January 1828]

MCDOUGALL, ALLAN, born 1718, tacksman of Kilchattan, Luing, died 26 October 1802, father of Allan McDougall tacksman of Ardlarach. [Kilchattan gravestone]

MCDOUGALL, ANN, a widow in Inveraray, was evicted by the Duke of Argyll on 28 March 1805. [NRS.B32.2.1.42]

MCDOUGALL, DUGALD, a spirit dealer, was admitted as a burgess of Dunbarton on 30 November 1837. [DBR]

MCDOUGALL, DUGALD, a merchant, was admitted as a burgess of Inveraray on 9 June 1842. [IBR]

MCDOUGALL, DUNCAN, a spirit dealer, was admitted as a burgess and guilds-brother of Dunbarton on 23 September 1826. [DBR]

MCDOUGALL, JOHN, born 1746, a former soldier of the 74th [Argyll Highlanders] Regiment, died in St David, New Brunswick, on 10 August 1826. [Acadian Recorder, 9 September 1826]

MCDOUGALL, JOHN, Major of the 91st Regiment of Foot, was admitted as a burgess of Inveraray on 21 October 1804. [IBR]

MCDOUGALL, MALCOLM, born 1802, died 1832, wife Ann, Livingstone born 1804, died 1873, parents of Duncan in Virginia City, died 28 April 1891 in Nevada. [Rothesay gravestone, Bute]

MCDOUGALL, MARGARET, relict of Lachlan McNeill a shipmaster in Campbeltown, wife of Hugh Sage a Corporal of the Argyll Militia, 7 November 1818. [NRS.JP36.5.62]

MCDOUGALL, MARY, from Oban, emigrated to Quebec, settled in Henryville by 1820. [NRS.NRAS.1190/52]

MCDOUGALL, PETER, from Inveraray, a merchant in New York from 1782, husband of Helen Robertson, died on 19 September 1798. [ANY.1.175][NRS.CS17.1.6/51]

MCDOUGALL, PETER, and Mary McDougall, in Ardinterny, Dunoon, were victims of theft in 1837. [NRS.AD14.37.192]

MCDOWALL, TURNBULL, possibly from Dunbarton, a shipwright in Halifax, Nova Scotia, died in March 1814, probate Halifax, N.S. on 7 March 1814.

MCDUFF, DUNCAN, born 1752, Mary McNeil born 1766, Janet born 1782, Nancy born 1787, Dugald born 1789, Catherine born 1797, Effy born 1801, Donald born 1803, emigrated via Oban aboard the Spencer of Newcastle bound for Prince Edward Island on 22 September 1806. [PAPEI, 2702]

MCDUFF, MARY, born 1734, Jane Currie born 1785, emigrated via Oban aboard the Spencer of Newcastle bound for Prince Edward Island on 22 September 1806. [PAPEI, 2702]

MCDUFFIE, FLORA, born 1765, Janet Bell born 1788, emigrated via Oban aboard the Spencer of Newcastle bound for Prince Edward Island on 22 September 1806. [PAPEI, 2702]

MCDUGALD, HEW, a merchant in Oban, testament, 30 November 1798, Comm. Argyll. [NRS]

MCEACHERN, ANGUS, born 1768 in Argyll, a mariner who was naturalised in Charleston, South Carolina, on 24 May 1811. [NARA.M1183.1]

MCEACHERN, ANGUS, born 1816, Margaret born 1830, Mary born 1842, Kate born 1844, Ann born 1846, and Isabella an infant, from Salen, Ardnamurchan, emigrated via Liverpool aboard the Allison bound for Melbourne, Victoria, Australia, on 13 September 1852. [NRS.HD4/5]

MCEACHERN, ARCHIBALD, born 1776, Malcolm born 1803, emigrated via Oban aboard the Spencer of Newcastle bound for Prince Edward Island on 22 September 1806. [PAPEI, 2702]

MCEACHERN, DONALD, an able seaman in Campbeltown in May 1795. [NRS.HCR.212]

MCEACHERN, JAMES, a shipmaster in Campbeltown, a bond, 1803. [NRS.CS271.589]

MCEACHERN, DONALD, an able seaman in Campbeltown in May 1795. [NRS.HCR.212]

MCEACHERN, JAMES, a shipmaster in Campbeltown, a bond, 1803. [NRS.CS271.589]

MCEACHRAN, JAMES, a shipmaster in Campbeltown, subscribed to a bond of caution for Malcolm McCallum a tidewaiter in Campbeltown in 1803. [NRS.CS271.589]

MCEACHRON, JOHN, born 1778, a labourer, his wife Margaret born 1773, Hugh born 1798, Alexander born 1801, Janer born 1803, and stepdaughter Catherine Lamont born 1794, emigrated via Oban on board the Clarendon of Hull bound for Charlottetown, Prince Edward Island, on 6 August 1808. [TNA.CO226.23]

MCEACHARN, MALCOLM, born 1748, Flora Buchanan born 1754, Mary born 1778, Donald born 1784, Ann born 1787, Angus born 1794, emigrated via Oban on board the Spencer of Newcastle bound for Prince Edward Island on 22 September 1806. [PAPEI.2702]

MCEACHERN, PATRICK, born 1750 in Argyll, died in North Carolina on 25 September 1828, buried in the Old Centre Cemetery, Maxton, North Carolina.

MCEACHY, ALEXANDER, from Campbeltown, married Elisabeth King, in St John, New Brunswick, on 6 February 1833. [Weekly Observer, 12 February 1833]

MCEWAN, JOHN, born 1796, a labourer from Dunbarton, with family, emigrated via Port Glasgow on board the Favourite of St John, bound for St John, New Brunswick, on 22 October 1815. [PANB.msRS23E.9798]

MCEWAN, JOHN, a grocer, was admitted as a burgess and guilds-brother of Dunbarton on 8 August 1821. [DBR]

MCEWING, MALCOLM, a fisherman at Lochgilphead, a petition, 1820. [NRS.AC20.2.52]

MCFADYEN, ARCHIBALD, born on Islay in 1754, died in North Carolina in 1830. [Longstreet, Fort Bragg, gravestone]

MCFARLAND, ALEXANDER, at Tarbert, a debtor of William Caldwell at Lochwinnoch, 5 November 1810. [NRS.JP36.5.55]

MCFARLAN, ALEXANDER, born 1760 in Aberfoyle, was educated at the University of Glasgow, minister at Kilfinan from1786, died 22 December 1808, inventory, 30 October 1811. [NRS.CC2.5.11][F4.30]

MACFARLANE, ALEXANDER, born 8 May 1786, son of Reverend John MacFarlane in Kilbrandon, educated at the University of Glasgow, minister at Kilbrandon from 1809 until his death on 11 May 1826. [F.4.90]

MCFARLANE, ALEXANDER, born 1806 in Argyll, settled in Caledon, Peel County, Upper Canada, died 29 November 1869, his wife Jane Hunter, born 1797 in Argyll, died on 6 April 1880. [Caledon gravestone]

MCFARLANE, ALEXANDER, in Milton, Bonhill, Dunbarton, was murdered in 1824. [NRS.AD14.24.201]

MCFARLANE, ANDREW, of Blairnairn, Rhu, settled in Bosnie Estate, Jamaica, by 1780. [GA.623T.MJ386/2] [NRS.NRAS.0623.TMJ365]

MCFARLANE, ANDREW, born 1794, from Luss, Dunbarton, emigrated on board a Hudson's Bay Company vessel bond for the Red River settlement in 1811. [PAC.m155, 145]

MCFARLANE, ANDREW, a grocer and spirit dealer, was admitted as a burgess and guilds-brother of Dunbarton on 15 May 1829. [DBR]

MCFARLANE, ARCHIBALD, a merchant, was admitted as a burgess and guilds-brother of Dunbarton on 25 July 1792. [DBR]

MCFARLANE, ARCHIBALD, the Sheriff Officer in Inveraray, petitioned to be admitted as a constable in 1801. [NRS.JP36.6.3]

MCFARLANE, ARCHIBALD, an innkeeper, was admitted as a burgess and guilds-brother of Dunbarton on 28 May 1804. [DBR]

MCFARLANE, ARCHIBALD, jr., a merchant, was admitted as a burgess of Dunbarton on 28 December 1833. As son of a burgess. [DBR]

MCFARLANE, COLIN, a tobacconist, was admitted as a burgess and guilds-brother of Dunbarton on 26 August 1817. [DBR]

MCFARLANE, DANIEL, a shoemaker in Renton, was admitted as a burgess of Dunbarton on 25 September 1818. [DBR]

MCFARLANE, DUGALD, born 1813, a crofter fisherman in Tobermory, Mull, with his wife Effy born 1817, and children Lachlan born 1839, Donald born 1841, Mary born 1843, Ann born 1845, Neil born 1847, Kate born 1849, and Sally born 1852, emigrated via Liverpool aboard the Panama bound for Van Diemen's Land, [Tasmania], Australia, on 8 January 1853. [NRS.HD.4/5]

MACFARLANE, DUGALD, son of Dugald MacFarlane [died in 1851] and his wife Janet Paton [1805-1844], died in Brisbane, Queensland, Australia, in 1857. [Arrochar gravestone]

MCFARLANE, DUNCAN, a messenger, was admitted as a burgess and guilds-brother of Dunbarton on 19 November 1821, by right of his wife the daughter of a burgess. [DBR]

MCFARLANE, GEORGE, a grocer, was admitted as a burgess and guilds-brother of Dunbarton on 29 January 1803. [DBR]

MCFARLANE, HELEN, daughter of P. McFarlane in Faslane, married Robert Smith, MD, in Berbice on 28 June 1839. [SG.8.809]

MACFARLANE, HUGH NORMAN, from Arrochar, Dunbartonshire, emigrated to America in 1784, settled in Chenanga County, New York. [CMF]

MCFARLANE, ISABELLA, born 1767?, died in Dunoon on 27 July 1850, wife of James Burns. [Dunoon gravestone]

MCFARLANE, JAMES, an able seaman in Campbeltown in May 1795. [NRS.HCR.212]

MCFARLANE, JAMES, a baker, was admitted as a burgess and guilds-brother of Dunbarton on 3 September 1798. [DBR]

MCFARLANE, JAMES DUNCAN, in Townend, was admitted as a burgess and guilds-brother of Dunbarton on 19 February 1836, as son of a burgess. [DBR]

MACFARLANE, JAMES, born 1820 in Arrochar, Dunbartonshire, a tannery manager in La Porte, Pennsylvania, died there on 10 September 1914. [ANY]

MACFARLANE, JEAN, relict of William Armour in Southend of Kintyre, testament, 12 June 1801. [NRS.CC2.3.13]

MCFARLAN, JEAN, spouse of Godfrey McIntaggart a wright in West Tarbert, died 23 July 1810, inventory, 20 October 1812. [NRS.CC2.5.11]

MACFARLANE, alias MCNEIL, JOHN, guilty of an assault in Dunbarton, was banished for life from Scotland, at Glasgow in September 1784. [Scots Magazine]

MCFARLANE, JOHN, a butcher, was admitted as a burgess of Dunbarton on 10 September 1800. [DBR]

MCFARLANE, JOHN, a shoemaker, was admitted as a burgess and guilds-brother of Dunbarton on 12 March 1801. [DBR]

MACFARLANE, JOHN, born 1756, son of Robert MacFarlane a farmer at the Port of Menteith, educated at the University of Glasgow, minister at Kilbrandon from 1788 until his death on 24 September 1806. [F.4.90],

MCFARLANE, JOHN, a grocer, was admitted as a burgess and guilds-brother of Dunbarton on 13 July 1822 as son of a burgess. [DBR]

MACFARLAN, JOHN, of Ballincleroch, was appointed factor to Elizabeth Haven Wardrobe in Portsmouth, Rockingham County, New Hampshire, on 3 May 1822. [NRS.RD5.227.363]

MCFARLANE, JOHN, a wright was admitted as a burgess and guilds-brother of Dunbarton on 21 September 1829, as married to the daughter of a burgess. [DBR]

MACFARLANE, JOHN, born 1798, farmer at Stronchullin, died 27 October 1847, husband of Jane Marquis, born 1810, died 21 August 1878. [Luss gravestone]

MACFARLANE, JOHN, died at Shawpark, Dunoon, on 27 April 1852. [Dunoon gravestone]

MACFARLANE, MALCOLM, born 1798, surgeon, died 8 May 1833, [Luss gravestone]

MCFARLANE, MARY, in Inveraray, was evicted by the Duke of Argyll on 28 March 1805. [NRS.B32.2.1.42]

MCFARLANE, MUNGO, minister at Tarbert from 1849 to 1850. [F.4.20]

MCFARLANE, P., in Old Kilpatrick, Dunbartonshire, applied to emigrate to Canada on 3 March 1815. [NRS.RH9]

MCFARLANE, PARLANE, born 1771, died in Faslane on 17 September 1846, his wife Helen Isabella Darroch, born 1790, died 22 January 1834. [Rhu gravestone]

MCFARLANE, PARLANE, at Aikebar, was admitted as a burgess and guilds-brother of Dunbarton on 29 January 1803. [DBR]

MCFARLANE, ROBERT, a butcher, was admitted as a burgess and guilds-brother of Dunbarton on 7 September 1824. [DBR]

MCFARLANE, THOMAS, an innkeeper, was admitted as a burgess and guilds-brother of Dunbarton on 1 July 1807. [DBR]

MCFARLANE, WALTER, a blacksmith, was admitted as a burgess and guilds-brother of Dunbarton on 11 August 1827. [DBR]

MCFARLANE, WILLIAM, a baker, was admitted as a burgess and guilds-brother of Dunbarton on 11 December 1811. [DBR]

MACFARLANE, WILLIAM, servant to John Dochart innkeeper at Dalmally, was accused of assault in 1815. [NRS.AD14.15.19]

MCFARLANE, WILLIAM, a grocer and spirit dealer, was admitted as a burgess and guilds-brother of Dunbarton on 15 May 1827, as son of John McFarlane a shoemaker burgess. [DBR]

MCFEE, JOHN, born 1840, son of Robert McFee and his wife Helen McKechnie, died at Pilgrim's Rest, South Africa, on 28 August 1878. [St Colmac's gravestone, Bute]

MCFIE, ARCHIBALD, born 1777, a shipmaster in Rothesay, died on 6 October 1816. [Rothesay gravestone, Bute]

MCFIE, JAMES, born 1820, son of John McFie and his wife Mary Thomson, died at Reedy Creek, Victoria, Australia, on 9 February 1887. [Kingarth gravestone]

MCFIE, JOHN, a mariner in Woodend, Rothesay, Bute, testament, 1790, Comm. Isles. [NRS]

MCFIE, ROBERT, shipmaster of the Mount Stuart of Rothesay, Bute, testament, 1792, Comm. Isles. [NRS]

MCFIE, ROBERT, born 1768, a shipmaster, died in May 1816. [Cumbrae gravestone]

MCGEACHIN, JAMES, a mason in Bonhill, was admitted as burgess of Dunbarton on 2 April 1794. [DBR]

MCGEACHY, ALEXANDER, from Kintyre, emigrated to America after 1783, settled in Robeson County, North Carolina, died 24 March 1844. [St Paul's Presbyterian Church records]

MCGEACHY, ALEXANDER, in Killean, a debtor to James McMillan a shoemaker in Killowcraw, 20 March 1811. [NRS.JP36.5.56]

MCGEACHY, ARCHIBALD, an able seaman in Campbeltown in June 1795. [NRS.HCR.212]

MCGHIE, GEORGE, a wright, was admitted as a burgess and guilds-brother of Dunbarton on 21 September 1802. [DBR]

MCGHIE, JOHN, a wright, , was admitted as burgess and guilds-brother of Dunbarton on 24 September 1813. [DBR]

MCGHIE, JOHN, an apothecary, was admitted as a burgess of Dunbarton on 26 June 1832. [DBR]

MCGHIE, JOHN, a skinner, was admitted as a burgess of Dunbarton on 10 January 1839. [DBR]

MCGILL, ANGUS, born 1749 in Kintyre, died in North Carolina on 22 December 1827. [Raleigh, N.C.....Weekly, 24 January 1828]

MCGILLVRAY, DUNCAN, born 1774 in Argyll, settled in Caledon, Peel County, Upper Canada, died in October 1858, his wife Mary McDonald, born 1781 in Argyll, died on 9 March 1865. [Caledon gravestone]

MCGILLEVRAY, JOHN, born 1798, son of Angus McGillevray, [1767-1828], and his wife Margaret Black, [1768-1847], settled at Colonel's Ridge, Jamaica, died in Kingston, Jamaica, on 12 December 1839. [Rothesay gravestone, Bute]

MCGLASHAN, ARCHIBALD, at Kinlochlaich, was accused of offences under the Excise Act, 12 October 1804. [NRS.JP36.5.49]

MCGLASHAN, ARCHIBALD, in Whitfield, Cowal, versus Archibald McIntyre, a tartan weaver at Gate House, near Cladich, 7 April 1824. [NRS.JP36.5.66]

MACGLASHAN, ARCHIBALD, in Shirdrim, versus Alexander MacNicol, schoolmaster at Furnace, 14 March 1825. [NRS.JP36.5.69]

MCGLASHAN, NICOL, and Dugald McGlashan, in Ardinterny, Dunoon, were victims of theft in 1837. [NRS.AD14.37.192]

MCGOWAN, ALEXANDER, a merchant, son of Alexander McGowan a baillie in Rothesay, Bute, died in Kingston, Jamaica, on 2 June 1795. [Scots Magazine. 57.612] [GM.65.791]

MCGREGOR, ALEXANDER, a vintner in Brodick, Arran, died in Kilbride on 7 March 1801, an edict of executry. [NRS.CC12.7.35.1]

MCGREGOR, ALEXANDER, a spirit dealer, was admitted as burgess and guilds-brother of Dunbarton on 8 March 1825. [DBR]

MCGREGOR, ANDREW, in Lower Dalinlongait, Dunoon, was accused of a hanging in 1828. [NRS.JC26.1828.400]

MCGREGOR, ARCHIBALD, born 1780, wife Christian born 1784, Alexander born 1805, from Appin, emigrated via Oban on board the Clarendon of Hull bound for Charlottetown, Prince Edward Island, on 6 August 1808. [TNA.CO226.23]

MCGREGOR, ARCHIBALD, born 15 May 1777, emigrated to America in 1804, settled in Barbecue, North Carolina, died 12 February 1859, buried at Cyress Church. [N. C. Presbyterian, 5.3.1859]

MCGREGOR, DANIEL, born 1832 on Lismore, son of John McGregor, emigrated to Texas in 1855, died in Austin, Arkansas, on 13 September 1862. [N.C. Presbyterian, 22.11.1862]

MCGREGOR, DUNCAN, born 1811, died on La Bonne Intention Estate, Demerara in July 1844. [Faslane gravestone]

MCGREGOR, DUNCAN, an innkeeper, was admitted as burgess and guilds-brother of Dunbarton on 3 September 1798. [DBR]

MCGREGOR, Mrs EFFIE, born 1783 in Argyll, wife of Archibald McGregor, settled in Cumberland County, North Carolina, died in Harnett County, N.C., on 10 April 1861. [N. C. Presbyterian, 20.4.1861]

MCGREGOR, JOHN, a hatter, was admitted as a burgess and guilds-brother of Dunbarton on 16 September 1814. [DBR]

MCGREGOR, JOSEPH, a cloth merchant, was admitted as a burgess and guilds-brother of Dunbarton on 13 July 1822 as husband of a daughter of a burgess. [DBR]

MCGREGOR, MALCOLM, a mariner in Charleston, South Carolina, son of Duncan McGregor on Lismore, Argyll, probate 1 October 1793, S.C.

MACGREGOR, MARGARET ELIZABETH STEWART, youngest daughter of Robert MacGregor in Campbeltown, married David L.Jolly of Real de Monte, in the British Consulate in Mexico on 2 April 1860. [S.1538][DC.23504][W/21.2196]

MCGREGOR, O. R., son of John McGregor and his wife Abigail McKenzie Martin [1799-1839], settled in Duntolm, Melbourne, Victoria, Australia. [Kilmartin gravestone]

MACGREGOR, THOMAS, born 6 November 1754, married Margaret McLaren on 11 October 1783, emigrated via Oban bound for Charlottetown, Prince Edward Island on 6 October 1808. [SG.39.2.84]

MCGUGAN, ARCHIBALD, an able seaman in Campbeltown in June 1795. [NRS.HCR.212]

MCGUGGAN, DUNCAN, born in May 1794 in North Knapdale, emigrated to America in 1801, died 15 January 1862, buried in McGuggan Cemetery, Shannon, Hoke County, North Carolina.

MCGUIRE, THOMAS, a provision dealer, was admitted as a burgess and guilds-brother of Dunbarton on 11 November 1822. [DBR]

MCHUTCHEON, JOHN, born 1717, shoemaker in Blarule, died in February 1802, husband of Janet Ewing, born 1722, died 14 March 1767. [Luss gravestone]

MCILEVIN, or LIVINGSTONE, MARGARET, relict of Archibald MacLachlan in Eurach, versus John MacLachlan at Auchayerran, a petition, 6 February 1792. [NRS.JP36.5.39]

MCILLERAND, JOHN, tenant in Kilmun, testament, 21 November 1797, Comm. Argyll. [NRS]

MCILLIRIACH, MARY, in Achlevan, versus Archibald Buchanan, a farmer in Baliveolan near Lismore, a petition,3 March 1820. [NRS.JP36.5.64]

MCILLIVAOIL, alias MCMILLAN, ALEXANDER, from Canna, guilty of shop-breaking, was sentenced to transportation for fourteen years, at Inveraray on 13 September 1811. [Scots Magazine.83.10/790]

MCILLONAN, EDWARD, an able seaman in Campbeltown in May 1795. [NRS.HCR.212]

MCILLVER, ANNABELLA, widow of Hugh McIllver tacksman of Rimmnel, a petition, 1824. [NRS.NRAS.1209.1942]

MCILROY, JOHN, a shoemaker, was admitted as a burgess and guilds-brother of Dunbarton on 23 September 1808 as son of Robert McIlroy a shoemaker. [DBR]

MCINDOE, DAVID, an innkeeper, was admitted as a burgess and guilds-brother of Dunbarton on 5 November 1793. [DBR]

MCINDOE, HUGH, an innkeeper, was admitted as a burgess and guilds-brother of Dunbarton on 16 May 1822. [DBR]

MCINDOE, JOHN, a grocer, was admitted as a burgess and guilds-brother of Dunbarton on 3 September 1798. [DBR]

MCINDOE, ROBERT, a weaver at Doveholm, was admitted as a burgess and guilds-brother of Dunbarton on 1 July 1807. [DBR]

MACINDOE, WALTER, son of Robert MacIndoe in Carbeth, Strathblane, a merchant in Virginia, died there in the early nineteenth century? [Strathblane gravestone]

MCINNIS, ..., born 15 February 1785 on Jura, died in North Carolina on 21 October 1849. [Longstreet gravestone, Fort Bragg]

MCINNES, DUNCAN, died 1795, wife Catherine did 1795, daughter Catherine McInnes born and died 29 June 1857, and son Alexander McInnes born 1785 and died in December 1853, emigrated from Appin to America in 1791, settled in Robeson County, North Carolina. [McInnes cemetery, Waikulla, Robeson County, N.C.]

MCINNIS, HECTOR, born in Argyll, died at Middle River, Pictou, Nova Scotia, on 24 February 1832. [Halifax Journal, 26 March 1832]

MCINNES, JOHN, a ship's carpenter, was admitted as a burgess and guilds-brother of Dunbarton on 28 April 1829. [DBR]

MCINTOSH, DONALD, a coppersmith, was admitted as a burgess and guilds-brother of Dunbarton on 3 September 1798. [DBR]

MCINTOSH, DONALD, an innkeeper, was admitted as a burgess and guilds-brother of Dunbarton on 17 May 1819, as married to a daughter of a burgess. [DBR]

MCINTOSH, DONALD, a proprietor in College Street, was admitted as a burgess of Dunbarton on 15 September 1843. [DBR]

MCINTOSH, THOMAS, a merchant, was admitted as a burgess and guilds-brother of Dunbarton on 19 June 1832. [DBR]

MCINTYRE, ARCHIBALD, a tailor, was admitted as a burgess and guilds-brother of Dunbarton on 4 August 1831. [DBR]

MCINTYRE, COLIN, a spirit dealer, was admitted as a burgess and guilds-brother of Dunbarton on 15 October 1836. [DBR]

MCINTYRE, MALCOLM, in Lochgilphead, victim of an assault in 1832. [NRS.AD14.32.161]

MCKEICH, ALEXANDER, a dealer in Dalnacarron, a petition concerning a consignment of potatoes in 1848. [NRS.SC50.5.1848.20]

MCKENDRICK, JOHN, a labourer in Kintyre, was accused of assault, trial papers, 1826. [NRS.JC26.1826.198]

MCKENZIE, or MCWHINNIE, MARGARET, in Shedog, Kilmory, Arran, died 8 September 1799, an edict of executry. [NRS.CC12.7.34.3]

MACKINTOSH, ALEXANDER, born 2 April 1801, son of Robert Mackintosh of Kirkmichael and his wife Marjory Robertson, educated at the University of St Andrews, minister at Craignish from 19 September 1844 until his death on 4 November 1857. [F.4.4]

MACINTOSH, ARCHIBALD, born 1798, shipmaster, died 1848, wife Isabella Gilchrist, born 1802, died 17 March 1874. [Rothesay gravestone]

MCINTOSH, DONALD, born in 1779, late in Jamaica, died in Dunbarton on 28 July 1845. [SG]

MCINTOSH, DUNCAN, born 1811, son of Peter McIntosh in Dunbartonshire, educated at the University of Glasgow, minister at Kilfinan from 1843 to 1860, died on 12 December 1873. [F.4.30]

MCINTOSH, DUNCAN, a merchant, was admitted as a burgess of Inveraray on 12 June 1848. [IBR]

MACINTOSH, ROBERTSON, a merchant, youngest son of Neil Macintosh in Rothesay, Bute, died in Montreal on 31 August 1843. [SG.1229]

MCINTYRE, ALEXANDER, born 15 April 1771, son of Reverend Joseph McIntyre in Glenorchy, minister of Kilchrennan and Dalavich from 4 May 1796 until 12 January 1802, died on 18 December 1823. [F.4.92]

MCINTYRE, ALEXANDER, a wright in Inveraray, was evicted by the Duke of Argyll on 28 March 1805. [NRS.B32.2.1.42]

MCINTYRE, ALEXANDER, a wright in Inveraray, a bond of caution, 9 June 1820. [NRS.CC2.9.7]

MCINTYRE, ANDREW, and family, from Slidderie, Arran, settled in Inverness Township, Lower Canada, in 1831. [TNA.CO384.28.fos.24-26, 341/2]

MCINTYRE, ANGUS, born 1791 in Morvern, settled in Charleston, South Carolina, in October 1822, naturalised on 1 January 1827 in Marlborough, S.C. [SCA]

MCINTYRE, ARCHIBALD, born 16 August 1774 in Glen Orchy, son of Reverend Joseph McIntyre and his wife Christian McVean, settled in Jamaica, he died on Kendal Estate, Hanover, Jamaica, on 18 December 1809. [F.4.87][PC.69]

MCINTYRE, ARCHIBALD, in Golchulin, was accused of offences under the Excise Act, 12 October 1804. [NRS.JP36.5.49]

MCINTYRE, DONALD, born 8 November 1778 in Glenorchy, son of Reverend Joseph McIntyre and his wife Christian McVean in Glenorchy, died in Jamaica in July 1797. [F.4.87]

MCINTYRE, DOUGALD, married Lilly Campbell in Lismore in 1820, then emigrated to South Carolina. [SHC]

MCINTYRE, GILBERT, born 1798 in Kintyre, emigrated to America in 1831, declaration of intent to naturalise on 17 December 1832. [Norfolk Circuit Court, Virginia]

MCINTYRE, HENRY, born 1811 in Argyll, of Gillespie, Moffat, and Company, died in Montreal on 17 June 1832. [GA.4258]

MCINTYRE, JOHN, born 12 August 1766 in Glenorchy, son of Reverend Joseph McIntyre and his wife Christian McVean in Glenorchy, settled in Jamaica. [F.4.87]

MCINTYRE, JOHN, born 21 August 1750 on Lismore, emigrated via Appin to Wilmington, North Carolina in 1791, a Presbyterian minister in Robeson County, NC, from 1820 to 1837, died in Wake County, NC, on 17 November 1853, buried in Antioch, NC. [St Paul's records] [Hoke gravestone, N.C.]

MCINTYRE, JOHN, born 7 March 1767 in Argyll, died in North Carolina on 9 March 1854. [Laurinburg gravestone]

MCINTYRE, JOSEPH, born 1735 in Breadalbane, educated at the University of Edinburgh, minister at Kilbrandon from 1763 1765, and at Glenorchy from 1765 until his death on 5 July 1823. [F.4.87]

MCINTYRE, PATRICK, born 14 February 1773, son of Reverend Joseph McIntyre and his wife Christian McVean, settled in Jamaica. [F.4.87]

MCINTYRE, DONALD, born 8 November 1778 in Glen Orchy, son of Reverend Joseph McIntyre and his wife Christian McVean, settled in Jamaica, he died in Jamaica, on 18 December 1797. [F.4.87]

MACINTYRE, Dr DONALD, was admitted as a burgess of Inveraray on 12 JuLY 1802. [IBR]

MACINTYRE, DONALD, Sheriff Officer in Inveraray, died 1 December 1814, inventory, 11 February 1815. [NRS.CC2.5.11]

MACINTYRE, DONALD, a shoemaker in the Newtown of Inveraray, a petition, 29 January 1821. [NRS.JP36.5.65]

MCINTYRE, DONALD, a tenant in Slidderie, Arran, with his family of six, emigrated to Canada in 1829. [TNA.CO384.22.fos.3-5]

MACINTYRE, DUNCAN, Sheriff Officer in Inveraray, versus Alexander MacNicol, schoolmaster at Furnace, 14 March 1825. [NRS.JP36.5.69]

MCINTYRE, ELIZABETH, in Inveraray, was evicted by the Duke of Argyll on 28 March 1805. [NRS.B32.2.1.42]

MCINTYRE, GILBERT, born 1797 in Argyll, landed in Norfolk, Virginia in September 1831, declared his intention to naturalise on 17 December 1832. [Norfolk Circuit Court]

MCINTYRE, JOHN, born on 12 August 1766 in Glen Orchy, son of Reverend Joseph McIntyre and his wife Christian McVean, an army officer who died in Bengal in February 1793. [F.4.87]

MCINTYRE, JOHN, born 7 March 1767 in Argyll, died in North Carolina on 9 March 1854, buried in the Carmichael-McIntyre Cemetery, Laurenburg, Scotland County, NC.

MCINTYRE, JOHN, born 29 March 1768 in Glen Orchy, settled in Jamaica on 4 June 1789, died 15 June 1842, buried in Kingston Cathedral, Jamaica. [Kingston Cathedral gravestone]

MCINTYRE, JOHN, a merchant in Inveraray, versus Dugald MacGregor, a petition, 31 October 1801. [NRS.B32.2.1.40]

MCINTYRE, MALCOLM, a mason in Inveraray, was evicted by the Duke of Argyll on 28 March 1805. [NRS.B32.2.1.42]

MCINTYRE, PATRICK, born 14 February 1773 in Glen Orchy, son of Reverend Joseph McIntyre and his wife Christian McVean, settled in Jamaica. [F.4.87]

MCINTYRE, PETER, schoolmaster of Cawdor, minister at Kilmore and Kilbride from 1819 to his death on 27 April 1834. [F.4.95]

MCINTYRE, WILLIAM, a butcher, was admitted as a burgess of Dunbarton on 15 June 1833. [DBR]

MCISAAC, DONALD, a servant in Campbeltown, was accused of the deforcement of the crew of an Excise cutter in 1815. [NRS.AD14.15.95]

MCISAAC, JOHN, born 1805, minister at Lochiel, Glengarry, Upper Canada, died in Oban on 15 January 1847. [Oban gravestone]

MCIVER, DAVID, a merchant in Glasgow, was admitted as a burgess and guilds-brother of Dunbarton on 12 December 1839. [DBR]

MACKAY, ARCHIBALD, born 1796, a farmer at Kerranashee, Kintyre, was accused of assault in 1821. [NRS.AD14.21.170]

MACKAY, DONALD, born 1791, a fisherman in Carradell, Kintyre, was accused of assault in 1821. [NRS.AD14.21.170]

MCKAY, DUNCAN, born 1744 in Knapdale, settled in Cumberland County, North Carolina, naturalised on Cape Fear, N.C. on 19 October 1803. [NARA]

MACKAY, JAMES, a mariner in Rothesay, Bute, testament, 23 May 1798, Comm. Isles. [NRS]

MACKAY, JAMES, in South Garrachty, Kingarth, Bute, testament, 23 March 1800, Comm. Isles. [NRS]

MACKAY, JAMES, a surveyor in Dunbarton, a plan, 1835. [NRS.NRAS.926.18]

MCKAY, JOHN, a buss-master later a merchant in Rothesay, Bute, testament, 7 August 1792, Comm. Isles. [NRS]

MACKAY, JOHN, a mariner in Rothesay, Bute, testament, 1798, Comm. Isles. [NRS]

MACKAY, JOHN, born 1774, a farmer at Kerranashee, Kintyre, was accused of assault in 1821. [NRS.AD14.21.170]

MACKAY, MACKINTOSH, born 18 November 1793 in Eddrachillis, son of Captain Alexander Mackay of Duartbeg and his wife Helen Falconer, educated at the Universities of St Andrews and of Glasgow, minister at Dunoon from 1832 to 1843 when he joined the Free Church, later a minister in Australia, died in Portobello, Midlothian, on 17 May 1873. [F.4.24]

MCKAY, MALCOLM, born 1769 in Argyll, naturalised on 8 August 1805 in Charleston, South Carolina. [NARA.M1183.1]

MCKEAN, BARTHOLOMEW, at Doveholm, was admitted as a burgess of Dunbarton on 27 July 1793. [DBR]

MCKEAN, JOHN, a merchant, was admitted as a burgess and guilds-brother of Dunbarton on 31 March 1806. [DBR]

MCKEAN, JOHN, a candlemaker in Dunbarton, brother and heir of James McKean in Jamaica, 1813. [NRS.S/H]

MCKEAN, WILLIAM, in Jamaica, later in Dunbarton, testament, 18 August 1814, Comm. Glasgow. [NRS]

MCKECHNIE, NEIL, a spirit dealer, was admitted as a burgess of Dunbarton on 1 May 1834. [DBR]

MCKEICH, ALEXANDER, a dealer in Dalnacarnan, 1848. [NRS.SC50.5.1848.20]

MCKELLAR, DUGALD, born in Argyll, settled in Abbeville, South Carolina, in 1816, naturalised on 21 March 1818 in S.C. [Citizenship book.78]

MCKELLAR, JOHN, born 1771 in Argyll, a partner of the firm McKellar and Ainsley in Augusta, Georgia, a resident of Cambridge, South Carolina, died 23 November 1812. [Augusta Chronicle, 22 February 1817]

MCKELLAR, JOHN, an able seaman in Campbeltown in May 1795. [NRS.HCR.212]

MCKELLAR, JOHN, a gabartman, was admitted as a burgess and guilds-brother of Dunbarton on 12 March 1801. [DBR]

MCKELLAR, JOHN, born 6 January 1788, minister at Glenorchy from 1824 until his death on 25 February 1837. [F.4.87]

MCKELLAR, JOHN, a spirit dealer, was admitted as a burgess and guilds-brother of Dunbarton on 3 December 1841. [DBR]

MCKELLAR, JOHN, born 1793, farmer in Auchdachiranmore, Glendaruel, died in Dunoon in January 1857, husband of Ann McNicol, born 1792, died in March 1848. [Dunoon gravestone]

MCKELLAR, JOHN, born at Finnart More on 21 August 1808, a boat builder at Strone, died at Kilmun on 4 February 1896. [Kilmun gravestone]

MACKELLAR, MARGARET, widow of Alexander MacDougall at Ardchuple, died 9 February 1810, inventory, 2 August 1811. [NRS.CC2.5.11]

MACKELLAR, PETER, born in Inveraray, a farmer who emigrated to Upper Canada in 1817.[Encyclopedia of Canada]

MCKELVIE, DUNCAN, and family of ten, from Knockew, Arran, emigrated to Quebec in 1831, [TNA.CO384.28.341.1/2]; settled in Inverness Township, Lower Canada, in 1831. [TNA.CO384.28.fos.24-26][AMC]

MCKELVIE, JOHN, a teacher in Drimlarborra, Arran, 1840. [BOA231]

MCKENDRICK, DONALD, in Knockrioch, a debtor of John McSporran a shoemaker in Campbeltown, a decreet, 3 June 1811. [NRS.JP36.5.56]

MCKENNON, JOHN, a vintner in Lagg, Arran, 1840. [BOA231]

MCKENNY, ..., born 1704 in Argyll, an indentured servant via London to Maryland in 1724. [London Guildhall Records]

MCKENZIE, ALEXANDER, an innkeeper in Lamlash, Arran, 1840. [BOA231]

MCKENZIE, ANDREW, from Argyll, a grocer in Charleston, South Carolina, was naturalised on 17 January 1792. [NARA.M1183.1]

MCKENZIE, ARCHIBALD, a tenant in Corrie, Arran, with his family of two, emigrated to Canada in 1829. [TNA.CO384.22.fos.3-5]

MCKENZIE, ARCHIBALD, and family, from Glen, Arran, emigrated to Quebec in April 1831, [TNA.CO384.28.341/2]; settled in Inverness Township, Lower Canada, in 1831. [TNA.CO384.28.fos.24-26]

MCKENZIE, DUGALD, a tenant in Mid Sannox, Arran, with his family of four, emigrated via Lamlash, Arran, on board the Caledonia bound for Quebec in 1829, laded on 25 June 1829, settled in Inverness township. [TNA.CO384.22.fos.3-5][AMC]

MCKENZIE, COLIN, a merchant, was admitted as a burgess of Inveraray on 29 September 1806. [IBR]

MCKENZIE, GEORGE, a vintner, was admitted as a burgess of Inveraray on 11 April 1848. [IBR]

MCKENZIE, JAMES, a butcher, was admitted as a burgess and guildsbrother of Dunbarton on 14 August 1812. [DBR]

MCKENZIE, JOHN, was admitted as a burgess of Inveraray on 24 November 1803. [IBR]

MCKENZIE, JOHN, born 1785 in Argyll, a merchant in Charleston, South Carolina, naturalised on 11 January 1808. [NARA.M1183.1]

MCKENZIE, JOHN, a tenant in North Sannox, Arran, with a family of five, emigrated on the Albion to Quebec in 1829, settled in Inverness township. [TNA.CO384.22.fos.3-5][AMC]

MCKENZIE, PETER, a tenant in Sannox, Arran, with his family of five, emigrated to Canada in 1829. [TNA.CO384.22.fos.3-5]

MCKENZIE, RODERICK, a merchant from Port Appin, Argyll, later in Halifax, Nova Scotia, in 1829. [NRS.CS17.1.46/471]

MCKENZIE, WILLIAM, a tenant in North Sannox, Arran, with a family of six, emigrated to Quebec in 1829, settled in Inverness township by 1831. [TNA.CO384.22.fos.3-5][AMC]

MCKENZIE, WILLIAM, and family, from Lochranza, Arran, emigrated to Quebec in April 1831, [TNA.CO384.28.341/2]; settled in Inverness Township, Lower Canada, in 1831. [TNA.CO384.28.fos.24-26]

MCKENZIE, WILLIAM, born1786 in Arran, died 5 April 1855, husband of Mary McKenzie born 1785 on Arran, died 15 March 1870. [St Andrew's Presbyterian cemetery, Inverness, Quebec]

MCKENZIE, WILLIAM, born 1788, a fisher in Lochranza, Arran, was accused of housebreaking in 1836. [NRS.AD14.36230]

MCKERILL, ARCHIBALD, in Polwinning, petitioned Captain Thomas Campbell the road surveyor for Kintyre, to be exempt from road work, on 16 May 1819. [NRS.SC54.17.5.3]

MACKICHAN, PETER, born 1804 in Oban, son of John MacKichan a merchant, educated at the University of Glasgow, minister at South Knapdale from 25 September 1828 until his death on 13 March 1842, father of John MacKichan who emigrated to Australia. [F.4.19]

MCKILLOP, ARCHIBALD, with a family of nine persons, in Lochranza, Arran, emigrated via Lamlash, Arran, aboard the Albion in 1829 bound for Quebec, settled in Inverness township. [TNA.CO384.22.3-5][AMC]

MCKILLOP, ARCHIBALD, with a family of seven in Lochranza, Arran, bound via Lamlash, Arran, for Quebec, aboard the Albion in 1829. [TNA.CO384.22.3-5]

MCKILLOP, Mrs CATHERINE, from Arran, with a family of five, settled in Inverness, Lower Canada, in 1831. [AMC]

MCKILLOP, DONALD, with a family of eight persons, in Sannox, Arran, bound via Lamlash, Arran, aboard the Caledonia, a brigantine, bound for Canada, landed at Quebec on 25 June 1829, settled in Inverness township. [TNA.CO384.22.3-5][AMC]

MCKILLOP, JOHN, born 1805 in Arran, emigrated with his family of six aboard the Albion to Quebec in 1829, settled in Inverness, Megantic County, Lower Canada, died 4 December 1871. [Inverness gravestone, Quebec] [AMC]

MCKILLOP, Mrs JOHN, in Arran, emigrated, with her family of nine, aboard the Albion to Quebec in 1829, settled in Inverness, Megantic County, Lower Canada. [AMC]

MCKILLOP, MALCOLM, tacksman of North Sannox, Arran, testament, 1807. [NRS.CC12.4.10.3]

MCKILLOP, NEIL, with a family of eight persons, in North Sannox, Arran, bound for Canada, aboard the Caledonia a brigantine, in 1829, landed at Quebec on 25 June 1829, settled in Inverness township. [TNA.CO384.22.3-5] [AMC]

MCKILLOP, PETER, with a family of nine persons, from Corrie, Arran, bound for Canada aboard the Caledonia a brigantine, in 1829, landed in Quebec on 25 June 1829. [TNA.CO384.22.3-5]

MCKILLOP, Mrs, a widow, and family, from Urinbeg, Arran, emigrated to Quebec in April 1831, [TNA.CO384.28.341/2]; settled in Inverness township, Megantic County, Quebec, in 1831. [TNA.CO384.28.24-26]

MCKILLOP, Mrs, a widow, from Corrie, Arran, aboard either the Albion or the Caledonia in 1829, settled in Inverness township Megantic County, Quebec, in 1831. [TNA.CO384.28.24-26]

MCKINLAY, DONALD, master of the gabart Jean of Dunbarton, was admitted as a burgess and guilds-brother of Dunbarton on 25 June 1825. [DBR]

MCKINLAY, DUNCAN, from Argyll, emigrated to Charleston, South Carolina, in December 1819, naturalised in Union, S.C. on 26 September 1840, naturalisation.46]

MCKINLEY, HANNAH GRACE, born 1844, daughter of John McKinlay and his wife Mary Mitchell, died in Newfoundland on 17 March 1850. [Rothesay gravestone, Bute]

MCKINLAY, JAMES, a clerk at the Dunbarton Glassworks, was admitted as a burgess of Dunbarton on 7 February 1839, by right of his wife the daughter of a burgess. [DBR]

MCKINLAY, or SHANKLAND, Mrs JANET, daughter and heir of Mungo McKinlay a heritor in Rothesay, Bute, 1832. [NRS.S/H]

MCKINLAY, JOHN, a boatman, was admitted as a burgess and guilds-brother of Dunbarton on 12 July 1791. [DBR]

MCKINLAY, JOHN, a gabartman, was admitted as a burgess of Dunbarton on 30 May 1801. [DBR]

MCKINLEY, JOHN, born in April 1850, son of John McKinlay and his wife Mary Mitchell, died in Newfoundland on 28 October 1850. [Rothesay gravestone, Bute]

MCKINLEY, JOHN EDWARD, born 1847, son of John McKinlay and his wife Mary Mitchell, died in Newfoundland on 14 December 1849. [Rothesay gravestone, Bute]

MCKINLAY, PETER, master of the SS Leven, was admitted as a burgess and guilds-brother of Dunbarton on 7 March 1825. [DBR]

MCKINLAY, PETER, a carrier between Dunbarton and Glasgow, was admitted as a burgess and guilds-brother of Dunbarton on 25 June 1825. [DBR]

MCKINLAY, ROBERT, a tailor, was admitted as a burgess of Dunbarton on 16 September 1795. [DBR]

MCKINLAY, THOMAS, land surveyor in Rothesay, Bute, testament, 7 December 1791, Comm. Isles. [NRS]

MCKINLAY, WILLIAM, jr., a weaver, was admitted as a burgess and guilds-brother of Dunbarton on 11 September 1790. [DBR]

MCKINLAY, WILLIAM, a farmer, was admitted as a burgess and guilds-brother of Dunbarton on 15 February 1820. [DBR]

MCKINLAY, WILLIAM, a writer, was admitted as a burgess of Dunbarton on 25 January 1830 as married to the daughter of a burgess. [DBR]

MCKINNON, ALASTAIR DOWNIE, born in 1827, son of A. K. McKinnon in Corry and his wife Flora Downie, died on Mocofferpore, East Indies, in 1860. [Cill Chriosd gravestone]

MACKINNON, ALEXANDER, born 1798 in Argyll, died 28 September 1860, his wife Elizabeth was born in Argyll 1795, died 4 December 1875, [North Lochaber Cemetery, Antigonish County, Nova Scotia]

MCKINNON, ALEXANDER, and family, from Corriecravie, Arran, emigrated to Quebec in April 1831, [TNA.CO384.28.341/2]; settled in Inverness Township, Lower Canada, in 1831. [TNA.CO384.28.fos.24-26]

MACKINNON, ALLAN, a prisoner in Inveraray Tolbooth, a petition, 15 October 1804. [NRS.B32.2.1.42]

MCKINNON, CATHERINE, born 1766 in Kintyre, died in Fayetteville, Cumberland County, North Carolina, on 13 July 1826. [Raleigh Register Weekly, 4 August 1826]

MCKINNON, DANIEL, from Corriecravie, Arran, emigrated to Quebec in April 1831, [TNA.CO384.28.341/2]; settled in Inverness township, Megantic County, Quebec, in 1831. [TNA.CO384.28.24-26]

MCKINNON, HECTOR, born in Largie, Tayinloan, Killean, Kintyre, with his wife Mysie MacEachrane, emigrated to Pictou, Nova Scotia, in 1822. [SG.39.161]

MCKINNON, JOHN, an able seaman in Campbeltown in May 1795. [NRS.HCR.212]

MCKINNON, JOHN, the elder, with his family of six, from Slidderie, Arran, emigrated via Lamlash, Arran, on board the brigantine Caledonia in 1829, landed in Quebec on 25 June 1829, settled in Inverness township, Megantic County, Quebec, in 1831. [TNA.CO384.28.24-26] [AMC]

MCKINNON, JOHN, from Corriecravie, Arran, with his family of eight, emigrated to Quebec in April 1831, [TNA.CO384.28.341/2]; settled in Inverness township, Megantic County, Quebec, in 1831. [TNA.CO384.28.24-26] [AMC]

MCKINNON, KATHERINE, relict of Alexander Currie a farmer in Corriecruvie, Arran, a petition, 1814. [NRS.CC12.6.8.3]

MCKINNON, WILLIAM, born 1827, son of Alexander McKinnon and his wife Jean Currie, died on 30 April 1890 in Victoria, Australia. [Clachan gravestone, Arran]

MCKINVEN, ALEXANDER, a shipmaster in Campbeltown, testament, 1794, Comm. Argyll. [NRS]

MCKINVEN, CATHERINE, born 1770 in Auchalaskin, Killean, emigrated via Campbeltown aboard the Monarch bound for Charleston, South Carolina, landed there on 20 November 1820. [NRS.AD14.20.112][NARA]

MCKINVEN, DONALD, an able seaman in Campbeltown in May 1795. [NRS.HCR.212]

MCKINVEN, JANET, born 1760, widow of Donald McBride a farmer in Auchalaskin, Killean, emigrated via Campbeltown aboard the Monarch bound for Charleston, South Carolina, landed there on 20 November 1820. [NRS.AD14.20.112][NARA]

MCKINVEN, NEIL, a ferryman at Tayinloan, Kilean, was accused of sheep stealing in 1820. [NRS.AD14.20.112]

MCKINZIE, DANIEL, born 1761, a mariner, died on 2 November 1803. [Dunbarton gravestone]

MCKIRDY, ALEXANDER, born 1794, died at Morant Bay, Jamaica, on 18 August 1823. [Cumbrae gravestone]

MCKIRDY, ANDREW, born 13 January 1796, died 28 April 1844, wife Isabella McKay born 20 May 1798, died 1 September 1880. [Rothesay gravestone, Bute]

MCKIRDY, DANIEL, master of the Peggy and Molly of Rothesay, Bute, testament, 15 December 1792, Comm. Isles. [NRS]

MCKIRDY, Reverend JAMES, born 1786, first pastor of the Baptist Church in Cumbrae, died 27 February 1854, husband of Barbara, born 1800, died 13 January 1856. [Cumbrae gravestone]

MCKIRDY, JAMES, a glassmaker in Dunbarton, was accused of the murder of Alexander McFarlane in 1824. [NRS.AD14.24.201]

MCKIRDY, JOHN, a mariner in Ascog, testament, 26 February 1790, Comm. Isles. [NRS]

MCKIRDY, MICHAEL, born 1757, a shipmaster in Rothesay, died on 20 January 1802. [Rothesay gravestone, Bute]

MCKIRDY, ROBERT, a farmer at Gallachan, Kingarth, Bute, testament, 2 December 1795, Comm. Argyll. [NRS]

MCLACHLAN, ALEXANDER, a wright, was admitted as a burgess of Dunbarton on 25 September 1829. [DBR]

MCLACHLAN, Major ARCHIBALD, of the Royal Marines, son of L. McLachlan in Levenmore, Argyll, died in London on 12 June 1820. [SM.86.191]

MCLACHLAN, CHARLES, a baker, was admitted as a burgess and guilds-brother of Dunbarton on 16 September 1814. [DBR]

MCLACHLAN, COLIN BELL, the younger of Craigenterve, a bond dated 17 May 1819. [NRS.CC2.9.7.8]

MCLACHLAN, DONALD, of MacLachlan, born 1757, died 11 November 1817, husband of Susan Campbell, born 1769, died 12 June 1842 in Southampton. [Edinburgh, Greyfriars, gravestone]

MCLACHLAN, DONALD, tenant of Salachan farm, Argyll, in 1795. [SHS.ns.1.184]

MCLACHLAN, DONALD, born 1800 in North Knapdale, son of Alexander McLachlan a weaver, educated at the University of Glasgow, minister at North Knapdale from 27 September 1836, died in Edinburgh on 28 May 1847. [F.4.17]

MCLACHLAN, DUGALD, late from Jamaica, residing in Callart, testament, 4 July 1800, Comm. Argyll. [NRS.CC2.3.12]

MCLACHLAN, DUGALD, a plumber, was admitted as a burgess of Dunbarton on 8 September 1834. [DBR]

MCLACHLAN, EWEN, tenant of Laudil farm, Argyll, in 1795. [SHS.ns.1.184]

MCLACHLAN, HUGH, son of Duncan McLachlan of Kilbryde, Ormaig, Kilmartin, testament, 23 May 1791, Comm. Argyll. [NRS]

MCLACHLAN, JAMES, of Caledonia Estate, Clarendon, Jamaica, son of Archibald McLachlan in Bannachra, Dunbartonshire, died in New York on 11 March 1812. [Scots Magazine, 74.479]

MCLACHLAN, JOHN, tacksman of Banachra, a contract, 1800. [NRS.NRAS.1209.44]

MCLACHLAN, JOHN, born in Auchriaclach, Kilbrandon, educated at the Universities of Glasgow and Aberdeen, also Theological Hall in Paisley, emigrated to Canada as a missionary, died in Beaverton, Ontario, on 3 June 1870. [RPC.124]

MCLACHLAN, LACHLAN, in Lochgilphead, a victim of crime in 1829. [NRS.AD14.29.302]

MCLACHLAN, NEIL, born 1753, married Sarah Leitch [1763-1851] in Kilmichael Glassary in 1785, settled in Cumberland County, North Carolina, in 1804, died there in 1833. [NCSA.2.8]

MCLARREN, DUGALD, an able seaman in Campbeltown in May 1795. [HCR.212]

MACLAREN, JAMES, son of Reverend John MacLaren and his wife Magdalene Cochrane [died 20 September 1823], died at Montego Bay, Jamaica in September 1823. [Kilbarchan gravestone]

MCLARTY, ALEXANDER, formerly at Blair Ferry, later at Argyll Furnace, versus Colin Campbell a writer in Inveraray, a petition, 3 May 1819. [NRS.AC20.2.51]

MCLARTY, ALEXANDER, MD, a physician in Kingston, Jamaica, in his will refers to his reputed daughter Eliza McLarty in Campbeltown, his sister Margaret, his sons Alexander and Colin, his daughter Isabella, his brother Colin McLarty in Campbeltown, his executors brother Colin, friends John and Richard Dick in Edinburgh, Dugald Campbell in St Andrews parish, Reverend Alexander Campbell in St Andrews parish, and Lewis Johnston a surgeon and physician in Kingston, subscribed on 13 December 1820. [NRS.SC53.56.3]; a will, 25 May 1821. [NRS.SC53.56.3.18]

MCLARTY, ALEXANDER, a blacksmith in Achonhew, Arran, 1840. [BOA231]

MCLARTY, CHARLES, was born in Campbeltown, graduated MD, married Isabella Campbell, died in Kingston, Jamaica, on 3 September 1812, testament, 1813, Comm. Edin. [NRS] [Edinburgh Advertiser, 5116.13]

MCLARTY, EDWARD, born 1814 in Argyll, a mariner in Charleston, South Carolina, was naturalised there on 2 October 1847. [NARA.M1183.1]

MCLAUCHLAN, DUNCAN, born 1796 in Argyll, son of Dugald McLauchlin, settled as a blacksmith and farmer in Moore County, North Carolina, died in 1852, buried at Moore County Presbyterian Church.

MACLAUGHLAN, DAVID, servant to Neil Campbell in Kerranmory, was accused of sheep stealing in 1813. [NRS.AD14.13.39]

MCLAUCHLAN, DUNCAN, born 1796 in Argyll, son of Dugald McLauchlin, settled as a blacksmith and farmer in Moore County, North Carolina, died in 1852, buried at Moore County Presbyterian Church.

MCLAURIN, ARCHIBALD, son of James McLaurin, a labourer in Dunoon, was victim of an assault in 1835. [NRS.AD14.35.154]

MCLAURIN, Mrs CATHERINE, born 1762 in Appin, daughter of Duncan Colquhoun, died 22 March 1841, buried in Stewartsville Cemetery, Laurinburg, Scotland County, N.C.

MCLAURIN, DUNCAN, born in Glenshiel in 1741, died in North Carolina on 18 July 1828, buried in Stewartsville Cemetery, Laurinburg, Scotland County, N.C.

MCLAURIN, HUGH, born 1751 in Ballachulish, Appin, emigrated to North Carolina in 1790, a farmer in Richmond County, died 12 January 1846, buried in Stewartsville Cemetery, Laurinburg, Scotland County, N.C. [Stewartsville gravestone, N.C.]

MCLAURIN, JOHN, was admitted as a burgess of Inveraray on 29 September 1806. [IBR]

MCLAURIN, MARY, born 1745 in Glenshiel, daughter of Hugh McLaurin, married Duncan McLaurin, died 25 October 1827, buried in Stewartsville Cemetery, Laurinburg, Scotland County, N.C.

MCLAURIN, NANCY, born 1780 in Appin, daughter of Duncan McLaurin, died in North Carolina on 23 November 1860, buried in Stewartsville Cemetery, Laurinburg, Scotland County, N.C.

MCLAURIN, NEILL, born 1772 in Appin, died in North Carolina on 16 October 1827, buried in Stewartsville Cemetery, Laurinburg, Scotland County, N.C.

MCLAURIN, NEILL, born in Glen Appin, Argyll, in September 1775, died in Wilmington, North Carolina, in June 1853, buried in Stewartsville Cemetery, Laurinburg, Scotland County, N.C.

MCLAURIN, NEILL, born in Glen Etive, Argyll, in September 1778, died in North Carolina in June 1853, buried in Stewartsville Cemetery, Laurinburg, Scotland County, N.C.

MCLAURIN, NEILL, born in Appin on 14 November 1779, died in North Carolina on 15 February 1840, buried in Stewartsville Cemetery, Laurinburg, Scotland County, N.C.

MCLAVERTY, Reverend COLIN, from Keill, Argyll, married Mary Elizabeth, daughter of Hinton East, in Jamaica on 1 January 1846, parents of a son born in Chestervale, Jamaica, on 27 July 1855; Rev. McLaverty, for '25 years the incumbent of St Peter's, Jamaica,' died at Clifton Passage, Jamaica, on 15 August 1869. [PC.2008][EEC.322788][S.8160]

MCLEA, Dr ARCHIBALD, minister of Rothesay, Bute, and Reverend Mr John Campbell minister of Dunoon, versus Peter Campbell, tenant of Gearhallow, 9 August 1803. [NRS.JP36.5.48]

MCLEA, DUNCAN, from Dunoon, was in Grenada in 1793. [NRS.NRAS.0876.18]

MCLEAN, ALEXANDER, in Balnagleck, Kilchenzie, a letter, 1817. [NRS.NRAS.1209.1836]

MCLEAN, ALLAN, a tenant farmer in Gerrach, Ardgour, executor to Donald McLean in 1786. [NRS.CC8.8.127]

MCLEAN, ALLAN, a wright in Clachan, a debtor to James McMillan a shoemaker in Killowcraw, 20 March 1811. [NRS.JP36.5.56]

MCLEAN, ALLAN, born 1798, a cottar in Arichonan, North Knapdale, was accused of rioting at a Highland clearance in 1848. [NRS.AD14.48.319]

MCLEAN, Captain ANDREW, born 1769 in Argyll, died in Charleston, South Carolina, on 5 October 1819. [Old Scots gravestone, Charleston]

MCLEAN, CHARLES, in St Mary's, Middlesex, Jamaica, nephew of Mary McLean in Pennycross, Mull, testament, 1823, Comm. Ed. [NRS]

MCLEAN, Captain CHARLES, born 1769 in Argyll, son of Hugh McLean, died in Shelburne, Nova Scotia, on 2 May 1840. [Acadian Recorder, 23 May 1840]

MCLEAN, DONALD, from Argyll, a planter and merchant in St Augustine, East Florida, died there in 1778, testament, 25 January 1786, Comm. Edinburgh. [NRS]

MCLEAN, DONALD, a merchant, was admitted as a burgess of Inveraray on 29 September 1806. [IBR]

MCLEAN, DONALD, in Old Kilpatrick, Dunbartonshire, applied to emigrate to Canada on 3 March 1815. [NRS.RH9]

MACLEAN, DONALD, a merchant in Inveraray versus Duncan Milloy, master of the Lark of Inveraray, 1809. [NRS.AC20.2.50]

MCLEAN, DOUGALD, born 1774, Allan born 1800, Alexander born 1804, and Gilbert born 1806, emigrated via Oban aboard the Spencer of Newcastle bound for Prince Edward Island on 22 September 1806. [PAPEI, 2702]

MCLEAN, DUGALD, at Gartloskin, a debtor of John McSporran a shoemaker in Campbeltown, a decreet, 3 June 1811. [NRS.JP36.5.56]

MCLEAN, DUNCAN, born 1795 in Killin, son of Archibald McLean a merchant, educated at the universities of Glasgow and Aberdeen, minister at Sale in 1828, at Kilbrandon in 1835 and at Glenorchy from 1837 until 1843 when he joined the Free Church, minister of Glenorchy Free Church from 1843 until his death on 26 December 1871. [F.4.87]

MCLEAN, DUNCAN, born 1783, a farmer in Glen Orchy, Argyll, with wife Janet McPherson, Effy born 1808, Malcolm born 1810, Catherine born 1812, and Alexander born 1814, emigrated via Greenock to Lower Canada in July 1815. [TNA.AO3]

MCLEAN, DUNCAN, born 7 January 1805 in Rothesay, Bute, educated at the University of Glasgow, minister at Kilmodan from 1838 until 1843 when he joined the Free Church, died 14 June 1858. [F.4.32]

MCLEAN, DUNCAN, born 1805, a tenant in Arichonan, North Knapdale, was accused of rioting at a Highland clearance in 1848. [NRS.AD14.48.319]

MCLEAN, HECTOR, fifth son of Hugh McLean of Kingairloch and his wife Mary Stewart, emigrated to Canada in 1812, a merchant in Pictou, late of Kingairloch, died in Pictou, Nova Scotia, on 28 April 1810. [Scots Magazine, 72.718]

MCLEAN, HUMPHREY, a merchant, was admitted as a burgess of Inveraray on 25 July 1820. [IBR]

MCLEAN, JAMES, a tenant farmer in Gerrach, Ardgour, executor to Donald McLean in 1786. [NRS.CC8.8.127]

MACLEAN, JAMES, a sailor in Daloman, Campbeltown, was accused of the deforcement of the crew of an Excise cutter in 1815. [NRS.AD14.15.95]

MCLEAN, JAMES, in St Mary's, Middlesex, Jamaica, nephew of Mary McLean in Pennycross, Mull, testament, 1823, Comm. Ed. [NRS]

MCLEAN, JOHN, a mariner from Islay, was admitted as a citizen of S.C. on 20 April 1796. [NARA.M1183.1]

MCLEAN, Ensign, JOHN, of the Argyll Militia, was admitted as a burgess of Inveraray on 10 June 1803. [IBR]

MCLEAN, JOHN, a boatman and spirit dealer, was admitted as a burgess of Dunbarton on 11 June 1840. [DBR]

MCLEAN, JOHN, a fisherman in Lochgoilhead, Dunbartonshire, was accused of housebreaking in 1845. [NRS.AD14.45.251]

MCLEAN, LACHLAN, an able seaman in Campbeltown in May 1795. [NRS.HCR.212]

MCLEAN, LAUCHLAN, born 1748, wife Catherine born 1752, Flora born 1778, Hugh born 1783, Ann born 1788, Hector born 1793, John born 1796, and Euphemia born 1798, emigrated via Oban, Argyll, on board the Clarendon of Hull bound for Charlottetown, Prince Edward Island on 6 August 1808. [TNA.CO226.23]

MCLEAN, LAUCHLAN, a tenant farmer in Gerrach, Ardgour, executor to Donald McLean in 1786. [NRS.CC8.8.127]

MCLEAN, LAUCHLAN, from Old Kilpatrick, Dunbartonshire, applied to settled in Canada on 3 March 1815. [NRS.RH15]

MCLEAN, MARY, from Pennycross, Mull, later in Edinburgh, heir to her nephew James McLean in St Mary's, Jamaica, 1826. [NRS.S/H]

MCLEAN, MURDOCH, born 31 December 1829, son of Reverend Duncan McLean and his wife Flora McLeod in Glenorchy, died in New Zealand on 16 June 1865. [F.4.87]

MCLEAN, SAMUEL, of Soroba, testament, November 1792, Comm. Argyll. [NRS]

MCLEAN, Captain, tenant of Scour farm, Argyll, in 1795. [SHS.ns.1.184]

MACLEAY, Dr KENNETH, in Oban, a bond, 1802. [NRS.CS271.35861]

MCLEISH, ALEXANDER, born 1788 in Argyll, emigrated to Caledon, Peel County, Upper Canada, died 2 March 1873; his wife Sarah Brown, born 1796 in Argyll, died 14 March 1874. [Caledon gravestone]

MCLEISH, ALEXANDER, born 1825 in Scotland, settled in Caledon, Peel County, Upper Canada, died 9 June 1895. [Caledon gravestone]

MCLEISH, DONALD, a carpenter and spirit dealer, was admitted as a burgess of Dunbarton on 3 May 1838. [DBR]

MCLEISH, HECTOR, born 1821 in Argyll, settled in Caledon, Peel County, Upper Canada, died 1 February 1894, his wife, Margaret Sinclair, born 1829 in Argyll, died on 29 January 1870. [Caledon gravestone]

MCLEISH, SARAH, born 1839 in Kilfinan, Argyll, wife of George W. Armstrong, settled in Caledon, Peel County, Upper Canada, died 26 December 1870. [Caledon gravestone]

MCLELLAN, ADAM, a grocer, was admitted as a burgess and guildsbrother of Dunbarton on 31 March 1806. [DBR]

MCLELLAN, ANDREW, a grocer, was admitted as a burgess and guildsbrother of Dunbarton on 16 May 1822 as married to a daughter of a burgess. [DBR]

MCLELLAN, DUGALD, born 1833, son of Duncan McLellan in Gallachelly, North Knapdale, was accused of rioting at a Highland clearance in 1848. [NRS.AD14.48.319]

MCLELLAN, DUNCAN, born 1798, tenant in Gallachelly, North Knapdale, was accused of rioting at a Highland clearance in 1848. [NRS.AD14.48.319]

MCLEOD, ALEXANDER, a Lieutenant of the Royal Navy, was admitted as a burgess of Inveraray on 24 April 1820. [IBR]

MCLEOD, JOHN, DD, minister at Kilmodan from 1806 until 1809. [F.4.32]

MCLEOD, JOHN, a gardener and innkeeper at Bridgend, was admitted as a burgess and guilds-brother of Dunbarton on 22 May 1819. [DBR]

MCLEOD, JOHN, born in Glen Fruin, Loch Lomondside, a resident of Washington, DC, died at 71 Irving Place, New York, on 28 June 1855. [W.XVI.1678]

MACLEOD, NORMAN, minister at Campbeltown from 1808 until 1825. [F.4.51]

MCLERAN, CATHERINE, in Inveraray, was evicted by the Duke of Argyll on 1 April 1802. [NRS.B32.2.1.41]

MCLERAN, CHRISTY, in Inveraray, was evicted by the Duke of Argyll on 1 April 1802. [NRS.B32.2.1.41]

MCLERAN, DUGALD, in Inveraray, was evicted by the Duke of Argyll on 28 March 1805. [NRS.B32.2.1.42]

MCLERAN, DUNCAN, born 1761 in Argyll, a merchant in Cross Creek, Cumberland County, North Carolina, died 6 December 1821. [Cross Creek gravestone, N.C.]

MCLEVEN, CHRISTIAN, born 1793 in Glassary, settled in Caledon, Peel County, Upper Canada, wife of Dugald Cameron, died 7 October 1823. [Caledon gravestone]

MCLINTOCK, JAMES, an engraver, was admitted as a burgess and guilds-brother of Dunbarton on 31 July 1795. [DBR]

MCLINTOCK, JAMES, a gardener, was admitted as a burgess of Dunbarton on 6 August 1795. [DBR]

MCLINTOCK, JAMES, a cloth merchant, was admitted as a burgess and guilds-brother of Dunbarton on 26 June 1834 as son of a burgess. [DBR]

MCLINTOCK, JOHN, a merchant, was admitted as a burgess and guilds-brother of Dunbarton on 25 July 1792. [DBR]

MCLINTOCK, ROBERT, a cloth merchant, was admitted as a burgess of Dunbarton on 28 December 1833. [DBR]

MCLIVER, ANGUS, a grocer, was admitted as a burgess and guilds-brother of Dunbarton on 25 August 1827. [DBR]

MCLULLICH, DUNCAN, in Kilbride, testament, 12 April 1800. [NRS.CC2.3.12]

MCLULLICH, DUNCAN, Sheriff Clerk Depute of Argyll, was admitted as a burgess of Inveraray in 1841. [IBR]

MCMARTINE, FINLAY, a Lieutenant of the Breadalbane Fencibles, was admitted as a burgess of Inveraray on 17 July 1800. [IBR]

MCMARTIN, FINLAY, a spirit dealer, was admitted as a burgess and guilds-brother of Dunbarton on 15 February 1825. [DBR]

MCMASTER, ANGUS, a spirit dealer, was admitted as a burgess and guilds-brother of Dunbarton on 9 June 1823. [DBR]

MCMASTER, ANGUS, a blacksmith in Shaddog, Arran, 1840. [BOA231]

MCMASTER, ARCHIBALD, son of Alexander McMaster, [1729-1812], a farmer in Feoline, and his wife Flora MacAlester, [1760-1843], settled in Canada West. [Clachan gravestone]

MACMASTER, DUNCAN, at Corrybeg, died 22 March 1811, inventory, 19 March 1812. [NRS.CC2.5.11]

MCMASTER, Reverend JOHN, born 1802, son of Alexander McMaster, [1729-1812], a farmer in Feoline, and his wife Flora MacAlester, [1760-1843], 'for 30 years in New Brunswick', died in Shedog, Bute, on 6 April 1886. [Clachan gravestone]

MCMASTER, MARY, from Oban, emigrated via Saltcoats to Quebec in June 1802. [LAC.mg24.183]

MCMATH, DONALD, an able seaman in Campbeltown in May 1795. [NRS.HCR.212]

MACMATH, DONALD, a merchant in Inveraray, a petition to evict Malcolm MacMath a merchant, 3 April 1804. [NRS.B32.2.1.42]

MCMATH, DUGALD, a shoemaker in Inveraray, testament, 8 June 1790, Comm. Argyll. [NRS]

MCMATH, DUNCAN, in Craigs, a debtor of John McSporran a shoemaker in Campbeltown, a decreet, 3 June 1811. [NRS.JP36.5.56]

MCMATH, PEGGY. At Mucklach, a debtor of John McSporran a shoemaker in Campbeltown, a decreet, 3 June 1811. [NRS.JP36.5.56]

MCMICHAEL, JOHN, a shipmaster and merchant in Campbeltown, testament, 1796, Comm. Argyll. [NRS]

MCMILLAN, ALEXANDER, born 1766, a mariner who was naturalised in South Carolina, on 26 July 1798. [NARA.M1183.1]

MCMILLAN, ANGUS, born 1801, son of Neil McMillan in Kilmory, North Knapdale, was accused of rioting at a Highland clearance in 1848. [NRS.AD14.48.319]

MCMILLAN, ARCHIBALD, an able seaman in Campbeltown in June 1795. [NRS.HCR.213]

MCMILLAN, DANIEL, tenant of Kilmichael, a memorandum in 1792. [NRS.NRAS.1209.1943]

MCMILLAN, DANIEL, born in Kintyre, died in North Carolina on 8 August 1812. [McMillan cemetery, Red Springs, N.C.]

MCMILLAN, DANIEL, a vintner in Lochranza, Arran, 1840. [BOA231]

MCMILLAN, DONALD, an able seaman in Campbeltown in May 1795. [HCR.212]

MCMILLAN, DONALD, son of Donald McMillan and his wife Barbara McKinlay, in Auchaloskin, Kintyre, with family, emigrated via Campbeltown to Canada in 1819, settled in Erin, Wellington, Upper Canada, in 1822. [CMM]

MACMILLAN, DONALD, tenant of Shengart, South Knapdale, was accused of assault in 1821. [NRS.AD14.21.155]

MCMILLAN, DUGALD, from Oban, emigrated to Quebec in June 1802. [LAC.mg24.183]

MACMILLAN, DUNCAN, a fisherman in Dalintober, Campbeltown, was accused of the deforcement of the crew of an Excise cutter in 1815. [NRS.AD14.15.95]

MCMILLAN, DUNCAN, born 1814, son of John McMillan a smith in Cardyhouse, Kilmun, was accused of forgery in 1832. [NRS.JC26.588]

MCMILLAN, DUNCAN, a shoemaker in South Killicraw, Kintyre, was accused of assaulting Revenue Officers in 1817. [NRS.JC26.1817.143]

MCMILLAN, DUNCAN, a blacksmith in Benecangan, Arran, 1840. [BOA231]

MCMILLAN, EWING, tenant in Laidnasery, Ardgour, with family, emigrated via Arisaig aboard the British Queen bound for Quebec on 16 August 1790. [PAC.RG4A1, Vol.48.15874-5]

MCMILLAN, JAMES, an able seaman in Campbeltown in May 1795. [NRS.HCR.212]

MCMILLAN, JAMES, a shoemaker in Killowcraw, a claim, 20 March 1811. [NRS.JP36.5.56]

MCMILLAN, JOHN, an able seaman in Campbeltown in May 1795. [NRS.HCR.212]

MCMILLAN, JOHN, late in Colasea now in Stockdale, a decreet, 1811. [NRS.JP36.5.56]

MCMILLAN, JOHN, son of Alexander McMillan a merchant in Campbeltown, a merchant in Cheraw, South Carolina, died 16 September 1827. [Scotsman.822.768]

MCMILLAN, JOHN, in Cardyhouse, Kilmun, was a victim of forgery in 1832. [NRS.JC26.588]

MCMILLAN, JOHN, a carpenter, was admitted as a burgess of Dunbarton on 7 February 1839. [DBR]

MCMILLAN, LAUCHLAN, tenant of Lower Shengart, South Knapdale, was accused of assault in 1820. [NRS.AD14.20.220]

MCMILLAN, MALCOLM, born 1753, emigrated from Argyll to Prince Edward Island in 1806, died there on 8 May 1847. [Woods Islands Pioneer Cemetery, PEI]

MCMILLAN, MALCOLM, born 1794, emigrated from Argyll to Prince Edward Island, died there on 28 July 1867. [Woods Islands Pioneer Cemetery, PEI]

MCMILLAN, MALCOLM, second son of Donald McMillan and his wife Barbara McKinley in Kintyre, emigrated to America in 1819. [CMM]

MCMILLAN, MARGARET, with her family of four, from Arran, emigrated via Lamlash, Arran, aboard the Caledonia bound for Quebec in 1829, landed there on 25 June 1829, settled in Inverness township. [AMC]

MCMILLAN, Mrs MARY, born 1753 in Argyll, died in North Carolina on 19 September 1825.[Raleigh, NC.....Weekly]

MCMILLAN or MUNRO, MARY, born 1783, wife of Neil McMillan in Kilmory, North Knapdale, was accused of rioting at a Highland clearance in 1848. [NRS.AD14.48.319]

MCMILLAN, MURDOCH, born 1751, Grizel McNeil born 1766, James born 1787, Betty born 1788, Alexander born 1792, Hector born 1793,

Malcolm born 1796, Flora born 1798, Duncan born 1802, Sophia born 1803, and Catherine born 1805, emigrated via Oban aboard the Spencer of Newcastle bound for Prince Edward Island on 22 September 1806. [PAPEI, 2702]

MCMILLAN, NEIL, a tenant in South Sannox, Arran, with his family of eight, emigrated via Lamlash, Arran, on board the Caledonia bound for Quebec in 1829, landed 25 June 1829, settled in Inverness township by 1831. [TNA.CO384.22.fo.3-5][AMC]

MCMILLAN, NEIL, jr, a farm servant of John Kerr an innkeeper and farmer at Crinan North Knapdale, was accused of rioting at a Highland Clearance in 1848. [NRS.AD14.48.319]

MCMILLAN, PEGGY, a debtor to James McMillan a shoemaker in Killowcraw, 20 March 1811. [NRS.JP36.5.56]

MCMILLAN, PETER, born 1826, son of Neil McMillan a crofter in Kilmorry, North Knapdale, was accused of rioting at a Highland Clearance in 1848. [NRS.AD14.48.319]

MCMILLAN, ROBERT, born 1837, son of Donald McMillan and his wife Catherine Stewart, died in Melbourne, Victoria, Australia, on 25 April 1862. [Kilbride gravestone, Arran]

MCMILLAN, SARAH, daughter of Neil McMillan a cottar in Kilmory, North Knapdale, was accused of rioting at a Highland clearance in 1848. [NRS.AD14.48.319]

MCMURCHIE, ALLEN, an able seaman in Campbeltown in May 1795. [NRS.HCR.212]

MCMURCHIE, ARCHIBALD, a writer, petitioned for a tenement to be used as a Masonic Lodge in 1832. [NRS.NRAS.1209.1977]

MCMURCHIE, JOHN, a wright in Gartvaich, versus Peter McDonald and Peter McDearmid workmen at Carsky, 12 May 1807. [NRS.JP36.5.52]

MCNAB, ANGUS, a merchant, was admitted as a burgess of Inveraray on 12 June 1848. [IBR]

MCNABB, DUNCAN, born 1798 on Islay, emigrated via Greenock to Charleston, South Carolina, petitioned to naturalise in Marlboro County on 11 March 1830. [SCA]

MACNAB, DUNCAN, born 14 February 1808 in South Knapdale, eldest son of Robert MacNab a farmer, educated at the University of Glasgow, minister in Dunoon from 1831 until 1841, then in Campbeltown from

1841 until 1843 when he joined the Free Church then minister of the Free Church in Campbeltown from 1843 until 1856, died in London on 12 June 1863. [F.4.51]

MACNAB, JAMES, born 1817, son of John MacNab, [1757-1837], and his wife Christine Buchanan, [1786-1845], died in Arthur township, Canada, on 29 March 1872. [Buchanan gravestone]

MCNAB, JOHN, at Barachastlan, driver of a horse and cart carrying unlicensed salt in Glenaray in 1804 petition, 14 November 1804. [NRS.JP36.5.49]

MACNAB, PETER, factor to James Forbes of Kingerloch, inventory, 17 September 1811. [NRS.CC2.5.11]

MCNAIR, ARCHIBALD, a wright in Campbeltown, papers, 1811. [NRS.NRAS.130.2]

MCNAIR, ARCHIBALD, born 1794 in Achaloscan, Killean parish, Kintyre, died at Laurel Hill, Richmond County, North Carolina, on 20 September 1839. [EEC.19979]

MCNAIR, DANIEL, sr., born 1731 in Kintyre, died in North Carolina in October 1800, buried in the Old Centre Cemetery, Maxton, N.C.

MCNAIR, DANIEL, a shoemaker, was admitted as a burgess of Inveraray on 29 September 1806. [IBR]

MCNAIR, DAVID, a mason at Littlemin, was admitted as a burgess of Dunbarton on 2 August 1808. [DBR]

MCNAIR, JOHN, born 1735 in Kilkenny, Argyll, youngest son of Neill McNair and his wife Sallie McGill, emigrated to America in 1770, settled in Robeson County, died 30 June 1819, buried in Richmond County, N.C.

MCNAIR, NATHANIEL, a wright in Campbeltown, papers, 1811-1841. [NRS.NRAS.130.2]

MCNAIR, RODERICK, born in Argyll in October 1764, son of John and Catherine McNair, died in North Carolina on 6 April 1839, buried at Old Laurel Hill Church, Rockingham, Richmond County, N.C.

MCNAUGHT, DANIEL, a cartwright and joiner, was admitted as a burgess and guilds-brother of Dunbarton on 21 September 1825. [DBR]

MCNAUGHT, JOHN, a shipmaster, was admitted as a burgess and guilds-brother of Dunbarton on 19 January 1833 as husband of a daughter of a burgess. [DBR]

MCNAUGHT, MORE or MARION, spouse of Alexander Alexander a seaman on HMS Zealand, was accused of rioting and attacking a ship loaded with grain attempting to sail from Campbeltown, a petition, 21 MSarch 1801. [NRS.JP36.5.46]

MCNAUGHT, NEIL, a shoemaker, was admitted as a burgess and guilds-brother of Dunbarton on 16 September 1814. [DBR]

MCNAUGHT, PETER, an innkeeper, was admitted as a burgess and guilds-brother of Dunbarton on 19 November 1821. [DBR]

MCNAUGHT, ROBERT, an able seaman in Campbeltown in May 1795. [NRS.HCR.212]

MCNAUGHTON, DONALD, from Cardross Moss, Dunbartonshire, emigrated via Greenock on board the Niagara bound for Montreal, with his wife Catherine, and children Duncan, John, Robert, Mary, and Alexander, in 1825, settled in McNab, Bathurst, Upper Canada.

MCNAUGHTON, DONALD, minister at Glencoe from 1813 until 1828; minister at Duror from 1828 until 1844. [F.4.84/85]

MCNAUGHTON, DUNCAN, an innkeeper at East Bridgend, was admitted as a burgess of Dunbarton on 20 September 1813. [DBR]

MCNAUGHTON, DUNCAN, a cloth merchant, was admitted as a burgess and guilds-brother of Dunbarton on 19 November 1821 as married to the daughter of a burgess. [DBR]

MCNAUGHTON, Captain JOHN, 'many years in the Bahamas', died in Campbeltown, Scotland, on 22 September 1808. [Bahamas Royal Gazette, 21,12.1808]

MCNAUGHTON, JOHN, a steward aboard the steamboat Ben Lomond, was admitted as a burgess and guilds-brother of Dunbarton on 25 June 1825 as son of a burgess. [DBR]

MCNEILL, ANGUS, born 1762 in North Knapdale, died in North Carolina on 13 September 1835, buried in the McNeill Cemetery, Wagram, Scotland County, N.C.

MCNEILL, ARCHIBALD, a blacksmith in Rothesay, Bute, testament, 1 June 1790, Comm. Argyll. [NRS]

MACNEIL, ARCHIBALD, a writer in Campbeltown, son of Archibald MacNeil a shipmaster in Campbeltown, was admitted as a Notary Public on 22 May 1792. [NRS.NP2.34.339]

MCNEILL, CHARLES, from Demerara, son of Captain Alexander McNeill of Colonsay, married Margaret, only child of Malcolm McNeill of Lossit, in Glasgow on 5 November 1840. [W.88]

MCNEIL, DONALD, a Captain of the 91st Regiment, was admitted as a burgess of Inveraray on 17 June 1801. [IBR]

MCNEIL, DONALD, born 1772, Malcolm born 1801, Donald born 1804, emigrated via Oban aboard the Spencer of Newcastle bound for Prince Edward Island on 22 September 1806. [PAPEI, 2702]

MCNEIL, DOUGALD, born 1746, Flora McMillan born 1755, Alexander born 1780, Margaret born 1785, Charles born 1791, and Dougal born 1794, Isabella born 1799, emigrated via Oban on board the Spencer of Newcastle bound for Prince Edward Island on 22 September 1806. [PAPEI.2702]

MCNEILL, DUNCAN, in Dunmore, testament, 23 July 1790, Comm. Argyll. [NRS]

MCNEILL, DUNCAN, the Lord Advocate, was admitted as a burgess of Inveraray on 7 September 1843. [IBR]

MCNEIL, Captain HECTOR, at Drimdrisshaig, was admitted as a burgess of Inveraray on 12 July 1802. [IBR]

MACNEIL, HECTOR, from Kingairloch, died in Pictou, Nva Scotia, in 1810. [GM.80.395]

MCNEILL, JAMES, an able seaman in Campbeltown in May 1795. [NRS.HCR.212]

MCNEILL, JOHN, a labourer in Achnafad, Kilcalmonell, Kintyre, was accused of sheep stealing in 1840. [NRS.AD14.40.3]

MCNEILL, LACHLAN, tacksman of Drumdrissaig, testament, 23 November 1790, Comm. Argyll. [NRS]

MCNEILL, LACHLAN, son of Hector McNeill and his wife Margaret in Saltpans, Machrahanish, a merchant who died in Jamaica in 1798. [SG.32.2.56]

MCNEILL, LAUGHLAN, an able seaman in Campbeltown in May 1795. [NRS.HCR.212]

MCNEILL, LACHLAN, born 22 April 1834, third son of Lachlan McNeill, a farmer in Kilmun, and his wife Jane Black, was educated at Glasgow University and at St Andrews University, a missionary and minister in Uruguay and in Argentina from 1866 to 1883, died in England on 18 December 1917. [F.7.683]

MCNEIL, MALCOLM, born 1755, Mary Livingstone born 1755, John born 1792, Janet born 1786, emigrated via Oban aboard the Spencer of Newcastle bound for Prince Edward Island on 22 September 1806. [PAPEI, 2702]

MCNEIL, MARGARET, born 1785, Catherine Munn born 1806, emigrated via Oban aboard the Spencer of Newcastle bound for Prince Edward Island on 22 September 1806. [PAPEI.2702]

MCNEILL, MARGARET, daughter of Hugh Spiers a constable in Campbeltown, a petition, 7 January 1822. [NRS.JP36.5.66]

MCNEAL, NEIL, born 1758 in Campbeltown, master and owner of the Isabella of Charleston died on 18 March 1823. [Old Scots gravestone, Charlest, S.C.]

MCNEILL, THOMAS, a weaver in Milton, was admitted as a burgess and guilds-brother of Dunbarton on 26 September 1805 as married to the daughter of a burgess. [DBR]

MCNEILL, THOMAS, a clothier, was admitted as a burgess of Dunbarton on 19 February 1836 as married to the daughter of a burgess. [DBR]

MCNEISH, DANIEL, a baker and grocer in Lamlash, Arran, 1840. [BOA230]

MCNERAN, MALCOLM, from Rosneth, was naturalised in Philadelphia's Court of Common Pleas on 14 October 1808, a gentleman in Philadelphia, Pennsylvania, in 1818, died 18 March 1836, testament, 1842. [NRS.SC53.56.2; SC70.1.61]

MCNICOL, ALEXANDER, in Sockoch, Glenurchy, inventory, 19 October 1812. [NRS.CC2.5.11]

MCNICOL, ARCHIBALD, a dyer in Lamlash, Arran, 1840. [BOA231]

MCNICOLL, CHARLES, a drover in Strathadally, testament, 22 November 1796, Comm. Argyll. [NRS]

MACNICOL, DONALD, Excise Officer at Rudile, died 27 February 1813, inventory, 15 August 1814. [NRS.CC2.5.11]

MCNICOL, DONALD, born 1800, Piermaster at Dunoon, died 23 February 1856, husband of Rebecca Clark, born 1803, died 10 January 1885. [Dunoon gravestone]

MACNICOLL, DONALD, born 1756 in Craignish, educated at the University of Glasgow, minister at Kilfinan from 1811 until his death on 15 March 1830. [F.4.30]

MCNICOLL, DUNCAN, a butcher, was admitted as a burgess of Inveraray on 29 September 1806. [IBR]

MACNICOLL, JOHN, Excise Officer in Lemnamuick, testament, 23 August 1800. [NRS.CC2.3.12]

MCNICOL, JOHN, a farmer in Gooseholm, was admitted as a burgess and guilds-brother of Dunbarton 19 January 1827 as married to the daughter of a burgess. [DBR]

MCNICOL, JOHN, a labourer, was admitted as a burgess and of Dunbarton on 12 September 1839. [DBR]

MACNICOL, LIZZY, daughter of Nicol McNicol in Polcheyline, Strachur, accused of infanticide, 1814. [NRS.AD14.14.55]

MCNICOLL, NICOL, late of Elrigmore, testament, 31 May 1792, Comm. Argyll. [NRS]

MCNICOL, SARAH, widow of John Ferguson in Inveraray, was evicted by the Duke of Argyll on 1 April 1802. [NRS.B32.2.1.41]

MCNICOL, WALTER, born 1810, a merchant in Dunoon, died 16 August 1847. [Dunoon gravestone]

MCNIDER, WILLIAM, born 1769, a shipmaster, died 29 December 1832. [Kirkbride gravestone]

MCNIVEN, JOHN, a wright, was admitted as a burgess of Inveraray on 29 September 1806. [IBR]

MCPHADEN, CHRISTIAN, born 1779, emigrated via Oban aboard the Spencer of Newcastle bound for Prince Edward Island on 22 September 1806. [PAPEI.2702]

MCPHADZEAN, ANGUS, a planter in Westmoreland parish, Jamaica, son and executor of Catherine McKewan, spouse of Donald McPhadzean in Cuilichnuick, Argyll, edict of executry, 1785. [NRS.CC2.8.88.6]

MCPHAIL, DONALD, son of Robert McPhail tenant in Laggar, was imprisoned in Inveraray Tolbooth accused of murder in 1804. [NRS.JC26.1804.11]

MCPHAIL, DUNCAN, a boatman, was admitted as a burgess and guilds-brother of Dunbarton on 27 May 1818. [DBR]

MCPHAIL, JOHN, an able seaman in Campbeltown in May 1795. [NRS.HCR.212]

MCPHAIL, JOHN, a shopkeeper, was admitted as a burgess of Dunbarton on 21 May 1803. [DBR]

MCPHAILL, ROBERT, in Laggan, a debtor of John McSporran a shoemaker in Campbeltown, a decreet, 3 June 1811. [NRS.JP36.5.56]

MCPHALE, JOHN, a dyke builder in Lergichoniemor, and Barra Cameron, a dyke builder in Kintraw, versus John Ferguson in Lergichoniemor, a petition, 6 February 1792. [NRS.JP36.5.39]

MACPHEE, CATHERINE, born 1801, John born 1822, Alexander born 1826, Mary born 1830, William born 1834, Donald born 1837, Duncan born 1843, and Ann born 1851, from Camuscharick, Ardnamurchan, emigrated via Liverpool on board the Allison bound for Melbourne, Victoria, Australia, on 13 September 1852. [NRS.HD4/5]

MCPHEE, DONALD, born 1775, a wright from Ardgour, wife Catherine born 1775, Alexander born 1800, Allan born 1805, John born 1809, Catherine born 1803, Ann born 1808, and Mary born 1813, emigrated via Greenock to Upper Canada in July 1815. [TNA.AO3; CO385/2]

MCPHEE, HUGH, an innkeeper, was admitted as a burgess and guilds-brother of Dunbarton on 16 March 1814. [DBR]

MACPHEE, MALCOLM, born 1821, died 10 January 1842, son of Janet Couan in Colipool. [Kilchattan gravestone]

MCPHERSON, ABRAHAM, a joiner, was admitted as a burgess and guilds-brother of Dunbarton on 23 September 1829 as the son of a burgess. [DBR]

MACPHERSON, ALEXANDER, a writer in Edinburgh, son of Duncan MacPherson at Lochfynehead, was admitted as a Notary Public on 25 June 1796. [NRS.NP2.35.345]

MCPHERSON, Mrs ANN, wife of Archibald McPherson in Dunoon, died in 1828. [Dunoon gravestone]

MCPHERSON, DUNCAN, a labourer, was admitted as a burgess and guilds-brother of Dunbarton on 23 April 1830. [DBR]

MCPHERSON, FINLAY, born 1796 in Strontian, son of John Macpherson an artificer, educated at Glasgow University, minister at Tobermory from 1834 to 1837, and at Kilbrandon from 1838 until 1843, minister of the Free Church there from 1852 until his death on 9 January 1852. [F.4.90]

MCPHERSON, JAMES, of Cour, Argyll, 'a most skilful and successful grazier and agriculturalist', emigrated, with 300 others from Islay and Kintyre, via Glasgow to Quebec on the Euclid of Liverpool in June 1847. [Aberdeen Journal.5188]

MCPHERSON, JOHN, born 1795, a baker, died 18 August 1835, husband of Jean Hunter. [Cumbrae gravestone]

MCPHERSON, JOHN, a grocer, was admitted as a burgess and guilds-brother of Dunbarton on 11 December 1811. [DBR]

MCPHERSON, MARGARET CAMPBELL, youngest daughter of Alexander McPherson of Achriach, married Donald Campbell a merchant in Glasgow on 5 June 1820. [SM.86.94]

MCPHERSON, PETER, born 1774, schoolmaster in Ardentinny, died 4 March 1829, husband of Elizabeth Douglas, born 1779, died 29 June 1867. [Kilmun gravestone]

MCPHERSON, SARAH, born 1809, Duncan born 1829, Alexander born 1834, Ann born 1836, Donald born 1842, Jane born 1844, and Dugald, from Laga, Ardnamurchan, emigrated via Liverpool, on board the Marmion bound for Moreton Bay, Queensland, Australia, on 28 August 1852. [NRS.HD4/5]

MCQUEEN, JAMES, a merchant, was admitted as a burgess and guilds-brother of Dunbarton on 6 May 1806. [DBR]

MCQUEEN, WILLIAM LENNIE, born 1833, died in Valparaiso, Chile, on 23 January 1879. [Drymen gravestone] [S.11092]

MCQUILKAN, ANGUS, in East Tarbert, a debtor of William Caldwell at Lochwinnoch, 5 November 1810. [NRS.JP36.5.55]

MCQUILKAN, ARCHIBALD, in Campbeltown, was admitted as a burgess and guilds-brother of Ayr on 12 June 1794. [ABR]

MCQUILKAN, JAMES, in West Tarbert, a debtor of William Caldwell at Lochwinnoch, 5 November 1810. [NRS.JP36.5.55]

MCRAE, ALEXANDER, born 1769, wife Margaret born 1776, John born 1794, Kenneth born 1800, Finlay born 1802, Archibald born 1805, Margaret born 1807, Catherine born 1809, Ann born 1812, Roderick born 1815, from Glen Orchy, emigrated via Greenock to Upper Canada in July 1815. [TNA.AO3]

MCRAE, ALEXANDER, born 1747, a farmer in Glen Orchy, his wife Catherine McIntosh born 1760, Archibald born 1793, Roderick born 1791, and grand-daughter Christian born 1805, emigrated via Greenock to Upper Canada in July 1815. [TNA.AO3]

MACSWAN, JOHN, died in Dunoon on 27 July 1842. [Dunoon gravestone]

MCSYMON, ARCHIBALD, a baker, was admitted as a burgess of Dunbarton on 9 August 1838. [DBR]

MCSYMON, JOHN, a baker, was admitted as a burgess and guildsbrother of Dunbarton on 9 August 1790. [DBR]

MCTAGGART, CATHERINE, spouse of Pinkerton Martin in Kilchenzie, a debtor of John McSporran a shoemaker in Campbeltown, a decreet, 3 June 1811. [NRS.JP36.5.56]

MCTAGGART, MALCOLM, son of Malcolm McTaggart, [1761-1831], died in Launceston, Van Diemen's Land, [Tasmania], Australia, on 28 March 1838. [Rothesay gravestone, Bute]

MCTAGGART, NEIL, from Campbeltown, emigrated via Londonderry on the Dispatch of Workington bound for Quebec on 29 May 1828, was shipwrecked off Ile aux Mort, Newfoundland, but was rescued and landed at Port aux Basques and taken to Halifax, Nova Scotia, on 26 July 1828. [NSARM] [Strabane Morning Post, 2.9.1828]

MACTAGGART, C & D, solicitors in Campbeltown, and Lochgilphead from 1813. [NRS.NRAS.2776]

MCTAGGART, MALCOLM, a merchant in Rothesay, Bute, versus Donald Munro a vintner in Inveraray, a petition, 22 July 1802. [NRS.JP36.5.47]

MCTAGGART, MALCOLM, son of Malcolm McTaggart, [1761-1831], died in Launceston, Van Diemen's Land, [Tasmania], Australia, on 28 March 1838. [Rothesay gravestone, Bute]

MCTAGGART, SCIPIO, Sheriff Clerk of Argyll, was admitted as a burgess of Inveraray on 27 November 1839. [IBR]

MACTAVISH, ALEXANDER, born 27 June 1800 son of the above Hugh Mactavish, was educated at the University of Edinburgh, minister at Dunoon from 15 July 1829 until his death on 29 September 1869. [F.4.28]

MACTAVISH, HUGH, born 15 February 1757, son of Archibald MacTavish minister of Torosay, educated at Glasgow University, minister at Inverchaolin from 1784 until 1828, died 24 March 1837. [F.4.28]

MACTAVISH, DUGALD, a Writer to the Signet in Campbeltown, father of William MacTavish in the service of the Hudson Bay Company, his heir in 1858. [NRS.S/H]

MACTAVISH, HUGH, born 15 February 1757, son of Reverend Archibald MacTavish on Mull, was educated at the University of Glasgow, minister at Dunoon from 1784 until 1828, died 24 March 1837. [F.4.28]

MACTAVISH, WILLIAM, of the Hudson Bay Company, son and heir of Dugald MacTavish, a Writer to the Signet in Campbeltown, Argyll, 1858. [NRS.S/H]

MACVANNELL, ARCHIBALD, a farmer in Lemnamuick, 1848. [NRS.SC50.5.1848.20]

MACVANNELL, JOHN, a farmer in Lemnamuick, 1848. [NRS.SC50.5.1848.20]

MACVANNELL, PETER, a farmer in Lemnamuick, 1848. [NRS.SC50.5.1848.20]

MCVEAN, JOHN, an innkeeper, was admitted as a burgess of Inveraray on 2 May 1836. [IBR]

MCVICAR, ARCHIBALD, born 1791 in Argyll, settled in Charleston, South Carolina, as a butcher, naturalised there on 19 October 1813. [NARA.M1183.1]

MCVICAR, ARCHIBALD, born 1797 in Minard, Argyll, settled in Charleston, South Carolina, in 1811, died 24 August 1823. [Old Scots gravestone, Charleston.]

MCVICAR, ARCHIBALD, born 1819, son of Neil McVicar of Ardishaig, died in Trinidad in April 1840. [Lochgilphead gravestone]

MCVICAR, DUNCAN, a grocer, was admitted as a burgess of Inveraray on 22 May 1848. [IBR]

MCVICAR, JOHN, from Argyll, emigrated via Bristol to Jamaica in 1793, settled on Good Hope Estate, Trelawney, Jamaica. [SRA.AGN.321]

MCVICAR, JOHN, a weaver in Inveraray, subscribed to a bond of caution for Donald McVicar, baron officer of North Knapdale, as a constable for Argyll, on 5 May 1795. [NRS.JP36.6.1]

MCVICAR, NEIL, born 1794 in Argyll, settled in Charleston, South Carolina, as a butcher, naturalised there on 29 January 1824. [NARA.M1183.1]

MACVICAR, PETER, son of Peter MacVicar miller at Smerby, Campbeltown, was accused of the deforcement of the crew of an Excise cutter in 1815. [NRS.AD14.15.95]

MCWALTER, JOHN, a baker, was admitted as a burgess and guilds-brother of Dunbarton on 29 July 1793. [DBR]

MCWALTER, ROBERT, jr., a boatman, was admitted as a burgess and guilds-brother of Dunbarton on 28 May 1792. [DBR]

MCWATTIE, ALEXANDER, son of Duncan McWattie a manufacturer in Bonhill, educated at Glasgow University in 1804, minister at Kennoway, Fife, from 1811 to 1820, emigrated to Canada. [MAGU.209]

MCWHIRTER, ELIZABETH, born 1822, died 1862, wife Dugald Kelly a baker in Innellan. [Dunoon gravestone]

MCWILLIAM, ANDREW, in Peninver, a debtor of John McSporran a shoemaker in Campbeltown, a decreet, 3 June 1811. [NRS.JP36.5.56]

MCWILLIAM, DONALD, tacksman of Smerby, died in February 1814, inventory, 9 August 1814. [NRS.CC2.5.11]

MCWILLIAM, MALCOLM, born 1758, emigrated via Oban aboard the Spencer of Newcastle bound for Prince Edward Island on 22 September 1806. [PAPEI, 2702]

MACOME, ROBERT, a writer, was admitted as a burgess of Dunbarton on 28 October 1842. [DBR]

MAINE, ELIZABETH, born 1831, from Camuscharik, emigrated via Liverpool on board the Allison bound for Melbourne, Victoria, Australia, on 13 September 1852. [NRS.HD4/5]

MAIN, HUGH, fisherman in Inveraray, was evicted by the Duke of Argyll on 28 March 1805. [NRS.B32.2.1.42]

MAIR, ANDREW, a mason, was admitted as a burgess and guilds-brother of Dunbarton on 23 September 1828 as son of Andrew Mair a burgess. [DBR]

MAIR, ROBERT, a mason, was admitted as a burgess and guilds-brother of Dunbarton on 25 September 1829 as son of a burgess. [DBR]

MAITLAND, JAMES, a baker, was admitted as a burgess of Inveraray on 12 June 1848. [IBR]

MAITLAND, MATTHEW, a grocer, was admitted as a burgess and guilds-brother of Dunbarton on 20 July 1819. [DBR]

MALCOLM, NEIL, of Poltalloch, an inventory of the Glebe of Inverlussa, papers dated 1 January 1812. [NRS.CH2.190.12.17]

MALLOY, ARCHIBALD, a weaver at Auchafarich, a debtor to James McMillan a shoemaker in Killowcraw, 20 March 1811. [NRS.JP36.5.56]

MALLOY, JOHN, from Kintyre, with his wife Catherine McCallum, emigrated to North Carolina in 1804, settled in Robeson County, died on 23 January 1839. [St Paul's records, NC]

MANNERS, JOHN, a weaver, was admitted as a burgess and guilds-brother of Dunbarton on 25 September 1818 as married to the daughter of a burgess. [DBR]

MARQUIS, JANET, spouse of James Stewart weaver at the Laggan, a decreet, 1811. [NRS.JP36.5.56]

MARQUIS, MARY, born 1791, died 5 November 1840, wife of Archibald Paterson a farmer at Ardluing. [Kilchattan gravestone]

MARSHALL, JOHN, eldest son of Dr Hugh Marshall in Rothesay, Bute, died in Charleston, South Carolina, on 8 June 1820. [SM.86.190]

MARSHALL, MARGARET W., born 1776 in Cardross, wife of Andrew Marshall, settled in Charleston, South Carolina, in 1821, died 24 September 1826. [2nd Presbyterian gravestone, Charleston]

MARSHALL, JOHN, eldest son of Dr Hugh Marshall in Rothesay, Bute, a merchant in Charleston, South Carolina, died there on 8 June 1820. [Blackwood's Magazine, 7.584] [Charleston City Gazette, 13.6.1820]

MARSHALL, MARK, born 1778 in Baldernock, son of James Marshall a farmer, educated at Glasgow University, minister at Kingarth from 1811 to his death on 14 December 1820. [F.4.35]

MARTIN, EZEKIAE, a shopkeeper, was admitted as a burgess and guilds-brother of Dunbarton on 29 July 1793. [DBR]

MARTIN, MARY, wife of Robert Brock a labourer in Corrieport, Kilbride, Arran, in Laigh Corrie, was accused of housebreaking and theft in 1842. [NRS.AD14.42.429]

MARTIN, PINKERTON, a shoemaker in Kilchenzie, a decreet, 1811. [NRS.JP36.5.56]

MAXWELL, JAMES, born 1765, son of James Maxwell in Kintyre, a shipmaster in Campbeltown, was drowned at Ayr on 29 January 1800. [Kirkoswald gravestone]

MAXWELL, JOHN, formerly a Lieutenant of the 8th West India Regiment, was admitted as a burgess and guilds-brother of Dunbarton on 25 June 1825 as married to the daughter of a burgess. [DBR]

MAXWELL, WILLIAM, was admitted as a burgess and guilds-brother of Dunbarton on 22 September 1814. [DBR]

MAXWELL, WILLIAM BEDWELL, a grocer, was admitted as a burgess and guilds-brother of Dunbarton on 13 July 1822. [DBR]

MAY, ALEXANDER, Customs Controller at Rothesay, Bute, was admitted as a burgess and guilds-brother of Ayr on 7 July 1790. [ABR]

MELVILLE, WILLIAM, a shopkeeper, was admitted as a burgess and guilds-brother of Dunbarton on 28 May 1804. [DBR]

MESSER, ALEXANDER, [1810-1857], an architect, husband of Jane who died in Andover, Massachusetts, aged 76, parents of Alexander born 185-, died 1861 in Andover, Elizabeth born 1852, died in Andover, and James who died in Andover in 189-. [St Clement's gravestone, Dingwall]

MICHAEL, WILLIAM, a merchant, was admitted as a burgess of Inveraray on 4 October 1813. [IBR]

MILLER, ALEXANDER, a hatter, was admitted as a burgess and guilds-brother of Dunbarton on 19 January 1791. [DBR]

MILLAR, ANDREW, a shipmaster, was accused of rioting and attacking a ship loaded with grain attempting to sail from Campbeltown, a petition, 21 March 1801. [NRS.JP36.5.46]

MILLAR, ANDREW, a gardener, was admitted as a burgess of Dunbarton on 20 June 1845. [DBR]

MILLER, DAVID, a mason, was admitted as a burgess and guilds-brother of Dunbarton on 20 September 1813. [DBR]

MILLER, JAMES, in Millburn, born 6 December 1780, died 9 May 1869, wife Catherine Angus born 1787, died 18 November 1862, son Robert Angus Millar, died in Trinidad on 26 February 1844. [Cumbrae gravestone]

MILLAR, JOHN, a bookbinder, was admitted as a burgess of Dunbarton on 3 September 1798. [DBR]

MILLAR, JOHN, a bookbinder, was admitted as a burgess and guilds-brother of Dunbarton on 8 March 1825. [DBR]

MILLER, JOHN, a carter, was admitted as a burgess and guilds-brother of Dunbarton on 31 May 1828. [DBR]

MILLER, JOHN, born 1828, died in Ovens, Victoria, Australia, on 9 April 1869. [Clachan gravestone, Arran]

MILLAR, JOHN, formerly a merchant in Glasgow, was admitted as a burgess of Dunbarton on 2 February 1836. [DBR]

MILLAR, ROBERT, a shoemaker, was admitted as a burgess of Dunbarton on 25 September 1818, having served an apprenticeship under a burgess. [DBR]

MILLAR, WILLIAM, from Dunoon, Argyll, a mason in New York, brother and heir of David Millar in Milton Mill, who died on 2 August 1865. [NRS.S/H]

MILLS, GEORGE, a wright, was admitted as a burgess of Dunbarton on 25 September 1829 as son of a burgess. [DBR]

MILLS, GEORGE, a shipbuilder at Little Milne, was admitted as a burgess of Dunbarton on 6 February 1837. [DBR]

MILNE, JAMES, a wright, was admitted as a burgess of Dunbarton on 25 June 1792. [DBR]

MITCHELL, DAVID, a weaver, was admitted as a burgess and guilds-brother of Dunbarton on 24 September 1818 by right of his father Peter Mitchell a shoemaker burgess. [DBR]

MITCHELL, JAMES, a shoemaker, was admitted as a burgess of Dunbarton on 20 September 1810. [DBR]

MITCHELL, JAMES, a shoemaker, was admitted as a burgess and guilds-brother of Dunbarton on 20 September 1810 by right of his father a burgess. [DBR]

MITCHELL, JOHN, a tanner, was admitted as a burgess and guilds-brother of Dunbarton on 22 June 1825 as son of a burgess. [DBR]

MITCHELL, JOHN, a copper and tin smith, was admitted as a burgess and guilds-brother of Dunbarton on 14 September 1827. [DBR]

MITCHELL, PETER HUTCHESON, a writer, was admitted as a burgess of Dunbarton on 29 September 1831 as son of a burgess. [DBR]

MITCHELL, ROBERT, a shoemaker, was admitted as a burgess of Dunbarton on 20 September 1810. [DBR]

MOFFAT, JOHN, a mason, was admitted as a burgess of Dunbarton on 16 November 1790. [DBR]

MOIR, ALEXANDER, a slater and mason, was admitted as a burgess and guilds-brother of Dunbarton on 4 July 1808. [DBR]

MONTEATH, WILLIAM, youngest son of Reverend J. Monteath in Killean, a surgeon who died on St Vincent on 16 August 1793. [SM.55.619]

MONTGOMERY, ALEXANDER, a grain merchant in Campbeltown, records 1813-1838. [NRS.NRAS.1370.3.1]

MONTGOMERY, GEORGE, a shoemaker a mason, was admitted as a burgess of Dunbarton on 13 October 1803 as son of George Montgomery a weaver burgess. [DBR]

MONTGOMERY, JOHN, a surgeon apothecary, a mason, was admitted as a burgess and guilds-brother of Dunbarton on 16 June 1827. [DBR]

MONTGOMERY, ROBERT, a weaver, a mason, was admitted as a burgess of Dunbarton on 26 July 1802. [DBR]

MOORE, ALEXANDER, in Dunoon, was the victim of an assault in 1835. [NRS.AD14.35.154]

MOOR, PATRICK, a weaver in Auchtyre, , testament, 22 July 1790, Comm. Argyll. [NRS]

MORRIS, JAMES, born 1789, a builder, died in August 1849, husband of Euphemia MacFarlane, born 1788, died in September 1850. [Dunoon gravestone]

MORRISON, CHARLES, and Robert Murphy, coopers, versus Peter MacArthur, a wright and fishcurer in Inveraray, a petition, 11 December 1800. [NRS.B32.2.1.40]

MORISON, DANIEL, born 1774, Customs Controller of Glasgow, died in Rothesay on 3 December 1844, wife Margaret Hall, born 1774, died 13 November 1853. [Rothesay gravestone, Bute]

MORRISON, HECTOR, a merchant, a mason, was admitted as a burgess and guilds-brother of Dunbarton on 20 July 1820. [DBR]

MORRISON, JOHN, a cooper, was admitted as a burgess of Inveraray on 29 September 1806. [IBR]

MORRISON, JOHN, a cooper, was admitted as a burgess of Inveraray on 21 May 1818. [IBR]

MORRISON, NEIL, born in Argyll before 1804, was naturalised in South Carolina on 20 November 1825. [SC. Citizens Book.109]

MORRISON, ROBERT, a grocer, was admitted as a burgess and guilds-brother of Dunbarton on 20 July 1820 as son of a burgess. [DBR]

MORTON, ALEXANDER, a shoemaker, was admitted as a burgess of Dunbarton on 22 October 1791. [DBR]

MOTHERWELL, WILLIAM, a china merchant, was admitted as a burgess and guilds-brother of Dunbarton on 13 July 1822. [DBR]

MUIR, ARCHIBALD, a merchant, younger son of Archibald Muir a wright in Rothesay, Bute, was admitted as a burgess and guilds-brother of Glasgow in 1787. [GBR]

MUIR, JOHN, son of James Muir a mason in Greenock, a writer in Rothesay, Bute, was admitted as a Notary Public on 9 July 1790. [NRS.NP2.34.195]

MUIR, JOHN, a vintner in Rothesay, Bute, testament, 21 May 1799, Comm. Argyll. [NRS]

MUIR, JOHN, born 1833, son of Thomas Muir and his wife Isabella McKinlay, died in Australia in March 1853. [Rothesay gravestone, Bute]

MUIR, JOHN, a mason in Campbeltown, 1848. [NRS.SC50.5.1848.43]

MUNN, DONALD, born 1785 in Rothesay, Bute, settled in St John, New Brunswick, in 1816, died there in June 1830. [City Gazette, 30 June 1830]

MUNN, DUNCAN, born 1746, wife Flora Brown born 1748, Angus born 1775, Neil born 1778, Malcolm born 1783, James born 1786, Ann born 1789, Effy born 1789, emigrated via Oban aboard the Spencer of Newcastle bound for Prince Edward Island on 22 September 1806. [PAPEI, 2702]

MUNN, JAMES, born 1784, emigrated from Argyll to Prince Edward Island in 1806, died there 5 June 1868, husband of Elizabeth McMillan, born 1786, died on PEI on 22 November 1873. [Woods Island Pioneer Cemetery, PEI].

MUNN, JOHN, a mariner in Dunbarton, testament, 19 July 1805, Comm. Glasgow. [NRS.CC9.7.76.197]

MUNN, ROBERT, a grocer, was admitted as a burgess and guilds-brother of Dunbarton on 1 August 1809. [DBR]

MUNN, WALTER, a hairdresser, was admitted as a burgess of Dunbarton on 9 May 1845. [DBR]

MUNRO, ALEXANDER, an innkeeper, was admitted as a burgess of Inveraray on 22 October 1838. [IBR]

MUNRO, CHARLES, in Campbeltown, petitioned for land opposite Machrimore, Southend, in 1845. [NRS.NRAS 1209.1981]

MUNRO, COLIN, a merchant, was admitted as a burgess of Inveraray on 27 June 1840. [IBR]

MUNRO, DONALD, an innkeeper, was admitted as a burgess of Inveraray on 24 November 1803. [IBR]

MUNRO, DUGALD, an innkeeper, was admitted as a burgess of Inveraray on 25 October 1813. [IBR]

MUNRO, DUGALD, a merchant, was admitted as a burgess of Inveraray on 11 September 1845. [IBR]

MUNRO, DUNCAN, in Inveraray, was evicted by the Duke of Argyll on 28 March 1805. [NRS.B32.2.1.42]

MUNRO, DUNCAN, a merchant, was admitted as a burgess of Inveraray on 29 September 1806. [IBR]

MUNRO, DUNCAN, jr., a merchant, was admitted as a burgess of Inveraray on 4 May 1837. [IBR]

MUNRO, JAMES, Sheriff Officer in Inveraray, died 1814, inventory, 23 November 1814. [NRS.CC2.5.11]

MUNRO, JOHN, a saddler and a merchant, was admitted as a burgess of Inveraray on 9 November 1850. [IBR]

MUNRO, PETER, an innkeeper, was admitted as a burgess of Inveraray on 25 October 1813. [IBR]

MUNRO, WILLIAM, son of Duncan Munro in Inveraray, a writer in Edinburgh, was admitted as a Notary Public on 6 March 1790. [NRS.NP2.34.157]

MURCHIE, DONALD, from Arran, emigrated to Quebec in 1829, settled in Inverness township by 1831. [AMC]

MURCHIE, JOHN, son of John Murchie, [1775-1853], a farmer in Kilpatrick, and his wife Catherine Bannatyne, [1790-1877], a merchant in Fiji. [Clachan gravestone, Arran]

MURCHY, ROBERT, a cooper, was admitted as a burgess of Inveraray on 29 September 1806. [IBR]

MURCHIE, WILLIAM, and family, from Ballymichail, Arran, emigrated to Quebec, settled in Inverness Township, Lower Canada, in 1831. [TNA.CO384.28.fos.24-26][AMC]

MURCHIE, Mrs, a tenant in Corrie, Arran, with her family of two, emigrated to Canada in 1829. [TNA.CO384.22.fos.3-5]

MURDOCH, CHARLES, a shoemaker in Lochranza, Arran, with his family of nine. emigrated to Canada in 1829. [TNA.CO384.22.fos.3-5]

MURDOCH, DAVID, a cloth merchant, was admitted as a burgess and guilds-brother of Dunbarton on 5 June 1808. [DBR]

MURDOCH, JAMES, a cloth merchant, was admitted as a burgess and guilds-brother of Dunbarton on 10 March 1810. [DBR]

MURPHY, MURDOCH, born in Kintyre, died in Robeson County, North Carolina, in 1814. [NCSA.2.36]

MURRAY, DUGALD, an innkeeper, was admitted as a burgess and guilds-brother of Dunbarton on 25 July 1792. [DBR]

MURRAY, DUNCAN, born 1840, son of James Murray, a planter in Fiji, and his wife Mary McConcely, died on 8 November 1842. [Kilkerran gravestone]

MURRAY, JAMES, a ferryman, was admitted as a burgess of Inveraray on 14 December 1844. [IBR]

MURRAY, WILLIAM, a slater in Glasgow, was admitted as a burgess and guilds-brother of Dunbarton on 2 August 1825. [DBR]

NAIRN, WILLIAM, a clothier, was admitted as a burgess of Dunbarton on 26 June 1832. [DBR]

NAPIER, ALEXANDER, a smith, was admitted as a burgess of Inveraray on 29 March 1845. [IBR]

NAPIER, JAMES, was admitted as a burgess and guilds-brother of Dunbarton on 20 August 1825. [DBR]

NAPIER, Lieutenant Colonel ROBERT JOHN, of Milliken, was admitted as a burgess of Inveraray on 17 June 1801. [IBR]

NAPIER, ROBERT, a smith, was admitted as a burgess of Inveraray on 29 September 1806. [IBR]

NAPIER, ROBERT, of Shandon, an engineer in Glasgow, a mason, was admitted as a burgess of Dunbarton on 12 December 1839 as son of a burgess. [DBR]

NASH, WILLIAM, a wright, was admitted as a burgess of Dunbarton on 25 September 1829. [DBR]

NEMMO, THOMAS, a mason in Lamlash, Arran, 1840. [BOA231]

NEWAL, JOHN, a shopkeeper, was admitted as a burgess and guilds-brother of Dunbarton on 9 August 1790. [DBR]

NICOL, DANIEL, and family, from West Bennan, Arran, emigrated to Quebec in April 1831, [TNA.CO384.28.341/2]; settled in Inverness Township, Lower Canada, in 1831. [TNA.CO384.28.fos.24-26] [AMC]

NIVEN, ARCHIBALD, a farmer at Silverton Hill, was admitted as a burgess of Dunbarton on 26 August 1843. [DBR]

NIVEN, PETER, a grocer, was admitted as a burgess and guilds-brother of Dunbarton on 23 September 1825. [DBR]

NOBLE, MARION, born 1805, 'dutiful servant to William Ewing in Ardvullin for 35 years', died in 1870. [Dunoon gravestone]

OGILVIE, FELICITY, born in Carricou, Grenada, in 1782, died in Auchenfree, Dunbartonshire, on 26 May 1831. [Cardross gravestone]

OGILVIE, JOHN, a carter and shopkeeper, was admitted as a burgess and guilds-brother of Dunbarton on 25 October 1798. [DBR]

OGILVIE, JOHN, a wright, was admitted as a burgess of Dunbarton on 25 October 1829. [DBR]

O'NEIL, JOHN, a travelling merchant, was admitted as a burgess of Inveraray on 5 December 1820. [IBR]

OREM, JOHN, a book seller and wright, was admitted as a burgess of Dunbarton on 16 September 1814. [DBR]

ORR, JAMES, MD, born 1809, died 19 June 1853. [Dunoon gravestone]

OTWAY, ABRAHAM, a confectioner, was admitted as a burgess and guilds-brother of Dunbarton on 31 March 1806. [DBR]

PARK, JOHN, Lieutenant Colonel of the 91st Regiment, was admitted as a burgess of Inveraray on 21 October 1804. [IBR]

PARK, JOHN, a slater in Old Kilpatrick, was admitted as a burgess of Dunbarton on 5 November 1810. [DBR]

PARK, MARY, born 1775, died 1 May 1803, daughter of Adam Park, farmer in Auchimor, and his wife Margaret Whyte. [Dunoon gravestone]

PARK, MARY, wife of Peter Headrick in Canada, sister and heir of Lillias Park, in Dunoon, Argyll, also to her sister Margaret there, 1863. [NRS.S/H]

PARLANE, JAMES, and his wife Mary Slack, in Bonhill, Dunbartonshire, parents of William Parlane who died in Brooklyn, New York, on 8 July 1875. [EC.28333]

PATERSON, ALEXANDER, a glass cutter, was admitted as a burgess and guilds-brother of Dunbarton on 18 September 1827 as son of James Paterson a sawyer burgess. [DBR]

PATERSON, ALEXANDER, jr., a wright, was admitted as a burgess and guilds-brother of Dunbarton on 23 September 1828 as son of Alexander Paterson a glass cutter burgess. [DBR]

PATERSON, ARCHIBALD, in Kilmory, Glassary, was accused of robbery in 1814. [NRS.AD14.14.54]

PATERSON, ARCHIBALD, a writer, was admitted as a burgess and guilds-brother of Dunbarton on 2 February 1836 as son of a burgess. [DBR]

PATERSON, CHARLES, born 1795, a mason, died 2 September 1849, wife Elizabeth Hunter, born 1804, died in September 1831. [Cumbrae gravestone]

PATERSON, DOLLY, born 1736, Catherine McLean born 1771, emigrated via Oban aboard the Spencer of Newcastle bound for Prince Edward Island on 22 September 1806. [PAPEI, 2702]

PATERSON, DUNCAN NUGENT, born 1795 in Campbeltown, a garden labourer in Glasgow, was accused of assault in 1835. [NRS.AD14.35.154]

PATERSON, JOHN, a wright, was admitted as a burgess and guilds-brother of Dunbarton on 20 September 1804. [DBR]

PATERSON, JOHN, a writer, was admitted as a burgess of Dunbarton on 13 August 1827. [DBR]

PATTERSON, JOHN, on Arran, a letter dated 22 July 1844. [NRS.NRAS.332.C4.449]

PATERSON, PETER, a wright, was admitted as a burgess and guilds-brother of Dunbarton on 25 September 1822 as a son of a burgess. [DBR]

PATERSON, WALTER, was admitted as a burgess and guilds-brother of Dunbarton on 13 Sptember 1828 as son of Alexander Paterson a glasscutter burgess. [DBR]

PATTEN, Mrs MARGARET, widow of Archibald Bell a baker, was admitted as a burgess of Inveraray in 1843. [IBR]

PAUL, JAMES, in Garshake, was admitted as a burgess and guilds-brother of Dunbarton on 12 March 1801. [DBR]

PAUL, ROBERT, a merchant, was admitted as a burgess and guilds-brother of Dunbarton on 13 May 1794. [DBR]

PAUL, WILLIAM, a grocer and a spirit dealer, was admitted as a burgess and guilds-brother of Dunbarton on 23 April 1830. [DBR]

PAXTON, JOHN, a weaver and ship's carpenter, was admitted as a burgess and guilds-brother of Dunbarton on 24 September 1818 as son of William Paxton a gardener burgess. [DBR]

PAXTON, WILLIAM, a gardener, was admitted as a burgess and guilds-brother of Dunbarton on 29 July1793. [DBR]

PEMBERTON, WILLIAM, a glass maker, was admitted as a burgess and of Dunbarton on 19 April 1844. [DBR]

PEREY, ANN, born 1812 in Argyll, died in Montreal or Quebec on 18 June 1832. [GA.4258]

PHILIPS, ARCHIBALD, emigrated via Oban to Quebec in 1819, settled in Argyle, Upper Canada, on 24 December 1819.

PHILIPS, DANIEL, born 1784 in Argyll, a mariner who was naturalised in Charleston, South Carolina, on 17 March 1806. [NARA.M1183.1]

PICKEN, JAMES, a merchant in Port Glasgow, was admitted as a burgess and guilds-brother of Dunbarton on 8 November 1796.[DBR]

PICKERING, WILLIAM, a merchant, was admitted as a burgess of Dunbarton on 25 January 1830. [DBR]

PLEAN, ANDREW, an able seaman in Campbeltown in May 1795. [NRS.HCR.212]

POLLOCK, JAMES, Procurator Fiscal of Kintyre, 1803. [NRS.JC26.1803.62]

POLLOCK, MATTHEW, a slater in Milton, was admitted as a burgess of Dunbarton on 23 July 1823. [DBR]

POLLOCK, PATRICK, possibly from Knapdale, a midshipman of the Royal Navy in 1794. [NRS.S/H]

POLLOCK, PATRICK, in Barnlangart, South Knapdale, an edict of executry, 1811. [NRS.CC2.8.115.5]

PORTEOUS, JAMES, from Bonhill, Dunbartonshire, died in Jamaica on 15 December 1821. [Scots Magazine.89.539]

PORTEOUS, Reverend WILLIAM, born 17 October 1837 in Napan, Miramachi, New Brunswick, died at Innellan on 28 November 1864. [Dunoon gravestone]

PORTER, JOHN, a baillie of Campbeltown, was admitted as a burgess and guilds-brother of Ayr on 12 June 1794. [ABR]

PRIMROSE, ADAM, a copper and tin smith, was admitted as a burgess and guilds-brother of Dunbarton on 20 September 1816. [DBR]

PRIMROSE, ADAM, jr., a tin smith, was admitted as a burgess and guilds-brother of Dunbarton on 4 September 1824 as son of a burgess. [DBR]

PRIMROSE, EDWARD, a copper and tin smith, was admitted as a burgess and guilds-brother of Dunbarton on 22 September 1802. [DBR]

PRIMROSE, WILLIAM, a tin smith, was admitted as a burgess and guilds-brother of Dunbarton on 20 September 1825 as son of James Primrose a tinsmith burgess. [DBR]

RALSTON, ANDREW, tenant of Knockstaplebeg, Southend of Kintyre, papers 1814-1833. [NRS.NRAS.1209.530]

RALSTON, JAMES, born 1784 in Argyll, a wine merchant in Charleston, South Carolina, was naturalised there on 9 August 1806, died there on 13 February 1810. [NARA.M1183.1] [Charleston City Gazette, 17.2.1810]

RALSTON, JOHN, a merchant in Jamaica, a sasine in 1813, grandson of Duncan Clyde a cooper in Campbeltown. [NRS.RS.Argyll.2329]

RALSTON, ROBERT, a grain merchant in Campbeltown, records 1813-1838. [NRS.NRAS.1370.3.1], his former servant, 15 July 1817. [NRS.AC20.2.51]

RAMAGE, THOMAS, a servant to John Napier a smith and founder, was admitted as a burgess and guilds-brother of Dunbarton on 8 April 1801. [DBR]

RAMSAY, JOHN, with six sons and two nephews, emigrated via Campbeltown on board the Annabella bound for Prince Edward Island in 1770. [NWI]

RANKIN, ALEXANDER, a slater, was admitted as a burgess of Dunbarton on 25 September 1829. [DBR]

RANKINE, ALEXANDER CAMPBELL, a writer, was admitted as a burgess of Inveraray on 8 November 1848. [IBR]

RANKIN, DANIEL, a slater at Little Milne, was admitted as a burgess and guilds-brother of Dunbarton on 18 September 1824. [DBR]

RANKIN, DANIEL, a shipmaster, was admitted as a burgess and guilds-brother of Dunbarton on 2 February 1836 as married to the daughter of a burgess. [DBR]

RANKIN, DUNCAN, born 1769 in Fort William, son of Duncan Rankin, educated at King's College, Aberdeen, minister at South Knapdale from 26 November 1805, died on 5 November 1842. [F.4.18]

RANKIN, JAMES, a merchant, was admitted as a burgess and guilds-brother of Dunbarton on 25 September 1829. [DBR]

RANKIN, WILLIAM, jr., a shipmaster, was admitted as a burgess and guilds-brother of Dunbarton on 11 February 1828, as son of a burgess. [DBR]

RATTRAY, DAVID, from Helensburgh, died in Hamilton, Canada West, on 5 September 1859. [GM.NS2/7.541]

RAY, DANIEL, born 1763 on Jura, emigrated to America in 1792 a farmer in Cumberland County, North Carolina in 1812, died on 9 March 1826. [Longstreet gravestone, Fort Bragg]

REID, ARCHIBALD, a wright, was admitted as a burgess and guilds-brother of Dunbarton on 31 March 1806. [DBR]

REID, GEORGE, a shoemaker, was admitted as a burgess and guilds-brother of Dunbarton on 24 September 1818 having served his apprenticeship under a burgess. [DBR]

REID, ROBERT, a smith, was admitted as a burgess and guilds-brother of Dunbarton on 25 June 1825, as a son of a burgess. [DBR]

REID, WILLIAM, a smith, was admitted as a burgess and guilds-brother of Dunbarton on 25 October 1796. [DBR]

REID, WILLIAM, a schoolteacher in Lubas, Kingarth, testament, 28 January 1799, Comm. Argyll. [NRS]

REID, WILLIAM, the younger, a grocer in Long Row, Campbeltown, a memorandum 1836. [NRS.NRAS.1209.1941]

RENNIE, JEAN, born 1794, died 17 June 1835, wife of William Campbell a wright in Glen Finnart. [Kilmun gravestone]

RENNIE, JOHN, a mason, was admitted as a burgess and guilds-brother of Dunbarton on 31 May 1828. [DBR]

RICHARDS, BENJAMIN, a surgeon and druggist, was admitted as a burgess of Dunbarton on 26 June 1832. [DBR]

RICHARDSON, JOHN, a clock and watchmaker, was admitted as a burgess of Dunbarton on 14 October 1793. [DBR]

RICHMOND, GEORGE, a wright, was admitted as a burgess of Dunbarton on 21 September 1802. [DBR]

RICHMOND, JOHN, a mason, was admitted as a burgess of Dunbarton on 1 September 1792. [DBR]

RICHMOND, JOHN, a shoemaker, was admitted as a burgess of Dunbarton on 25 September 1818 as son of a burgess. [DBR]

RICHMOND, JOHN, a joiner, was admitted as a burgess and guilds-brother of Dunbarton on 23 September 1829 as son of a burgess. [DBR]

RIDDELL, Sir JAMES, Lieutenant Colonel of the Argyll Militia, was admitted as a burgess of Inveraray on 6 July 1809. [IBR]

RISK, JAMES, a grocer and spirit dealer, was admitted as a burgess and guilds-brother of Dunbarton on 20 January 1824. [DBR

RISK, JAMES, was admitted as a burgess and guilds-brother of Dunbarton on 9 February 1836 as son of a burgess. [DBR]

RISK, WILLIAM, a grocer, was admitted as a burgess and guilds-brother of Dunbarton on 10 March 1810. [DBR]

RITCHIE, ARCHIBALD, born on Cumbrae in 1767, died on Trinidad in 1822, wife Sarah Tucker, born 1763, died in Ardrossan on 14 February 1837. [Cumbrae gravestone]

RITCHIE, Reverend HUGH, born in Millport in 1840, died in Taiwanfoo, Formosa, on 29 September 1879. [Cumbrae gravestone]

RITCHIE, JAMES, born 1771, formerly in Craignish, Argyll, died in De Pere, Wisconsin, on 2 April 1855. [IC.1952]

RITCHIE, JOHN, jr., a shoemaker, was admitted as a burgess and guilds-brother of Dunbarton on 26 September 1796. [DBR]

RITCHIE, SUSANNA, spouse of John Mackay a cooper in Rothesay, Bute, testament, 16 May 1798, Comm. Argyll. [NRS]

RITCHIE, WILLIAM, a shoemaker, was admitted as a burgess of Dunbarton on 4 March 1802. [DBR]

RITCHIE, WILLIAM, jr., a shoemaker, was admitted as a burgess and guilds-brother of Dunbarton on 24 Septembr 1818 as son of John Ritchie a shoemaker burgess. [DBR]

ROBB, JAMES, painter in Inveraray, versus Alexander Young, a petition in November 1803. [NRS.B32.2.1.41]

ROBB, WILLIAM, a mason, was admitted as a burgess of Dunbarton on 25 September 1829. [DBR]

ROBERTSON, ANGUS, and family, from Urinbeg, Arran, emigrated to Quebec in April 1831, [TNA.CO384.28.341/2]; settled in Inverness Township, Lower Canada, in 1831. [TNA.CO384.28.fos.24-26]

ROBERTSON, ARCHIBALD, a weaver, was admitted as a burgess of Dunbarton on 25 April 1790. [DBR]

ROBERTSON, JAMES, a shoemaker, was admitted as a burgess of Dunbarton on 20 September 1810. [DBR]

ROBERTSON, JAMES, in Glen Loin, Arrochar, Dunbartonshire, nephew and heir of George Ogilvie, formerly in Jamaica, lately in Dundee, 1842. [NRS.S/H]

ROBERTSON, JOHN, a shoemaker, was admitted as a burgess of Dunbarton on 25 September 1818, having served his apprenticeship under a burgess. [DBR].

ROBERTSON, JOHN, and family, from Kilpatrick, Arran, emigrated to Quebec in April 1831, [TNA.CO384.28.341/2]; settled in Inverness Township, Lower Canada, in 1831. [TNA.CO384.28.fos.24-26]

ROBERTSON, JOHN, a saddler, was admitted as a burgess of Inveraray on 3 November 1835. [IBR]

ROBERTSON, MALCOLM, born 1796, son of Donald Robertson, [1755-1809], and his wife Mary McColl, died 1804, died in Canada in 1818. [Isla Munda, Ballachulish, gravestone]

ROBERTSON, NEIL, a vintner in Shaddog, Arran, 1840. [BOA231]

ROBERTSON, PETER, a shopkeeper, was admitted as a burgess and guilds-brother of Dunbarton on 28 May 1792. [DBR]

ROBERTSON, ROBERT, MD, was admitted as a burgess of Inveraray on 18 December 1800. [IBR]

ROBERTSON, WILLIAM, an innkeeper, was admitted as a burgess and guilds-brother of Dunbarton on 20 July 1820. [DBR]

ROBERTSON, WILLIAM, a boot and shoemaker in Lamlash, Arran, 1840. [BOA230]

ROBERTSON, Mrs, born in the parish of Port, died in Dunoon on 5 June 1859. [Dunoon gravestone]

ROBINSON, JAMES, born in Argyll in 1761, died near Salisbury, North Carolina, on 23 July 1821. [Western Carolinian, 31 July 1821]

ROCHEAD, DAVID, a saddler, was admitted as a burgess and guilds-brother of Dunbarton on 28 September 1822 as son of a burgess. [DBR]

ROCHEAD, JAMES, jr., a saddler, was admitted as a burgess and guilds-brother of Dunbarton on 24 September 1829 as son of James Rochead a saddler burgess. [DBR]

ROCHEAD, JOHN, a baker, was admitted as a burgess and guilds-brother of Dunbarton on 8 March 1825 as son of a burgess. [DBR]

RODGER, JOHN, a farmer at Bishopton, was admitted as a burgess and guilds-brother of Dunbarton on 8 March 1825. [DBR]

ROSS, JOHN, a watchmaker in Inveraray, versus Janet McBrain, relict of Thomas Robertson grieve to the Duke of Argyll, 11 July 1806. [NRS.B32,2.1.43]

ROSS, JOHN, a merchant in Glasgow, married Ann McKail, daughter of Angus McKail of Prospect, Montego Bay, Jamaica, in Campbelltown, Argyll, on 1 November 1824. [S.504.802]

ROWAN, JAMES, a cottar in Ballanach, North Knapdale, was accused of hamesucken in 1823. [NRS.AD14.23.20]

ROWAN, JOHN, son of Robert Rowan a cottar in Achayerron, Glassary, was accused of hamesucken in 1823. [NRS.AD14.23.20]

ROY, ALEXANDER, a watchmaker, was admitted as a burgess and guilds-brother of Dunbarton on 13 June 1800. [DBR]

ROY, ROBERT, a baker, was admitted as a burgess of Dunbarton on 4 October 1846. [DBR]

SALMOND, DUNCAN, son of James Salmond in Inveraray, Argyll, a merchant who was admitted as a burgess and guilds-brother of Glasgow in 1845. [GBR]

SALMON, JAMES, a shoemaker, was admitted as a burgess of Inveraray on 29 September 1806. [IBR]

SCOTT, ALEXANDER, a writer, was admitted as a burgess and guilds-brother of Dunbarton on 10 March 1836 as married to the daughter of a burgess. [DBR]

SCOTT, JAMES, a mason, was admitted as a burgess and guilds-brother of Dunbarton on 19 September 1791. [DBR]

SCOTT, JOHN, born 1812, a millwright in Clachaig, Glenlean, Dunoon, was accused of assaulting Robert Sheriff of Selma Cottage, Cowal, in 1832. [NRS.AD14.32.226]

SCOTT, THOMAS, son of C. Scott in Woodbank, Dunbartonshire, died in Jamaica in 1813. [EA.5204.13]

SCOTT, WALTER, an advocate, interim Sheriff of Argyll, 1818. [NRS.NRAS.1209.63]

SEMPLE, JOHN, born 1800, died 9 December 1852. [Rothesay gravestone, Bute]

SERVICE, ROBERT, a wright, was admitted as a burgess of Dunbarton on 11 January 1800. [DBR]

SHANNAN, Captain NEILL, late of Sephenstraw, testament, 19 April 1799, Comm. Argyll. [NRS]

SHARP, JOHN, an able seaman in Campbeltown in May 1795. [NRS.HCR.212]

SHARP, ROBERT, master of the Fortune of Rothesay, Bute, testament, 28 June 1794, Comm. Isles. [NRS]

SHAW, ARCHIBALD, a tailor in Lamlash, Arran, 1840. [BOA231]

SHAW, DAVID, a shipping agent in Montreal, Quebec, son and heir of Agnes Shaw or Jamieson, in Helensburgh, Dunbartonshire, who died on 19 May 1862. [NRS.S/H]

SHAW, DONALD, an able seaman in Campbeltown in May 1795. [NRS.HCR.212]

SHAW, DONALD, an ordinary seaman in Argyll in June 1795. [NRS.HCR.212]

SHAW, MARY, postmistress and grocer in Brodick, Arran, 1840. [BOA230]

SHAW, MATHEW, born in Bute, was naturalised in South Carolina on 4 April 1820. [SC. Circuit Court Journal, 9.54]

SHAW, THOMAS, a wright, was admitted as a burgess and guilds-brother of Dunbarton on 24 June 1795. [DBR]

SHAW, THOMAS, born 1794, a labourer from Dunbarton, emigrated via Port Glasgow on board the Favourite of St John bound for St John, New Brunswick, on 22 October 1815. [PANB.ms.RS23E/9798]

SHAW, THOMAS, born 1790 in Dunbarton, died in Halifax, Nova Scotia, on 13 February 1827. [AR.17.2.1827]

SHAW, WILLIAM, a sawyer, was admitted as a burgess and guilds-brother of Dunbarton on 16 May 1822, as son of a burgess. [DBR]

SHEARER, JAMES, born in Innellan in 1762, late of Waimate, Otago, New Zealand, died in Dunoon on 29 November 1840. [Dunoon gravestone]

SHEARER, JANET CURRIE, born 1819, died in Ardyne, Waimate, Otago, New Zealand, on 7 July 1902. [Dunoon gravestone]

SHEARER, WILLIAM, born 1753, a seaman who was lost at sea in September 1806. [Cumbrae gravestone]

SHEPHERD, Mrs EFFIE, born 1790 in Argyll, married Augustus Shepherd in Virginia, died in Anson County, North Carolina, on 19 February 1863. [Wadesboro gravestone, N.C.]

SILLARS, DONALD, and family, from Monyquil, Arran, emigrated to Quebec in April 1831, [TNA.CO384.28.341/2]; settled in Inverness Township, Lower Canada, in 1831. [TNA.CO384.28.fos.24-26] [AMC]

SILLARS, DUNCAN, a weaver in Campbeltown, was accused of rioting and attacking a ship loaded with grain attempting to sail from Campbeltown, a petition, 21 March 1801. [NRS.JP36.5.46]

SILLARS, DUNCAN, and family, from Monyguil, Arran, settled in Inverness Township, Lower Canada, in 1831. [TNA.CO384.28.fos.24-26]

SILLER, ELIZABETH, born 1741 on Arran, widow of D. M. Neish, died in Dalhousie, New Brunswick, on 18 February 1842. [Halifax Journal, 28 March 1842]

SILLARS, JOHN, with family, from Maryquil, Arran, settled in Inverness Township, Lower Canada, in 1831. [TNA.CO384.28.fos.24-26]; born 1793, died 1859. [Chemin du Cimeriere gravestone]

SILLARS, PETER, a tenant in South Sannox, Arran, with his family of eight, emigrated on board the Albion bound for Quebec in 1829, settled in Inverness township by 1831. [TNA.CO384.22.fos.3-5] [AMC]

SILLARS, PETER, a boot and shoemaker in Lamlash, Arran, 1840. [BOA230]

SILLARS, PETER, a grocer in Lamlash, Arran, 1840. [BOA230]

SIMSON, ANN, born 1764, widow of William Lyon in Halifax, Nova Scotia, died in August 1850. [Rothesay gravestone, Bute]

SINCLAIR, ARCHIBALD, eldest son of Alexander Sinclair of Kilchamaig, Argyll, died at Mount Irvine, Tobago, on 11 September 1823. [Blackwood's Magazine, 15.131]

SINCLAIR, DUGALD, in Glasgow, was admitted as a burgess of Inveraray on 23 April 1849. [IBR]

SINCLAIR, DUNCAN, in Bellanoch, son of the deceased Neil Sinclair late church officer in Daill, South Kintyre, a bond dated 17 May 1819. [NRS.CC2.9.7.8]

SINCLAIR, JAMES, in Boston, New England, son and heir of his mother Isobel Lamont, wife of Donald Sinclair a merchant in Inveraray, in 1790. [NRS.S/H]

SINCLAIR, JAMES, a carrier, was admitted as a burgess of Dunbarton on 29 January 1803. [DBR]

SINCLAIR, JOHN, an innkeeper, was admitted as a burgess of Dunbarton on 21 May 1803. [DBR]

SINCLAIR, JOHN, in Inveraray, was evicted by the Duke of Argyll on 28 March 1805. [NRS.B32.2.1.42]

SINCLAIR, JOHN, a merchant, was admitted as a burgess of Inveraray on 29 September 1806. [IBR]

SINCLAIR, JOHN, a baker in New York, brother and heir of Mary Sinclair, Agnes Sinclair, and Janet Sinclair, daughters of Graham Sinclair in New Kilpatrick, Dunbartonshire, 1827. [NRS.S/H]

SINCLAIR, JOHN, born 1822, a servant of Donald McKellar a grocer and spirit dealer in Lochgilphead, was accused of theft and embezzlement in 1842. [NRS.AD14.42.435]

SINCLAIR, JOHN, born 1816, with his wife Ann born 1817, and son John, from Strontian, emigrated via Liverpool aboard the Allison bound for Melbourne, Victoria, Australia, on 13 September 1852. [NRS.HD4/5]

SINCLAIR, MARGARET, a chambermaid at the New Inn of Inveraray, a petition, 1810. [NRS.B32.2.1.45]

SINCLAIR, NEIL, born 1794 in Tarbert, Kintyre, emigrated to Wilmington, North Carolina, in August 1804, settled in Robeson County, NC, died 18 August 1880. [St Paul's records]

SINCLAIR, NEIL, in Daill, South Kintyre, an edict of executry, 1808. [NRS.CC2.112.2]

SINCLAIR, PETER, a fish-curer, was admitted as a burgess of Inveraray on 4 July 1837. [IBR]

SKINNER, ALEXANDER, the Tax Collector in Inveraray, was admitted as a burgess of Inveraray on 3 October 1818. [IBR]

SKINNER, HUGH, born 9 April 1784, son of Reverend Donald Skinner and his wife Mary in Ardnamurchan, a lighthouse-keeper in Cape Breton, Nova Scotia. [F.4.107]

SKINNER, JAMES, born 17 October 1781, son of Reverend Donald Skinner and his wife Mary in Ardnamurchan, a physician in Pictou, Nova Scotia. [F.4.107]

SKINNER, Mrs MARY, born 1752, widow of Reverend Donald Skinner in Ardnamurchan, died in Pictou, Nova Scotia, in 1831. [EEC.18635]

SMITH, DONALD, born 31 May 1802, son of Reverend John Smith in Campbeltown, minister of Campbeltown from 1826 until his death on 3 April 1841. [F.4.51]

SMITH, FLORA, and Jane McKellar, residing at Kilmory, on returning from the Low Countries, had put a chest aboard ship which had been lost, versus Neil Clark, 1806. [NRS.CC20.2.49]

SMITH, HECTOR, with Mary Campbell his wife, emigrated from Argyll to North Carolina in 1803, settled in Moore County. [NCSA.2.47]

SMITH, JAMES, a grocer, was admitted as a burgess and guilds-brother of Dunbarton on 18 June 1825. [DBR]

SMITH, JOHN, born 1765, died 23 December 1840, husband of Ann Samuel, born 1761, died 9 July 1812, parents of Donald Smith, a feuar in Dunoon. [Dunoon gravestone]

SMITH, JOHN, an ordinary seaman in Campbeltown in June 1795. [NRS.HCR.213]

SMITH, JOHN, born at Croft Brackley in Glenorchy in July 1747, son of John McLulich or Smith and his wife Mary Campbell, educated at Edinburgh University, minister at Campbeltown from 1781 until his death on 26 June 1807. [F.4.50]

SMITH, JOHN, born 1789 in Argyll, died in Charleston, South Carolina, on 15 October 1816. [Charleston City Gazette, 16.10.1816]

SMITH, JOHN, a tanner, was admitted as a burgess and guilds-brother of Dunbarton on 12 January 1828. [DBR]

SMITH, JOHN, a provision dealer, was admitted as a burgess and guilds-brother of Dunbarton on 30 April 1835. [DBR]

SMITH, JOHN, jr., a carter, was admitted as a burgess and guilds-brother of Dunbarton on 4 December 1846. [DBR]

SMITH, JOHN PATRICK, born 1838 in Argyll, son of Reverend Colin Smith and his wife Ann Campbell, died in Australia in 1905. [F.4.10]

SMITH, MALCOLM, a coach driver, was admitted as a burgess of Dunbarton on 10 October 1845. [DBR]

SMITH, PATRICK, a merchant in Brackley, Glen Orchy, son of the late John Smith, was admitted as a burgess of Inveraray on 25 September 1820. [IBR]

SMITH, PATRICK DUGALD, born 1851 in Argyll, son of Reverend Colin Smith and his wife Ann Campbell, possibly died in Australia. [F.4.10]

SMITH, PETER, born 1768 in Campbeltown, a mariner who was naturalised in South Carolina on 9 July 1806. [NARA.M1183.1]

SMITH, WILLIAM, a mariner in Inveraray, versus Hugh McLean master of the Inveraray Castle of Inveraray in 1821. [NRS.AC20.2.53]

SMITH, WILLIAM, a mason, was admitted as a burgess and guilds-brother of Dunbarton on 10 November 1842. [DBR]

SMITH, Reverend Professor, of Queen's College in Canada, died in Garelochhead on 8 August 1856. [GM.NS2/1.390]

SMOLLETT, JOHN ROUET, of Bonhill, born 9 May 1767, a Rear Admiral of the Red, died on 16 May 1842. [Alexandria gravestone]

SMYLIE, ARCHIBALD, at Tayinloan, a debtor to James McMillan a shoemaker in Killowcraw, 20 March 1811. [NRS.JP36.5.56]

SMYLIE, JAMES, with his wife Jane Watson, from Upper Barr in the parish of Killean and Kilkenzie, Kintyre, emigrated to North Carolina in 1776, settled in Scotland County, N.C, and by 1810 were in Amite County, Mississippi. [NCSA.2.26]

SPENCER, WILLIAM, an innkeeper, was admitted as a burgess and guilds-brother of Dunbarton on 12 July 1791. [DBR]

SPENCER, WILLIAM, an innkeeper, was admitted as a burgess of Inveraray on 4 October 1813. [IBR]

SPENCER, WILLIAM, an innkeeper, was admitted as a burgess of Inveraray on 22 March 1821. [IBR]

SPIERS, MATTHEW, a distiller in Lagg, Arran, 1840. [BOA231]

STALKER, DUNCAN, formerly in Tobago, late in Killean, Kintyre, testament 19 October 1798, Comm, Argyll, edict of executry, 1798. [NRS.CC2.8.102/7]

STALKER, EFFIE, born 1804 in Argyll, wife of John McLaurin, died 18 September 1881. [Laurinburg gravestone, North Carolina]

STALKER, JOHN, from Argyll, emigrated to America in 1824, buried in Sutherland Cemetery, South Carolina. [SHC]

STARK, JOSEPH, born 1801 in Cumbernauld, educated at the Universities of Glasgow and of Edinburgh, minister at Kilfinan from 1832 until 1843 when he joined the Free Church, then minister of the Free Church in Kilfinan from 1843 until his death on 24 August 1877. [F.4.30]

STEELE, JAMES, born 1794 son of William Steele schoolmaster in Dunbartonshire, educated at Glasgow University, settled in Jamaica as a minister in Kingston from 1821 until his death in September 1822. [F.7.670]

STEELE, JAMES, a wheelwright, was admitted as a burgess and guilds-brother of Dunbarton on 12 March 1798. [DBR]

STEELE, WILLIAM, a schoolmaster, was admitted as a burgess and guilds-brother of Dunbarton on 3 September 1792. [DBR]

STEPHEN, ALEXANDER, born 1801, a surgeon in Dunoon, died 10 September 1847. [Dunoon gravestone]

STEPHEN, WILLIAM, a grocer, was admitted as a burgess and guilds-brother of Dunbarton on 14 August 1812. [DBR]

STEVEN, or RUSSELL, JEAN, in Garbethill, Cumbernauld, Dunbartonshire, brother and heir of John Steven a millwright in Trinidad, 1845. [NRS.S/H]

STEVEN, JOHN, an innkeeper, was admitted as a burgess and guilds-brother of Dunbarton on 25 October 1796. [DBR]

STEVEN, JOHN, a cooper, was admitted as a burgess and guilds-brother of Dunbarton on 19 September 1806 as son of John Steven a burgess. [DBR]

STEVENSON, Lieutenant HUGH, of the Argyll Militia, admitted as a burgess of Inveraray on 10 June 1803. [IBR]

STEVENSON, JAMES, late miller at Kilchoan, imprisoned in Inveraray Tolbooth, a petition, 28 January 1811. [NRS.B32.2.1.46]

STEVENSON, JAMES, a surgeon in Glasgow, was admitted as a burgess and guilds-brother of Dunbarton on 29 September 1825. [DBR]

STEVENSON, JOHN, merchant in Oban, a contract, 1800, [NRS.NRAS.1209/44]; died 27 December 1812, inventory, 19 April 1813. [NRS.CC2.5.11]

STEWART, ALEXANDER, at Auchnacon, former tacksman of Keill, Appin, testament, 3 June 1796, Comm. Argyll. [NRS]

STEWART, ALEXANDER, of Invernahyle, Appin, testament, 16 October 1801. [NRS.CC2.3.13]

STEWART, ALEXANDER, son of Dugal Stewart a surgeon in Kintyre, 1803. [NRS.JC26.1803.62]

STEWART, ALEXANDER, of Achnaon, Argyll, died on his estate of Lorn, Jamaica, in March 1806. [SM.68.486]

STEWART, ALEXANDER, in Darachmhor, born 1803, died 10 March 1857, husband of Mary Ann Miller, born 1800, died 24 May 1890. [Dunoon gravestone]

STEWART, ALEXANDER, and family, from Corriecravie, Arran, emigrated to Quebec in April 1831, [TNA.CO384.28.341/2]; settled in Inverness Township, Lower Canada, in 1831. [TNA.CO384.28.fos.24-26]

STEWART, ALLAN, in Taycharnan, testament, 22 November 1796, Comm. Argyll. [NRS]

STEWART, ALLAN, tacksman of Shuna, testament, 28 July 1801. [NRS.CC2.3.13]

STEWART, ARCHIBALD, a mariner in Rothesay, Bute, testament, 24 June 1790, Comm. Argyll. [NRS]

STEWART, ARCHIBALD, born 10 September 1805, son of Reverend Francis Stewart and his wife Margaret Campbell, minister at Craignish from 1 September 1831 to 25 April 1844. [F.4.4]

STEWART, CHARLES, a hairdresser, was admitted as a burgess and guilds-brother of Dunbarton on 6 August 1795. [DBR]

STEWART, CHARLES, born 1757 in Campbeltown, emigrated with his father and family, a senior magistrate and Colonel of the 1st Battalion of Militia, died in Dalhousie, New Brunswick, on 2 November 1838. [The Gleaner, 20 November 1838]

STEWART, CHARLES, born 1759 in Campbeltown, son of Peter Stewart, emigrated to Prince Edward Island in 1775, a lawyer and administrator, died in Charlottetown, P.E.I., on 6 January 1813. [DCB]

STEWART, DONALD, born 1764, a labourer from Glencoe, emigrated via Oban on board the Clarendon of Hull bound for Charlottetown, Prince Edward Island, on 6 August 1808. [TNA.CO226.23]

STEWART, DONALD, a tenant in Margarioch, Arran, wth his family of nine, emigrated via Lamlash, Arran, on the Caledonia bound for Quebec, landed there on 25 June 1829, settled in Inverness township. [TNA.CO384.22.fos.3-5][AMC]

STEWART, DUNCAN, seaman in Kilduskland, inventory, 22 August 1812. [NRS.CC2.5.11]

STEWART, FRANCIS, born 12 December 1753, son of Archibald Stewart tenant in Upper Ardroscadale and his wife Elizabeth Bannatyne, educated at Edinburgh University, minister at Craignish from 1795, died 13 February 1832. [F.4.2]

STEWART, FREDERICK CAMPBELL, of Ascog, married Maria Smith, second daughter of Judge Smith of the Supreme Court of Pennsylvania, in Philadelphia, Pa., on 30 May 1820. [BM.7.705]

STEWART, HUGH, a weaver in Bracklet, Southend, Kintyre, was accused of theft in 1830. [NRS.AD14.30.107]

STEWART, JAMES, born 1775 in Appin, husband of Margaret McEachin, settled in North Carolina, died on 29 December 1821, buried in Stewartville Cemetery, Laurinburg, NC. [NCSA.2.82]

STEWART, JAMES, born 1778, son of Andrew Stewart of Invernahyle, died in New York in 1813.

STEWART, JAMES, and family of four, from North Kiscadale, Arran, emigrated to Quebec in April 1831, [TNA.CO384.28.341/2]; settled in Inverness Township, Lower Canada, in 1831. [TNA.CO384.28.fos.24-26] [AMC]

STEWART, JOHN, born 1759, emigrated from Kintyre in 1766, died at Mount Stewart, Prince Edward Island, on 22 June 1834. [New Brunswick Courier, 12 July 1834]

STEWART, JOHN, an innkeeper, was admitted as a burgess and guildsbrother of Dunbarton on 15 May 1792. [DBR]

STEWART, JOHN, born 1766 in Argyll, a merchant, died in Georgia on 24 April 1806. [Savanna Death Register]

STEWART, JOHN, a sailor on Cumbrae, 1794. [NRS.S/H]

STEWART, JOHN, an able seaman in Campbeltown in May 1795. [NRS.HCR.212]

STEWART, JOHN, schoolmaster of the Campbeltown Poor School, a petition dated September 1822. [NRS.NRAS.1209.516]

STEWART, JOHN, of Levenbank, was admitted as a burgess and guildsbrother of Dunbarton on 8 March 1825. [DBR]

STEWART, JOHN, an innkeeper, was admitted as a burgess and guildsbrother of Dunbarton on 16 May 1827, as husband of a burgess's daughter. [DBR]

STEWART, JOHN, a teacher at Whiting Bay, Arran, 1840. [BOA231]

STEWART, JOHN, of Glen Buckie, petitioned for land opposite Machrimore, Southend, in 1845. [NRS.NRAS 1209.1981]

STEWART, Reverend JOHN, born 1826, eldest son of Archibald Stewart, Dunamuck, Lochgilphead, died in Kincardine, Ontario, on 29 December 1898. [S.17337]

STEWART, JULIET, a baker, was admitted as a burgess of Inveraray in May 1843. [IBR]

STEWART, MARGARET, wife of Donald Colquhoun on Mull, sister and heir of Duncan Stewart in Jamaica, 1814. [NRS.S/H]

STEWART, MARY, born 1803 in Argyll, wife of Dougald McGibbon, settled in Caledon, Peel County, Upper Canada, died in December 1863. [Caledon gravestone]

STEWART, NEIL, born 1773, a labourer from Glencoe, wife Mary born 1781, Christian born 1803, Margaret born 1805, and Mary born 1807, emigrated via Oban on board the Clarendon of Hull bound for Charlottetown, Prince Edward Island, on 6 August 1808. [TNA.CO226.23]

STEWART, ROBERT, a sailor in Cumbrae, 1794. [NRS.S/H]

STEWART, ROBERT, Captain in the Royal Navy, residing in Glackeriska, Appin, a bond of caution, 10 March 1817. [NRS.CC2.9.7]

STEWART, ROBERT, a fisher in Largiebeg, Arran, was accused of running down a vessel and causing death in 1824. [NRS.AD14.24.262]

STEWART, ROBERT, from Arran, emigrated via Lamlash, Arran, on the Caledonia bound for Quebec, landed there on 25 June 1829, settled in Inverness township. [AMC]

STEWART, Mrs WILLIAM, from Arran, with her family of seven, emigrated via Lamlash, Arran, bound for Quebec, settled in Inverness township, 1829. [AMC]

STEWART, WILLIAM, a weaver in Bracklet, Southend, Kintyre, was accused of theft in 1830. [NRS.AD14.30.107]

STODDART, ANDREW, a surgeon in Brodick, Arran, 1840. [BOA231]

STODDART, JOHN, a surgeon in Brodick, Arran, 1840. [BOA231]

STATHEARN, DONALD, a watchman, was admitted as a burgess and guilds-brother of Dunbarton on 5 July 1842 as son of a burgess. [DBR]

STRATHEARN, WILLIAM, a shoemaker, was admitted as a burgess of Dunbarton on 5 February 1790. [DBR]

STRAWHORN, ANDREW, born 1785 in Argyll, settled in New Brunswick in 1816, died in Bathurst, N.B. on 6 September 1830. [Gleaner, 21 September 1830]

STUART, Colonel CHARLES, son of the Earl of Bute, was admitted as a burgess of Ayr on 7 July 1790. [ABR]

STUART, JAMES COULTER, youngest son of Captain Stuart of Dullatur, died at Ardoch Pen, St Anne's, Jamaica, on 19 April 1826. [EA.6539.449]

STUART, JOHN FISH, born 1821, second son of Robert Stuart in Gortinean House, Kilean, Argyll, died in Kingston, Canada, on 2 September 1844. [SG.1347][W.5.515]

STUART, JOSEPH, born 24 March 1798, son of Reverend John Stuart in Luss, educated at the University of Glasgow, minister at Kingarth from 1825 until his death on 1 September 1826. [F.4.35]

SWAN, JOHN, a witness at the murder trial of Alexander McFarlane in 1824. [NRS.AD14.24.201]

STUART, WILLIAM SWAN, a surgeon, was admitted as a burgess and guilds-brother of Dunbarton on 9 February 1836 as married to a burgess's daughter. [DBR]

SYME, JOHN, a merchant, was admitted as a burgess and guilds-brother of Dunbarton on 4 December 1807. [DBR]

SYME, SAMUEL, from Old Kilpatrick, Dunbartonshire, applied to settle in Canada on 3 March 1815. [NRS.RH9]

TAGG, JOHN, formerly at Lennox Miln, Campsie, was admitted as a burgess and guilds-brother of Dunbarton on 22 May 1824. [DBR]

TAIT, WILLIAM, a weaver, was admitted as a burgess of Dunbarton on 25 September 1818. [DBR]

TAYLOR, ANDREW, a mason, was admitted as a burgess of Dunbarton on 19 September 1804. [DBR]

TAYLOR, ANGUS, in Brackley, South Knapdale, an edict of executry, 1818. [NRS.C2.8.123.2]

TAYLOR, ARCHIBALD, a carter, was admitted as a burgess and guilds-brother of Dunbarton on 8 November 1796. [DBR]

TAYLOR, DANIEL, a wright, was admitted as a burgess and guilds-brother of Dunbarton on 31 July 1810. [DBR]

TAYLOR, JAMES, at Beaucharr, a debtor to James McMillan a shoemaker in Killowcraw, 20 March 1811. [NRS.JP36.5.56]

TAYLOR, JOHN, in Corslett, was admitted as a burgess and guilds-brother of Dunbarton on 12 March 1801. [DBR]

TAYLOR, JOHN, a wright, was admitted as a burgess and guilds-brother of Dunbarton on 26 September 1845, son of a burgess. [DBR]

TAYLOR, ROBERT, an innkeeper, was admitted as a burgess and guilds-brother of Dunbarton on 26 July 1802. [DBR]

TAYLOR, ROBERT, a carter, was admitted as a burgess and guilds-brother of Dunbarton on 18 May 1841 as married to the daughter of a burgess. [DBR]

TAYLOR, Dr ROBERT FRAZER, born 1826, died 12 October 1866. [Dunoon gravestone]

TELFORD, FRANCIS, born 1740 possibly in Dunbarton, a shipmaster in Greenock in 1786, was admitted as a burgess of Dunbarton in 1780, settled in New York, died there on 22 August 1836. [DBR] [ANY]

TEMPLETON, ROBERT, with his family of five, from Rothesay, Bute, emigrated via Greenock on board the Portaferry bound for Quebec in May 1832, landed there in June 1832. [QM.13.6.1832]

THOM, ELIZA, in Ascog, Bute, heir of William Thom in Dundas, Canada West, who died 4 May 1860. [NRS.S/H]

THOM, ROBERT, in Ascog, Bute, heir of William Thom in Dundas, Canada West, who died 4 May 1860. [NRS.S/H]

THOMSON, ARCHIBALD, born 1737, a sailor on the Cumrees cutter, died 12 December 1790. [Cumbrae gravestone]

THOMSON, DUGALD, cottar in Drumalea, Kintyre, was accused of looting a wrecked vessel in 1817. [NRS.AD14.17.86]

THOMSON, DUNCAN, a tailor, was admitted as a burgess and guildsbrother of Dunbarton on 25 January 1836. [DBR]

THOMSON, GEORGE, a watchmaker, was admitted as a burgess of Inveraray in July 1842. [IBR]

THOMSON, HUGH, a merchant and mariner in Rothesay, Bute, testament, 9 June 1796, Comm. Argyll. [NRS]

THOMPSON, JAMES, [1], an able seaman in Campbeltown in May 1795. [NRS.HCR.212]

THOMPSON, JAMES, [2], an able seaman in Campbeltown in May 1795. [NRS.HCR.212]

THOMPSON, JAMES, a carpenter in Lamlash, Arran, in 1840. [BOA230]

THOMSON, JAMES, a carter, was admitted as a burgess of Dunbarton on 18 May 1841. [DBR]

THOMSON, JAMES, a baker, was admitted as a burgess of Inveraray in July 1842. [IBR]

THOMSON, JOHN, in Ballochcroy, a debtor of William Caldwell at Lochwinnoch, 5 November 1810. [NRS.JP36.5.55]

THOMSON, JOHN, a carter, was admitted as a burgess and guilds-brother of Dunbarton on 20 March 1819 as son of a burgess. [DBR]

THOMSON, JOHN, from Inveraray, married Margaret Campbell from Caithness, in St John, New Brunswick, on 27 February 1827. [City Gazette, 1 March 1827]

THOMSON, JOHN, a surgeon in the Royal Navy, in Sierra Leone, testament, 19 July 1826, Comm. Argyll. [NRS.SC51.32.2.163A]

THOMSON, JOHN M., son of Henry Thomson a soldier in Dunbarton, was educated at Marischal College, Aberdeen, in 1844. [MCA]

THOMSON, JOHN, a tinsmith, was admitted as a burgess of Dunbarton on 10 March 1836. [DBR]

THOMSON, MARY, daughter of James Thomson from Argyll, married William Clarke, in Lancaster, New Brunswick, on 30 September 1825. [NBC.1.10.1825]

THOMSON, WILLIAM, a carter, was admitted as a burgess and guilds-brother of Dunbarton on 18 January 1802. [DBR]

THOMSON, WILLIAM, a spirit dealer, was admitted as a burgess and guilds-brother of Dunbarton on 29 October 1833 as married to the daughter of a burgess. [DBR]

THORBURN, WILLIAM, a farmer at Storfield, late in Bute, testament, 26 June 1793, Comm. Argyll. [NRS]

TOLMIE, JOANNA, second daughter of James Tolmie in Campbeltown, married Montague William Drake, in Victoria, Vancouver Island, British Columbia, on 12 March 1862. [GM.ns2/13.222]

TOWART, ROBERT, a wright, was admitted as a burgess and guilds-brother of Dunbarton on 18 November 1805. [DBR]

TOWIE, THOMAS, a fishmonger, was admitted as a burgess of Dunbarton on 10 August 1834. [DBR]

TROTTER, GEORGE, from Dunbarton, died in Springfield, Illinois, on 18 May 1842, testament Edinburgh, 1843. [NRS]

TURNBULL, WILLIAM, a labourer in Dunoon, was accused of assault in 1835. [NRS.AD14.35.154]

TURNER, ARCHIBALD, born 1791, died at Orimdrishaig, on 30 July 1883, husband of Janet Whyte, born 1799, died 30 October 1885. [Kilmun gravestone]

TURNER, CATHERINE, versus Janet Bell, spouse to Archibald Sinclair a tailor in Inveraray, 15 October 1806. [NRS.B32.2.1.43]

TURNER, Major General CHARLES, was admitted as a burgess of Inveraray on 27 October 1821. [IBR]

TURNER, COLIN, born 1791, coal merchant in Dunoon, died 14 June 1839. [Dunoon gravestone]

TURNER, DUNCAN, a butcher, was admitted as a burgess and guilds-brother of Dunbarton on 18 June 1825. [DBR]

TURNER, DUNCAN, a butcher in Duntochter, Dunbartonshire, was tried for sheep stealing in 1847. [NRS.AD14.47.334]

TURNER, JOHN, in Kirkton of Muckairn, testament, 13 April 1801. [NRS.CC2.3.12]

TURNER, JOHN, from Savannah, Georgia, married Elizabeth Galbraith in Luss, Dunbartonshire, on 17 August 1821. [EA.6025.127]

TURNER, PETER, master of the Mally of Rothesay, Bute, testament, 17 October 1795, Comm. Isles. [NRS]

TURNER, PETER, an innkeeper, was admitted as a burgess and guilds-brother of Dunbarton on 23 March 1804. [DBR]

TURNER, WILLIAM, a spirit dealer, was admitted as a burgess and guilds-brother of Dunbarton on 18 September 1824. [DBR]

URE, JOHN, born 1815, died in Oakland, California, on 12 May 1897. [Dunbarton gravestone]

URIE, JAMES, born 1789, from Cowal, emigrated on board a Hudson's Bay Company vessel bound for the Red River settlement in 1811. [PAC.m155, 145]

WADDELL, WILLIAM, a shopkeeper, was admitted as a burgess and guilds-brother of Dunbarton on 16 July 1804. [DBR]

WALKER, ADAM WILLIAMSON, a shoemaker, was admitted as a burgess and guilds-brother of Dunbarton on 22 September 1820 as son of George Walker a burgess. [DBR]

WALKER, DOUGALD, an innkeeper, was admitted as a burgess and guilds-brother of Dunbarton on 16 March 1814. [DBR]

WALKER, JOHN, born 1790, from Bonhill, Dunbarton, emigrated on board a Hudson's Bay Company vessel bound for the Red River settlement in 1811. [PAC.m155, 145]

WALKER, JOHN, of the George Inn in Inveraray, was admitted as a burgess of Inveraray on 20 July 1827. [IBR]

WALKER, ROBERT, at Lochus, was admitted as a burgess and guilds-brother of Dunbarton on 1 November 1802. [DBR]

WALKER, ROBERT, an innkeeper, was admitted as a burgess and guilds-brother of Dunbarton on 11 February 1803. [DBR]

WALKER, ROBERT, a baker in Luss, Dunbartonshire, was tried for housebreaking in 1842. [NRS.AD14.42.122]

WALKER, WILLIAM, born 1754, a butcher, died 11 January 1845, wife Jane Boyd born 1750, died 22 March 1845, son John born 1804, died in Queensland, Australia, in January 1845. [Cumbrae gravestone]

WALLACE, ROBERT, flax-dresser in Kilmory, Kilean, 1816. [NRS.NRAS.1209.1942]

WALLACE, WALTER, a carpenter, was admitted as a burgess and guilds-brother of Dunbarton on 15 August 1794. [DBR]

WALLACE, WILLIAM, born 1759, died 9 June 1833, wife Janet Stewart, born 1764, died 12 February 1852, parents of Francis drowned in Demerara in 1827. [Rothesay gravestone, Bute]

WARRY, NICKALL, an able seaman in Campbeltown in May 1795. [NRS.HCR.212]

WATSON, ALEXANDER, a shoemaker, was admitted as a burgess and guilds-brother of Dunbarton on 1 July 1807. [DBR]

WATSON, ARCHIBALD, a merchant in Campbeltown, versus Archibald Huie a wright, decreet, 6 May 1811. [NRS.JP36.5.56]

WATSON, JAMES, a sailor, was admitted as a burgess of Dunbarton in 1792. [DBR]

WATSON, JOHN, a weaver, was admitted as a burgess and guilds-brother of Dunbarton on 25 September 1818 having served his apprenticeship under a burgess. [DBR]

WATSON, THOMAS, a tailor, was admitted as a burgess and guilds-brother of Dunbarton on 11 September 1790. [DBR]

WATSON, WILLIAM, probably from Old Kilpatrick, Dunbartonshire, a stonemason in Pittsburgh, Pennsylvania, letters dating between 1801 and 1817. [NLS.Acc.7439]

WATSON, WILLIAM, the younger, a merchant in Main Street, Campbeltown, 1820. [NRS.NRAS.1209.940]

WEIR, ARCHIBALD, born 1777, a farmer from Argyll, with his wife, landed in America on 13 September 1807, settled in Herkimer County, New York. [1812]

WEIR, JAMES, a weaver, was admitted as a burgess and guilds-brother of Dunbarton on 25 September 1818 as husband of a burgess's daughter. [DBR]

WEIR, JAMES, a mason, was admitted as a burgess and guilds-brother of Dunbarton on 23 September 1833 as son of a burgess. [DBR]

WEIR, JAMES, a mason, was admitted as a burgess and guilds-brother of Dunbarton on 23 September 1833 as son of a burgess. [DBR]

WEIR, ROBERT, a mason, was admitted as a burgess and guilds-brother of Dunbarton on 21 May 1795. [DBR]

WHITE, JANET, wife of James Culbertson, late tenant in Bulloch, later in Cheskan, Campbeltown, was accused of theft and fire-raising in 1820. [NRS.AD14.20.173]

WHITE, ROBERT, a mason, was admitted as a burgess of Dunbarton on 21 September 1802. [DBR]

WHITEFORD, ROBERT, miller at Lopit, son of Robert Whiteford a miller at Lopit, later at Marypans, Kintyre, was accused of murder, papers 9 May 1805. [NRS.JC26.1805.16]

WHITELAW, CHARLES, was accused of theft from the Dunlocher Grain Mill, Dunbartonshire, in 1834. [NRS.AD14.34.7]

WHITELAW, ROBERT, born 1795, forester at Castle Toward, died 20 December 1849, husband of Jean Park, born 1797, died 7 January 1879. [Dunoon gravestone]

WHITY, PETER, a seaman from Argyll, was killed by lightning during a voyage on the schooner Loyalist en route from Wilmington to St John on 17 April 1839. [St Andrews Standard]

WHYTE, DANIEL, born 1779 in Argyll, a butcher in Charleston, South Carolina, was naturalised there on 28 December 1813. [NARA.M1183.1]

WHYTE, JOHN, born 1845, son of John Whyte [1804-1891], a farmer in Ballochyle and Corruisk, and his wife Catherine Clark [1801-1866], died in North America. [Kilmun gravestone],

WHYTE, WILLIAM, a brewer, was admitted as a burgess and guilds-brother of Dunbarton on 2 February 1836. [DBR]

WILES, JOHN WOOTEN, a tailor and clothier, was admitted as a burgess of Dunbarton on 9 December 1833. [DBR]

WILKIE, DOUGLAS, born 1793 in Campbeltown, deserted from HMS Talbot at St Johns, Newfoundland, on 26 August 1813. [Royal Gazette, Newfoundland Advertiser, 23 September 1813]

WILKINSON, JOHN, a teacher in Sliddre, Arran, 1840. [BOA231]

WILLIAMSON, ARCHIBALD, born 1782 in Campbeltown, a shipwright, died in St John, New Brunswick, on 4 September 1827. [City Gazette, 5 September 1827]; probate, 22 September 1827, Halifax, Nova Scotia.

WILLIAMSON, JAMES, a grocer, was admitted as a burgess and guilds-brother of Dunbarton on 22 July 1816. [DBR]

WILLIAMSON, THOMAS, born 1791, possibly from Arran, died in Halifax, Nova Scotia, on 27 March 1848, probate, 1848, Halifax, N.S.

WILSON, JAMES, a shoemaker, was admitted as a burgess and guilds-brother of Dunbarton on 4 July 1808 as son of William Wilson a wright burgess. [DBR]

WILSON, JAMES, a spirit dealer, was admitted as a burgess and guilds-brother of Dunbarton on 10 January 1839. [DBR]

WILSON, JOHN, a mason, was admitted as a burgess of Dunbarton on 21 September 1809. [DBR]

WILSON, JOHN, master of a steamboat, was admitted as a burgess and guilds-brother of Dunbarton on 2 June 1846. [DBR]

WINGATE, THOMAS, from Stirling, was admitted as a burgess of Inveraray on 16 August 1799. [IBR]

WOOD, CHARLES, a ship builder, was admitted as a burgess of Dunbarton on 15 October 1836. [DBR]

WOOD, WILLIAM, a shopkeeper, was admitted as a burgess of Dunbarton on 18 March 1836. [DBR]

WRIGHT, ANGUS, a grocer in Lamlash, Arran, 1840. [BOA230]

WRIGHT, ARCHIBALD, born 1764 in Argyll, died in Fredericton, New Brunswick, on 8 July 1830. [New Brunswick Courier, 17 July 1830]

WRIGHT, Provost JAMES, a writer, was admitted as a burgess of Inveraray in 1843. [IBR]

WRIGHT, PETER, an innkeeper, was admitted as a burgess of Inveraray on 19 October 1802. [IBR]

WYLIE, ARCHIBALD, a seaman in Stragel, Kilmorrie, Arran, testament, 25 March 1784, Comm. Isles. [NRS]

WYLLIE, JAMES, in Toledo, USA, second son of Alexander Wyllie a distiller in Campbeltown, married Jane, eldest daughter of William Greenlees a farmer in Ardnacross, Argyll, in Haarlem, Winnebago County, Illinois, on 18 December 1852. [W.XIII.1301]

YOUNG, ALEXANDER, a wright in Inveraray, versus Peter MacArthur a wright in Inveraray, 23 July 1802. [NRS.B32.2.1.40]

YOUNG, ALEXANDER, a painter, was admitted as a burgess of Inveraray on 29 September 1806. [IBR]

YOUNG, JAMES, jr, a tailor, was admitted as a burgess and guilds-brother of Dunbarton on 23 September 1818 as son of James Young a tailor burgess. [DBR]

YOUNG, JAMES, a grocer, was admitted as a burgess and guilds-brother of Dunbarton on 20 July 1820. [DBR]

YOUNG, ROBERT, a tailor, was admitted as a burgess and guilds-brother of Dunbarton on 10 December 1816. [DBR]

YOUNG, WILLIAM, a saddler, was admitted as a burgess and guilds-brother of Dunbarton on 1 August 1810. [DBR]

www.ingramcontent.com/pod-product-compliance
Lightning Source LLC
Chambersburg PA
CBHW050820160426

43192CB00010B/1835

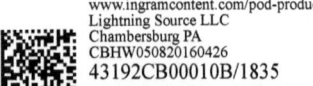